What others are saying about this book:

Virtual Assistant – The Series is a complete reference guide and more for new and experienced virtual assistants. Diana Ennen and Kelly Poelker have successfully touched upon all aspects being a virtual assistant.

Mona Lisa Safai, TCM Reviews

When I first started my virtual assistant business I came into a completely new environment. Thanks to Kelly and Diana's book, *Virtual Assistant – The Series,* I got all the information I needed at my fingertips, and I still refer back to it at all times.

Vera Regelbrugge

As a VA that's been around the block a few times, I have to give *Virtual Assistant - The Series* a big thumbs up. Out of all of the other "how to" books I've found out there for Virtual Assistants, this book is the one that gets my highest recommendation. Whether you're new and just entering the VA Industry, or a VA that's been in business for a while and just needs some good, sound advice and instruction regarding how to grow and manage a successful business, this book is for you! Kelly and Diana have, again, outdone themselves in this newest edition of what I deem to be the best VA book on the market!!

Terry Green, Fastype VA Services, Inc.

I could not have started my VA business without this book. I was so overwhelmed with where to start and what to do first, I almost didn't get started period. This book is easy to follow, enjoyable to read, and has a wonderful step-by-step plan for putting it all together. Success will surely follow all its readers.

Leisa Bain Good, Gemstone Business Solutions

Virtual Assistant – The Series not only opened the door to a new career path for me, it greeted me, guided me through the door and led me down the path! My sincere gratitude goes to Kelly and Diana for showing me how to take 30 years of knowledge and experience in the face-to-face world and turn it into a *virtual* success story. I'm loving it!

Marilyn Stafford, Alliance Virtual Services

Diana Ennen and Kelly Poelker capture and provide you with all the information you need to be armed with to be a highly successful Virtual Assistant. The information they provide is based on their real life experiences, making this book a must have for anyone considering this field. If you only purchase one book to guide you or help you decide if being a VA is for you, this is it. Use this book as you decide to become a VA, as you set up your office, as you market your services, and as you run your business. Everything you need it right here in one easy to follow format.

-Michelle Dunn, Author / Consultant

About the Authors

Diana Ennen – Author and President of Virtual Word Publishing since 1985, Diana has been actively involved in the virtual assisting industry.

One of her main passions is helping others start their own business. She offers online consulting and mentoring, and is extremely active on Twitter and Facebook groups. She also is able to help others with their start-up questions by responding via e-mail and sending out a free booklet that she has written, and sample letters, etc. that she has found useful in her own business. Visit her website at: http://www.virtualwordpublishing.com.

Diana is the mother of three amazing kids: Jeremy, Amanda, and Amber; and the wife of a very supportive husband, Greg. Her greatest accomplishment is raising such wonderful kids and having the opportunity to work at home with them.

Kelly Poelker – Author and President of Another 8 Hours®, which was founded in 2000. She started her practice part-time while working full-time, and in just ten months was able to leave that full-time job to pursue her dream as an entrepreneur.

Kelly shares her knowledge and expertise in the virtual assistant industry as a coach through the Academy of Virtual Professionals LLC (http://www.AcademyVP.com), through Twitter and Facebook, and as an industry speaker. She has also served on the Executive Board of International Virtual Assistants Association (IVAA). She is the co-founder of the first-ever annual VA Conference held from 2001 - 2006.

Kelly is the mother of two wonderful children, Kelsey and Kory, and wife to a very supportive husband, Randy.

Other books by Diana Ennen and Kelly Poelker
- *Virtual Assistant – The Series: Become a Highly Successful, Sought After VA Workbook Edition* (recommended to accompany this book)
- *Virtual Assistant – The Series: Working Virtually*
- *Virtual Assistant – The Series: Become a Highly Successful, Sought After VA* (first and second editions published as *"Up Close and Virtual"*)
- *Virtual Assistant Solution Pack (Microsoft® Word Edition)*
- *The Bizymoms Cookbook*
- *Bizy's Guide to Starting Your Own Virtual Assistant Business*

Other books by Diana Ennen
- *Words From Home: How To Start and Operate a Successful Home-Based Word Processing Business*
- *Success From Home: The Word Processing Business* (published by Adams-Blake Publishing)
- *Virtual Assistant Solution Pack (WordPerfect Office Ready® Edition)*
- *So You Want to Be a Work-At-Home Mom: A Christian Guide to Starting a Home-Based Business* (Beacon Hill Publishing)

Virtual Assistant – The Series

Become a Highly Successful, Sought After VA

Diana Ennen and Kelly Poelker

Fourth Edition

Foreword by
Mary Goulet

Visit us online at:
http://www.VA-TheSeries.com

Another 8 Hours Publishing • O'Fallon, Illinois

Virtual Assistant – The Series:
Become a Highly Successful, Sought After VA

By Diana Ennen and Kelly Poelker

Published by:
Another 8 Hours Publishing
A division of Another 8 Hours, Inc.
O'Fallon, IL 62269
orders@VA-TheSeries.com
http://www.VA-TheSeries.com

ISBN, print ed.   978-0-9742790-8-4
ISBN, PDF ed.   978-0-9742790-9-1

First edition published in 2001 as Up Close and Virtual (ISBN 0-9742790-1-3)
Second edition published in 2003 as Up Close and Virtual (ISBN 0-9742790-2-1 paperback)
                                                                                        (ISBN 0-9742790-3-X pdf)
Third edition revised published in 2004 as Virtual Assistant – The Series: Become a Highly Successful, Sought After VA (ISBN, print ed. 0-9742790-5-6; PDF ed. ISBN 0-9742790-6-4)

Printed in the United States of America

Original Cover Design: Nancy Cleary
Revised Design: Killer Covers

Library of Congress Control Number: 2010910581

Table of Contents

Foreword

When I first heard of the virtual assistant industry, I was hosting an Internet talk radio show for entrepreneurs. Many segments of the show were formatted to include online components. It seemed a natural evolution to highlight news on the Web, people who made their living with an online business and others who augmented their offline business with an online marketing component. Virtual assistants, I have found, do all three. For a year, the VA Industry was profiled each month on my show to educate the public on the benefits of hiring a VA, or becoming one. During that year I became even more convinced it is the wave of the secretarial future.

VA's are resourceful, motivated, educated and probably the most willing entrepreneurs I have met. They take pride in providing a multitude of services for those who have burgeoning brick and mortar businesses; speaking, consulting and coaching careers that take them on the road; and for business people in general that need an extra hand from time to time.

There are countless business arenas a virtual assistant with technical, writing, organizing and facilitating specialties can find to grow a healthy client base. With that said, the proper business structure needs to be in place for the virtual assistant to be successful. Virtual Assistant – The Series is "the" book on starting and growing a successful virtual assistant practice.

I have been an enthusiastic believer in the role VA's play. I am an advocate for this industry. It allows men and women to choose their career based on their skills, passion and expertise. Being a virtual assistant affords one the opportunity to be an entrepreneur while staying home with their children, and customize their work schedule to suit the demands of daily life.

Kelly and Diana have taken the lead in the VA Industry and written a comprehensive and practical step-by-step guide to ensure your success. It is becoming the industry bible. If you want to be successful as a virtual assistant, buy this book, read it and let it work for you.

Mary Goulet
Author, Speaker, Spokesperson, TV & Radio Show Host
MomsTown.com, Co-Founder

Contributors to this edition of *Virtual Assistant – The Series: Become a Highly Successful, Sought After VA*

Contributing Editor,
Creating a Business Plan and Marketing Strategies
Steve Windhaus
Windhaus & Associates
Port Lucie, FL
http://www.windhaus.com

Determining Pricing
Robert Brenner
Brenner Information Group
http://www.brennerbooks.com/
brenner@brennerbooks.com

Financial Statements
Sheryl Michilli
Kaisana Administrative Support
http://www.kaisana.net
sheryl@kaisana.net

Proofreading and Editing
Marilyn Stafford
Alliance Virtual Services
http://www.alliancevs.com
marilyn@alliancevs.com

Christine Cavagnaro
administratorsRus
www.administratorsrus.net
ccavagnaro@administratorsrus.net

••

NOTE: Throughout this book, the authors share their experience, ideas, tips, and suggestions both collectively as the authors and as individual business owners. Though not always grammatically correct, it was found that writing in their own voices allows the readers to gain the most impact from the information presented, and get the viewpoint of how they each handle different matters in their respective lives and businesses. So, rather than writing "this is Kelly's" or "this is Diana's" input, you'll find the use of I/we/me/us and so forth dependent upon the context of the material. We trust you will find the value in presenting the information in this manner. Enjoy!

Diana's Acknowledgments

I want to thank all the many virtual assistants who continually support me and motivate me to continue on and be the best I can be. It's such a blessing to be a part of such a passionate industry and to learn and grow from you throughout the years. I'm looking forward to the years ahead.

I want to thank my co-author, Kelly Poelker, for all her hard work and wisdom in putting together another edition of our book. We now have had the pleasure of meeting several times, and it's always great to connect personally. It's been a pleasure to be on this journey with you.

I also want to thank my wonderful family, Jeremy, Amanda and Amber. I'm so proud of the people you are becoming and am grateful that I got to work at home all these years and be an active part of your lives. I wish this for all those who wish to be an entrepreneur. It's one of the true perks of being a work-at-home mom.

And to my husband, Greg, again thanks for always listening and constantly encouraging. Thanks for supporting me once again, through another edition, and always saying the right things when I need them most. You totally rock!

Kelly's Acknowledgments

Sincerest thanks to my wonderful and supportive family. I wouldn't be where I am today without your love, support, patience, and encouragement. You are my inspiration to be the best that I can be. Thank you all for believing in me.

Very special thanks to Diana Ennen for being such a wonderful co-author. The success achieved with our books has far exceeded anything I'd ever imagined. It's been a terrific journey and I look forward to our continued success.

To Steve Windhaus and Sheryl Michilli, and all of our other wonderful contributors, my deepest gratitude for all of your efforts in making this book such a valuable resource.

Special thanks to my "desk buddy," the late Janet Jordan for her many words of encouragement and advice. I'll always remember that no matter how many doors may close, a new one will open. You were an asset to the virtual assistant industry and I'll remember you, always.

And finally, thanks to my clients, for without them I would not have these experiences to share with you.

Introduction

Virtual assistants are an extremely proud group. Many of us endured years of office politics, constantly ringing phones, demanding bosses, hours upon hours of endless office work, long commutes to work, and precious time spent away from those dearest to us, our families.

According to Key Facts About Women-Owned Businesses 2008-2009 Update, the Center for Women's Business Research reports there are an estimated 10.1 million firms owned by women (75% or more). And, women-owned firms (50% or more), account for 40% of all privately-held firms in the United States. Astonishing, isn't it? No longer are we sitting behind the desk taking orders. We are aspiring to be leaders. We are teaching our children that no dream is beyond their reach. We embrace the future and welcome all of the challenges of the new technologies. The advent of the Internet was but a beginning to a world of hope and opportunity. We continue to seize the challenge and we never plan on letting it go. The more we learn, the more eager we are for more.

As Lesley Spencer-Pyle, founder of Home-Based Working Moms, states, "Working at home has become a popular choice for moms in the millennium. Not only does a home business give moms the opportunity to be at home with their children and earn additional income; it also gives stay-at-home parents a new sense of accomplishment and self-worth. Working from home enables parents to gain more self-respect while taking charge of their future."

You can change your destiny. You can make it happen. We are here to guide you along the way to becoming a highly successful, sought after virtual assistant. As we share our own personal experiences and those of other industry professionals, our hope is that you will gain an appreciation for believing in yourself and your success as a business owner. Read…take notes…dream. ***Aspire To Be The Best That You Can Be***.

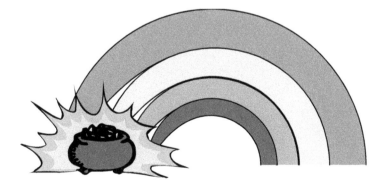

"If you love your job, you haven't worked a day in your life."
–Tommy Lasorda

Understanding The Concept

What is a Virtual Assistant?

A virtual assistant, or VA, is a highly-skilled professional who provides administrative support and other specialized services to businesses, entrepreneurs, executives, sales professionals, and others who have more work to do than time to do it.

VAs work as independent contractors, most from their own home, some from outside the home. VAs use leading-edge technology to communicate work assignments via the Internet, e-mail, disk transfer or such traditional methods as regular mail, overnight shipping, and even pick-up and delivery in local areas. A VA's services typically include Internet research, word processing, medical or legal transcription, database management, e-mail handling, reminder service, bulk mailings, information processing, and any other tasks typically given to the office secretary. Many VAs also provide web development, design and maintenance; meeting and event planning; desktop publishing; bookkeeping; social media, PR, marketing, shopping cart setup and maintenance; and business start-up consultations. The services are endless, depending upon the VA's knowledge, skills and creativity.

The late Thomas Leonard, who founded Coach U and later Coachville coined the term "virtual assistant." Thomas Leonard was a nationally recognized coach and speaker who bought a Winnebago and traveled all over the U.S. from meeting to meeting; and therefore, no longer had a brick and mortar building. Kelly interviewed him via telephone and was able to learn the following: Thomas had an assistant whom he had never met who managed his business, and his life, from afar. Since he had never met this assistant, he once referred to her as his "virtual assistant." From then on he used this term when encouraging other coaches and speakers to utilize the services of a virtual assistant. Before he passed away in 2003, he had partnered with several virtual assistants—most, if not all, of whom he never had the pleasure of meeting face-to-face.

While there seems to be no dispute over who coined the term "virtual assistant," you might find controversy over who was the first "official" virtual assistant. There have obviously been home-based secretaries and word processors dating back to the 1980s. However, when you consider the meaning of the word "virtual" in the computer science sense of the word, you think "computer." Until the popularity of computers, home-based secretaries may not have been thought of as being virtual until the mid-1990s, and that is only if they began to utilize this powerful tool called the Internet or if they even knew the term existed. The word "virtual" would also indicate no physical presence, therefore adding more meaning since we are not physically located in our client's office.

When comparing the role of a secretary to that of a virtual assistant, you will see similarities. However, the two can differ greatly. A secretary is thought to always be at the beck and call of her boss to administer such tasks as handling correspondence, maintaining files, fetching coffee, etc. It took many years for secretaries to begin getting the recognition they deserved as assistants to executives and other levels of management. As time goes on, more and more assistants are developing their skills, allowing them to become vital and trusted members of the business team. A virtual assistant working remotely doesn't allow the boss the luxury of having someone right outside his office door or to get his coffee, but they can become a vital part of the business team if the VA manages their business and the client relationship properly.

In Their Own Words:

Alyssa Gregory: A business owner who may provide a variety of skills that enable him/her to support their clients' businesses so they can become more organized, productive and profitable.

Andrea Pixley: In the traditional office, they are known as administrative assistants, but in the online community, they are known as virtual assistants. VAs work from their own offices, use their own equipment, and provide services to businesses, entrepreneurs, executives, or busy people. Assignments are usually communicated through e-mail, phone, fax, or mail. Whatever the project, information is easily transferred between client and virtual assistant.

Nora Rubinoff: Outsourced, off-site, administrative and technical support.

Nancy Seeger:Businesses providing assistive or specialized services contractually to independent and small businesses, artists, writers and other solo practitioners.

Donna Toothaker: My definition of a VA is someone who supports a small business owner or entrepreneur, virtually.

Susan Totman: Virtual assistants are administrative professionals providing administrative support virtually, sometimes globally, utilizing the technological age to its fullest to enable the businessperson to focus on their priority – growing their business.

Benefits to Clients

The benefits to your clients are numerous, as a good VA can actually make or break a business. You will be instrumental in your clients' marketing and promotional work, and also in keeping their office running smoothly and effectively. Many clients realize that they are spending too much time taking care of busy-work that they can't bill clients for, but still needs to be done, such as scheduling trips, planning meetings, researching the Internet for information, tracking expenses, paying bills and taxes, balancing the books, maintaining files, screening calls, and answering e-mails. A VA can save the clients' time because they will be spending less time doing that work and more time growing their business, having quality time with their family, or just plain relaxing. It's important for you to realize these benefits so that when asked, you can outline these benefits to your clients.

Scott Stratten is a speaker, trainer, and coach who encourages the use of VAs to his clients, in addition to utilizing his own VA. Scott had this to share with us: "It amazes me when I talk to some clients about hiring a VA to help ease their stress and time-management issues. They usually throw up the wall of 'can't afford it' or 'I don't have time to find one.' In reality, those are the reasons WHY YOU NEED ONE! I teach people to value their time and delegate tasks that aren't crucial to be a part of. If they have too much on their plate, they need a VA to sit at the table with them and help clear it or they'll never finish." Scott is the president of Un-Marketing (http://www.un-marketing.com) and Work Your Life (http://www.workyourlife.com).

Additionally, your clients can escape the hidden costs of having an employee, such as payroll taxes, sick time, chatting around the water cooler time, down time, and breaks. Since all VAs have their own office, clients don't have to pay for additional office equipment, computers or software. Also, clients no longer have to pay vacation time, holiday pay, and expensive benefit packages.

My clients have realized the importance of having someone outside the office handle all those tasks they can't seem to get done with their current staff, if they even have a staff. I have built partnerships that allow my clients to put their faith in me to handle routine tasks while they concentrate on what they do best.

If you're ever faced with a potential client that can't decide if having a VA is a good idea, ask them to take some time and jot down a list of what they like and dislike doing in their office. Review the list with them and explain how having a virtual assistant to take over all those tasks frees up their valuable time for more important matters, like generating business. Further explain that VAs can also take on tasks that clients don't mind doing, but should probably be delegated. We also recommend having potential clients complete a Client Self-Assessment form; see the Appendix for a sample.

Once a client realizes the benefits of partnering with a VA, the question then becomes "where do I find a VA?" Many clients who are seeking long-term help look for a VA who has graduated from one of the VA training programs. Other great places to find VAs are virtual assistant organization member directories. The following is a sample listing of directories. This list is not meant to be exhaustive by any means. Head over to your favorite search engine and search on the keywords "virtual assistant directories." There, you will find the most current and accurate listing.

- International Virtual Assistant Association (http://www.ivaa.org)
- Worldwide Directory of Virtual Office Assistants (http://www.eliteofficesupport.com)
- A Clayton's Secretary (http://www.asecretary.com.au/)
- Canadian VA Network (http://www.canadianva.net)
- Canadian Virtual Assistant Connection (http://www.cvac.ca)
- Alliance of UK Virtual Assistants (http://www.allianceofukvirtualassistants.org.uk)
- Virtual Assistant Forums (http://www.virtualassistantforums.com/directory/)

You will want to list your company in most, if not all, of these directories. Additionally, there may be a virtual assistant member group in your area you can get involved with that may also provide a directory for its membership.

Additional benefits to clients in partnering with a virtual assistant include:

- Saving them money by eliminating the expenses associated with hiring in-house staff. These expenses would include things like office space, equipment, payroll taxes, medical benefits, and paid vacation.
- Saving them time by providing support to complete the non-revenue generating tasks, affording the client time to focus on revenue-generating tasks.
- Saving them money because they only pay for time spent on task.
- Giving them access to experienced support with no training required. Training on proprietary systems can typically be minimized.
- Access to a professional business owner who is dedicated to helping them grow their business.

When speaking to prospective clients, keep in mind these specific tasks that VAs can do to benefit their clients. Of course, these benefits will vary based upon your particular service offering, but this will give you an idea.

- Type all correspondence, transcription, etc.
- Bookkeeping: invoice customers, receive and pay bills, reconcile bank statements, and keep track of expenses and tax records.
- Create and maintain electronic mailing lists for e-newsletters and correspondence.
- Maintain the company website and blog.
- Receive, screen, and send e-mail, faxes, and regular mail.
- Make and return phone calls.
- Schedule business and personal appointments and interviews.
- Maintain files for vendors and clients.
- Research and plan both business and personal trips.
- Create efficient office systems to create more space and streamline tasks.
- Make marketing calls and do other promotional work.
- Send reminders of important dates.
- Send out cards and gifts.
- Submit articles to online directories.
- Submit press releases to the media outlets.

Andrea Pixley states, "Who can benefit from using a virtual assistant?"

Small and home-based businesses

Your office will run more smoothly with scheduling and reminder services, and you can concentrate on expanding (instead of catching up) when you let us do your data entry and word processing.

Non-profit organizations

You can have your events planned, publicized, and organized for you.

Students

You no longer need to spend time researching topics or typing papers.

New parents

You don't have to make time to send out your personalized birth announcements and your family members can view your family photos on your own website.

Engaged couples

You can receive help with your wedding and reception planning and organizing. Have your announcements sent to local newspapers, invitations designed, printed, and mailed, thank-you notes written, and travel arrangements for the honeymoon taken care of.

Family, alumni, and military members

You can have your reunions planned and organized, video slide shows created as mementos, and newsletters sent out so you stay in touch.

Other types of businesses who can benefit from your service offering may include:

- **Churches** – presentations, newsletters, welcome packets, posting audio recordings to the web.
- **Consultants** – contact management, scheduling and calendar maintenance, mass mailings, newsletter production and distribution, social media management.
- **Architects and general contractors** – proposal management, scheduling, answering phones, contact management, payroll, bookkeeping.
- **Internet marketers** - article and blog management, linking, bookmarking, pay-per-click management, affiliate marketing and management, online advertising, content writing, proofreading, keyword searches, podcast editing and submission, etc, etc.
- **Training company** – transcription, podcast editing, marketing assistance.
- **Salon or Spa** – newsletter management, data entry, blog updates.

Here's what a couple of clients had to say about the benefits they have experienced in partnering with a virtual assistant:

John Finch, President, Resolve Associates, Int., an International Recruiting Firm

John, what are the main benefits of hiring a VA?

The first is time. Essentially it frees me up to do other things. Also, I don't have to be in the office. Whether I'm interviewing a client in Mexico, or composing a

Candidate Profile here at home, it doesn't matter. I can leave with confidence knowing that all my business obligations will be fulfilled.

The second is image. In today's environment you can't afford to make mistakes. Having a professional proofing my documents and also recommending changes when necessary is extremely beneficial. It's like getting a second opinion on your work. They can provide you with comments and suggestions on how to make the best impression.

They also get to know your business personally and are eager to help you succeed.

Overhead: I don't need to have an office set-up.

Having someone 24/7.

John, what services does your VA provide?

Well, I don't type. I have her handling all correspondence and other important word processing. Responding to e-mails for me.

I can call-forward my phones when I'm out of the country, and she can keep my business running successfully from her own office.

As I have a specialized program made specifically for my profession, I needed someone who could work with the program. Through PCAnywhere she is able to connect right into my computer.

Any disadvantages:

The camaraderie. Not having someone in the office to chat with.

Immediate projects. If something comes up that you need typed immediately, it can be a problem if she isn't home or working on another project for another client.

Sharon Simoncini, Vice-President, S&R Transfer

Sharon, what are the main benefits of hiring a VA?

I always receive high-quality work and I don't have to spend time correcting mistakes or overlooking the work that goes out. Also, she knows our business (sometimes even better than I think we do), and provides ideas and suggestions on how we can best succeed.

Also, she has all the equipment she needs so I don't have to worry if something breaks down that I'll need to fix it. Since it's her own business, she keeps everything in running order.

Plus, our business is seasonal, and we only have to pay for the time she works. In the summer, we don't have a lot of work, but, come January we are extremely busy. It's nice not to have to pay someone for time we don't need them.

In Their Own Words:

Tess Strand Alipour: Having a skilled service provider who has bootstrapped her own business to success, as a partner invested in growth is such an incredible asset to any business.

Alyssa Gregory: Clients are able to offload "outsourceable" work, create systems so that much of this work can be completed on autopilot, and free up time to focus on growing their business.

Nora Rubinoff: I talk about how my clients can "free themselves to work on their high payoff activities." We all know how important administrative and technical tasks and projects are to our business. But, small business owners and entrepreneurs are often working with a lean staffing structure. They need to be free to work in their area of subject matter expertise – that's where the money is for their business!

Nancy Seeger: Being able to choose more high-qualified, experienced contractors for only the time and services they need without the overhead of employer expenses associated with employees.

Donna Toothaker: Clients benefit from using a VA by having more time to focus on income-producing activities in their business when they let some more technical or administrative work go. They may also benefit from the VA's area of expertise, which could be anything from online marketing to bookkeeping.

Susan Totman: Lowers the overall cost of administrative support because they only pay for time used, and do not have to pay for benefits and other expenses as they would for a traditional employee.

Top 8 Ways a VA Can Save Time for Sales Professionals
How a VA can give you 225 more hours in front of your clients...

As a sales professional, you are faced with the daunting tasks of meeting sales quotas, satisfying clients, putting out client fires, preparing call reports, sending out literature, and following up on leads—just to name a few. Achieving these tasks while managing your life can be challenging at times. Achieving success in the world of sales is a challenge unto itself.

Making effective use of your time and resources is the key to overcoming these challenges and achieving success. Effective time management can offer a substantial increase in your revenue; not to mention a reduction in your stress level.

So how do you overcome these challenges and implement effective time management? Consider partnering with a virtual assistant. A virtual assistant, or VA, is an independent business professional offering administrative support and other specialized services to those who want to achieve growth in their business while saving time and money.

By partnering with a virtual assistant to keep you on track and to handle some, if not all, of those daunting tasks I touched on earlier, you can quickly save yourself as little as five hours per week – or more. That's right, just five hours a week, one hour per day! What could you do with that extra five hours per week? Make a few more sales calls, take a customer out to lunch, or maybe…take a day off for yourself. And, you'll save money in the process.

"Excessive and redundant paperwork is one of the biggest time wasters for sales people. Even if the paperwork is necessary, nothing is more wasteful than having a $150k salesperson spending selling time doing paperwork that could be done better by a much less expense administrative professional," states Barry Maher, author of "No Lie: Truth Is the Ultimate Sales Tool" (McGraw-Hill, 2003).

Let me give you an example:
- You make $100,000 a year (combined annual salary, bonuses, and commissions) = $55.55 per hour based upon a 225 day work year.
- You spend one hour per day, or 225 hours annually, on tasks that you shouldn't be handling yourself, which costs you $12,498.75 per year.
- Take that 225 hours and partner with a virtual assistant, at an average cost of $35 per hour, and you save over $4,600 per year PLUS you gain an extra 225 hours of time annually.

It's a win-win situation!

Now let's look at the specific tasks your VA can handle for you while you spend your time generating revenue, or taking some much-needed time for yourself. These Top 8 Ways were developed based on what I have identified as some of the biggest time-wasters for sales professionals. This list is in no particular order.

1. E-mail management
E-mail can be both beneficial and detrimental in conducting business today. It can be a distraction and a major time-hog. Turn your e-mail off and let your VA screen your e-mail. The VA can get rid of all the unwanted messages, handle routine responses and designate a special folder, or even a separate e-mail address, where messages are placed that need your attention.

2. Paperwork
Paperwork comes in many shapes and sizes. Aahhh...the vision and grandeur of a paperless office – NOT! While we'd like to think we could do away with paper, it's not as easy as it might sound. Your VA can be instrumental in organizing your mail, call reports, sales reports, faxes, and forms. Your VA can even do your filing. Yep, believe it or not, the filing—it really can be done without the VA being in your office.

3. Following up on leads
How many times have you gone to a trade show, returned to the office with a pile of leads, and never took the time to follow up on those leads? My hope for you is never, but, unfortunately, it does happen. Don't let those leads fall through the cracks. Your VA can enter them into your database as well as work with you to qualify the leads and organize them accordingly for follow up in person, or otherwise.

4. Sales meetings – planning and preparation
Meetings, meetings, and more meetings; at times, you think you're meeting to talk about the meeting. The good news is you don't have to spend the 48 hours prior to start time (with no sleep) preparing for the meeting. Call on your VA to prepare your presentation, put together any handouts, and do whatever research needs to be done. If you're the one running and planning the meeting, your VA can be instrumental in making all the arrangements, coordinating attendees, and ensuring that all attendees get the most out of the meeting in the least amount of time.

5. Literature fulfillment and mailings
Satisfying literature requests can take up a great deal of time. Your VA can prepare and ship your literature packets to potential or existing clients. Maybe you have a new product or service to announce? Let your VA prepare the mailing list, assemble the information packet, create the mailing, and take it to the post office for you.

6. Contact management
Contact management systems are great, but it takes a lot of time to keep them updated in order to remain effective. Let your VA maintain your database while you spend your time meeting with your contacts.

7. Marketing materials
Creating just the right look and feel of your marketing materials can be both costly and time consuming. Your VA can be instrumental in coordinating your brand across all marketing material. Whether it be coordinating the work with your vendor of choice or utilizing the expertise of your VA, you can be sure that you will look good in the eyes of prospects and clients.

8. Sample management
If a prospect requests a sample, then chances are you've generated a solid lead. No time to spend following up on those samples? Unsure of whether a sale was generated? Not a problem. Your VA can implement a system for tracking and following up to ensure you're getting the most out of your samplings.

Do You Have What It Takes?

Self-Employment Considerations

Here are some things you need to consider before you decide to start a business. We in no way want to discourage you from following your dream. However, we want you to be aware of these considerations, make sure they are not a problem, or if there is a problem, it's one that you can deal with and have the solution for prior to your starting date.

Even though your pay rate might be higher if you work at home, which it definitely should be, you won't have paid benefits, a pension plan, sick days, paid holidays, and other traditional employee perks. You will also be responsible for your own taxes. Let's examine some of these issues.

- **Taxes**—you will be responsible for your own taxes. It's important to be able to put money aside regularly for this. At some point, you will probably need to be paying quarterly taxes. You need to be disciplined in doing this. Many fall into this trap. You will be receiving payment for the work done. If you continually spend that full amount, come tax-time, you won't have the money put aside that you will need to pay your taxes and then your wonderful business becomes an overnight nightmare.

- **Insurance**—for many, you don't need to worry about insurance, as you will be covered under your spouse's plan. However, if this is not the case, then it is a consideration that you want to address prior to starting your business. I know many insurance plans for a couple and one child can run $500.00 to $600.00 a month. That is a major expense. We go more into detail later on in this book. However, for this chapter, this is another consideration.

- **Time**—you have to be disciplined. Many find it hard to leave work when it is only a few feet away or right down the hall. Most of the time, you can still hear the phone ringing and the tendency is to go look and see whose calling. What if you didn't finish something? Can you let it go and enjoy dinner with the family? These are things you want to address. You'll find that those "just a few minutes" add up. Soon you're spending the night in your office and your family is feeling neglected.

- **Family Support**—your decision to be self-employed is something that you should discuss in detail with all family members, not just your spouse, as it does affect everyone. Naturally, more time should be spent with your spouse. Don't get defensive. Keep in mind that although this is your dream come true; to them this is a paycheck that isn't coming in, a different lifestyle than they are accustomed to, and perhaps sacrifices that they aren't ready to make. If you go into this as a team, your chances of success are all the greater.

- **Office Space**—you'll have to provide your own office. Do you have sufficient space in your home or will you need outside office space? Maintaining an outside office will add to your overhead. You need space for equipment, filing, a desk area, office supplies and phone lines.

- **Isolation**—working in an office all day with a lot of people around can satisfy the human need for social interaction, even if you're not very fond of your co-workers.

Heading home to work in a bedroom converted to an office where no one is home all day is a totally different experience. When the clients are virtual and your new industry colleagues are hundreds of miles away, you can't meet in the break room for lunch. Are you prepared for less human interaction throughout the day? Can you stay focused on your work and avoid turning on the television for company?

- **Capital and Cash Flow**—getting into any kind of business requires some type of cash investment. Even if you have money saved or there is little needed for start up money, you're going to need money to live on while you ramp up your business. It is suggested you have three-six months reserve on hand. Take the time now to examine your available resources and any capital required.

- **Technical Support**—you won't have an IT department to run to for support when your computer crashes or you can't get a program to work properly. You may be one of the lucky ones who is very tech savvy and this isn't an issue at all. If you're not, you'll need to determine to whom you will look to for support on the technical side of business.

- **You Are The Boss**—when you go solo, you go solo. You're it—the chief cook and bottle washer. Are you prepared to make the decisions you need to make in your business and make them with confidence? Unless you are starting out with some kind of staff or a partner, chances are you are going to be responsible for running every aspect of your business by yourself. That's a huge responsibility. If you look at an organizational chart of a business, you will fill every role – marketing, sales, accounting, administration – and that's on top of doing the client work. Your responsibilities as a business owner go much deeper than just doing the work you love to do.

- **Feast or Famine**—one of the challenges of being in business is surviving the times when you are so busy you go absolutely insane to the times when the phone is just not ringing and the bank account dwindles down to nothing. The good news is that you can control this. Prepare now and have subcontractors and back-ups for when you get busy. Also, setup your business practices and procedures so that you can spend time doing what makes you money. Avoid the lean times by always marketing your business and networking. Try and have some extra money set aside for times that are routinely slow (like the holidays). Always focus on the positive.

Are You VA Material?

We're asked this question a lot. Someone is eager to start a business, but skeptical that they have what it takes. One of the first questions we reply with is, "Are you motivated and want to make this work?" If the answer is, "You betcha!" then we proceed to ask about their skills and knowledge of the business world. With the right motivation, most **CAN** succeed—(especially with the help of our book)! However, if the answer is, "Well, I own a computer, I have access to the Internet, and I own a few software programs with a printer—I can be a virtual assistant, everyone else is doing it," then we have to question the motivation for becoming a VA.

I think the dream of owning your own business and the freedom that comes along with it can sometimes cloud the reality that you might not be choosing the right business to start. Now is the time to do some real soul-searching and determine if becoming a VA is really what you want to do in life. A better way to look at it is to ask yourself, "If money were no object, am I choosing a career that allows me to do what I love to do?" Further, when you choose to start your own business it should not be considered a hobby. Yes, you might start part-time, but the commitment and desire for being a long-term viable business is highly important. If you don't take your business seriously, how can you expect others to do the same?

The virtual assistant industry is rapidly expanding and the desire to become a virtual assistant is fast becoming reality for a great many people. For this, we are thrilled. But, how many of those businesses are still around after six months, a year, or even two years? Did those who didn't make it take their business seriously? Did they constantly improve their skills, seek the proper training, and partake in the necessary networking opportunities? We have to remember that other professionals rely on us to help their business grow. Are you ready for that responsibility?

Not only do you need to have the skills to handle the services you will offer, but you must also have what it takes to be an entrepreneur. Let's first take a look at the characteristics of an entrepreneur:

- Do you have a strong desire to achieve?
- Are you willing to take risks?
- Do you possess self-confidence?
- Do you have a "passion for the business?"
- Can you accept challenges?
- Do you strive to be the best?

Next, consider the following personal traits:

- Are you a self-starter?
- Do you like to work with dynamic people?

- Are you confident about your ability to get the job done?

- Are you creative?

- Can you adapt to rapid change?

- Do you have good problem-solving skills?

- Can you set goals and follow them to completion?

- Can you handle multiple tasks at one time?

- Can you anticipate the needs of others?

- Are you a leader?

- Can you learn from your past mistakes?

- Can you work through problems and not dwell on them?

How did you do? Now would be a good time to ask yourself what additional positive traits you have and how you can best put them to use.

Here are some things you might ask yourself when you're contemplating whether or not to start a VA practice:

- **Are you a good time manager?** The impact of those two words will amaze you. Talk to any virtual assistant in business today and they will tell you just what an impact it can have on your business. You have to know how to manage your time. DEADLINES!! INTERRUPTIONS!! FAMILY CRISES!! SHOPPING!!! (Only kidding, just wanted to see if you were listening!) It's crucial to have your day planned out in advance, while at the same time not crumble when someone throws a wrench in your schedule. You need to be the type of person who can do this.

- **Do you have excellent typing and proofing skills?** This is very important to your business. You are your business; therefore, you want to do your absolute best in ensuring that all documents are as close to perfection as possible. That includes correspondence with potential or existing clients, as well as your VA associates. Don't feel that you need to be a super fast typist—that's not necessary. The main key is to be a good typist and a good proofreader. Your speed will increase with time.

- **Do you already know several people who could utilize your services?** Many VAs are fortunate to already know clients who want to utilize their services. It can be past employers, friends or acquaintances at church. This is definitely an added plus because you then have money coming in immediately.

- **Are you capable of making a great income and will stop at nothing to make it happen?** I always knew when I was working at my secretarial positions that I should be making more than I was, and I wanted to make more. However, in the typical secretarial jobs you were lucky to get a $1.00 to $2.00 raise a year. I loved it when I was finally able to make the kind of income I deserved. Now that's what I'm worth. How about you? With your skills and experience, how much do you think you're worth?

- **Do you enjoy helping people?** What a wonderful feeling it is to help other businesses succeed. I have always targeted new businesses and in doing so I am able to see them grow and become great successes. My experience enables me to help develop their business image in a positive manner.

- **Do you have self-discipline?** Working solo means you will be accountable to yourself and to your clients to complete the necessary assignments in a timely fashion all on your own. You'll be relied upon to be the highly skilled professional with the right knowledge and expertise to do the work. If you're accustomed to working with a team headed by a manager that keeps you on track, or if you're typically reliant on co-workers to complete a project, you'll need to adjust your work habits and your mindset accordingly.

- **Can you work in isolation?** Working in an office environment with any number of co-workers around provides a necessary human social interaction. When you're the only one at home all day with work to do and no one to talk to, it can be quite challenging. You'll need to be mentally prepared to not have the same interaction. Of course, you will have the freedom of no office politics to look forward to!

- **Are you a decision maker?** As a business owner you will have you and only you to rely on for making decisions about your business. You have to think on your feet and stand by your decisions, good or bad. You're undoubtedly going to make mistakes, and that's okay, the key is to learn from them and adjust as needed. The good news is you won't have anyone there to question or judge your decisions.

- **Are you a good communicator?** When working in a virtual environment, you'll find that good communication is even more critical. You won't always have the benefit of face-to-face conversations where body language is visible or voice inflection is present. You'll be providing services to clients you've never even met in person. Having the ability to communicate clearly, succinctly, and professionally, in both written and verbal forms will keep you on the road to success.

- **Do you know how best to utilize your talents to keep systems up and running?** You wear many hats as an entrepreneur. You need to know how to manage things when they go right and wrong.

According to a 2009 study by the U.S. Small Business Administration Office of Advocacy, there are 29.6 million small businesses across the country. Of that, 52% are home–based businesses. Are you ready to join this growing population?

Keep reading!

Skills Required

Naturally, the more skills you have, the better off you are. However, keep in mind that you can customize your business to fit your individual skills. The good thing about owning your own VA business is you get to choose your clients. What clients could best use your particular skills?

Every virtual assistant has his or her own unique skills and experience that enables them to start their business. The right skills are those that you have perfected and can perform well. As you further develop your skills, you can expand your service offering. It is not recommended that you offer services you are not able to support. Should a client ask you to perform a task that you are not proficient at, consider one of the following:

- Advise the client that you do not offer that service but you would be happy to find them a VA who can.

- Establish a network of other virtual assistants with complementary services and subcontract the work.

- Advise the client that you do not offer the service but you are willing to learn. Leave it up to them if they are willing to go through the learning process with you. You'll also want to consider lowering your rate or not charging the client at all for the learning time if it is a skill that will benefit your overall service offering—not if it's something exclusive to this client's line of work.

Accepting a job that you do not have the skills to support can get you into trouble. It's often hard to say no when we are desperately seeking income and that first client. To be up front with the client and offer alternative solutions, like referring to another VA, is much more professional. They will respect you for not entering into a task you cannot perform.

VA skills range from the basics, such as typing, to highly specialized areas like:
- Web design
- Graphic arts
- Technical writing
- Social media management
- Shopping cart setup and maintenance
- Internet marketing
- Accounting
- Copywriting
- Search engine optimization
- Article marketing
- Legal and medical transcription
- Project management
- IT support
- Business consulting

A professional VA will be proficient in the Internet, computers, software, word processing and spreadsheet applications. In addition to the technical skills, a professional VA will have good business management skills as well as knowledge of:

- Marketing
- Advertising
- Record keeping
- Public relations
- Collections
- Budgeting
- Customer Service

Business management skills not only help you in operating your own business, but also allow you to aid your clients in running theirs.

If you are re-entering the workforce after an extended leave, you might find that a few of your skills are a little rusty, but you still excel in other areas. Start off by offering only those services you excel in while you catch up on those rusty skills, and learn some new ones.

For assistance, for assessing your skill set in a variety of areas we recommend a visit to Brainbench, http://www.brainbench.com. Brainbench is a skills testing site offering certification in areas such as MSWord, MSExcel, Business Writing, Written English, and so on. The tests are timed and taken right over the Internet with the results returned to you immediately. The results of the test will reveal your strengths and weaknesses in the topic chosen, as well as how you ranked against others that have taken that test. And, you can retake the test to improve your score. Brainbench keeps a transcript of your test scores that you can send to potential clients. Once you have passed a test, you can receive a certificate by mail and you will have access to graphics that can be placed on your website attesting to your certification. You can also add a link to your online transcript.

VAs must be motivated. You can't get discouraged when you experience minor setbacks. Start fresh each day. If the phone didn't ring yesterday, make it ring today. Failure is not an option. You need to know that you're going to make it and stop at nothing short.

Jan Melnik says it so well in her book, *How To Start a Home-Based Secretarial Services Business,* "High energy level and good health should accompany your own motivation and drive to succeed."

Good organizational skills are also important. You will need the ability to juggle multiple priorities, work assignments and often children at the same time. The key is to stay focused. Don't jump ahead to the other assignments that need to be done or think about your son's baseball game. Manage your social networking time and don't let it become a distraction in your day. Concentrate only on the work you are working on now. Once you complete that, you can move on.

Barbara Rowen: I have worked as a word processor, litigation secretary and legal assistant for sole practitioners as well as small and medium-sized law firms for more than 25 years. I was confident I could provide the kind of services small business owners needed. Once I finally decided who I really wanted to work for (and who I didn't want to work for), the rest was easy. I've always had the ability to pick up computer concepts and programming quickly, which has definitely worked to my advantage in this ever-changing environment.

Nora Rubinoff: I had been in business administration, office management, personal computing skills, and computer networking (LAN) prior to starting my business.

Nancy Seeger: Former arts administration manager with orchestras, 16 years including ticket sales, personnel, finance, programs, concert touring, marketing, website & graphics layout work. In a small orchestra, you learn to do a little of everything and specialize as you rise in the ranks.

Donna Toothaker: I had little administrative experience, but had superb organizational skills, as well as customer service/support skills and experience.

Susan Totman: Prior to 1987, I had several years of administrative experience and had taken college business courses as well as completed a two-year program of vocational training specifically in office support. Throughout the 80s and 90s I worked for several years in office administration in both the legal and automotive arenas.

Making the Switch to the Mac
By Nora Rubinoff

Interest in the Mac platform is growing in the virtual assistant industry. More VAs are exploring either a switch to Mac or adding a Mac to their office network. Some VAs have come to this decision because they don't want to implement the new Windows Vista operating system. Some are at this point because they have more clients who own Macs. Some are influenced by Apple's aggressive and successful Mac and PC commercials. And some, like me, reach this point because they are tired of spending so much time tweaking Windows, keeping things secure and rebooting after lock ups.

According to Apple Watch on eWeek, "Apple's retail market share is 14 percent, and two-thirds for PCs costing $1,000 or more." "Windows desktop PC sales are way down," writes Joe Wilcox. Stephen Baker, NPD Group vice president of industry analysis states, "in notebooks they're [Apple] growing two times the market. Windows notebooks are pretty much flat right now." According to Baker, for the first quarter, Windows notebooks had "zero percent" growth year over year, while by comparison, Apple notebooks had "50 to 60 percent growth."

In February 2007, I decided I was fed up with Windows. Vista's launch was imminent, and I knew I did not want to implement it on my office computers. I bought an iMac.

I will not lie — the first week of migrating data from my legacy PC to my iMac was time consuming, and moving Outlook, even with Little Machines' inexpensive O2M application, was a real pain. A fundamental mistake that I made: I stayed "open" during the migration time. This meant I was bouncing between iMac and legacy PC, since some data was moved and some was not yet there. If you make the switch, I strongly recommend you don't do it that way. Close your office for a few days until you are all set.

I still have my PC connected to my network, and I use a KVM switch between my iMac and PC so that I can share a mouse and keyboard. Occasionally — very, very occasionally — I still use my legacy PC. For the most part though, it's been retired to act as a TiVO server for our household.

Here are 5 reasons why I'm happy I've switched to Mac:

1. **Every day I come into my office and get to do much more of what I'm there to do each day — work!** Windows requires constant vigilance to keep your system buttoned up tight. Even though I used the best security protection available for anti-virus, anti-ad and spy ware as well as a firewall, new challenges pop up almost daily on the PC platform as new viruses etc. are released and the security software companies must keep up. I also spend less time "tweaking" my system for performance issues and can go <u>weeks</u> without needing to reboot.

It's simple math: **More Work + Less Fussing With My System = More Billable Hours**. Mac computers, by and large, just work, they are lower maintenance and have a much greater mean time between failures. What a concept!

2. Many of my clients are PC-based. If a client's security is not as tight as mine, I might receive the "gift" of a virus or trojan on work files they send. Most viruses and trojans are written for Windows. My alternate operating system adds an extra layer of security. (Note to Mac users — just because most viruses, etc. are written for PCs doesn't mean you shouldn't have good anti-virus and firewall projection installed on your Mac!)

3. I can do everything I need to do on a Mac. Office apps are compatible, for the most part. I can track time for my VA business using OfficeTime, an equivalent of TraxTime, a time tracking app many PC-based VAs use. I can use Mac versions of most software VAs are already familiar with, such as Dreamweaver, FTP programs like CuteFTP, Adobe Acrobat, Photoshop, web browsers like Firefox and Opera, instant messenger and so forth. More companies are realizing the importance of offering software on both the Mac and PC platform. And, with the rise of Web 2.0 and SAAS (Software As A Service) apps like Google Documents, Basecamp and Salesforce.com, operating system boundaries are becoming a thing of the past.

4. When I need a PC, I can launch Parallels or VMWare Fusion and emulate a PC in a window on my Mac. This has come a long way in recent years on the Mac platform. Parallels will set you back a mere $80, and VMWare Fusion is about the same price. Both let you do anything you need without having to fire up your old legacy PC. In Parallels on my iMac, I have my scanner, printers, microphone, video camera and other peripherals installed as well. With just a few clicks, you can be using Windows if you need it. Sharing files between Windows in Parallels and my iMac is a breeze using Parallels Tools.

5. Applications are in some cases cheaper. Sure, as a PC user you may not have heard of Acorn (a nimble image editing app for small, quickie edits), OmniGraffle Pro (which runs circles around Visio, in my humble opinion — and exports in Visio XML format) or Yep (imaging for small offices — think PaperPort only not nearly as much of a system resource hog), but in my office, those apps, as well as others, keep me productive without being hogs on my Mac or drains on my wallet. All the function — and in some cases even *more* function — for a fraction of the price and a fraction of the bloat on my system.

Whether you are thinking about making the switch to the Mac or you are just considering adding a Mac to your existing office network, you'll find a wealth of resources online to help ease the transition. With more virtual assistants making the switch, you'll find a growing connection with colleagues who are finding enhanced productivity and therefore increased billable time for their practices.

At Your Service Cincinnati principal Nora Rubinoff's core virtual assistant services include project management, customer relationship management, customized e-mail marketing campaigns and productivity enhancement. Nora holds the IVAA EthicsCheck™ certification and serves as a board member for IVAA. www.aysweb.com

Training

There are many avenues you can take with regard to training. Let's first focus on getting training as a virtual assistant. Most VAs have received a great deal of training through current or past employers. Some have received formal education through secretarial schools as well as accredited colleges. A great many of us have gained a vast amount of knowledge through numerous channels, including the school of hard knocks. It could be that you know everything you may need to know about being a business owner, and an assistant, but you just aren't sure how to apply your knowledge and skills to the "virtual" world. Don't fret—there is hope!

At the time of writing our first book there were just a few VA training programs. Today, there are a great number of training resources dedicated to becoming a virtual assistant. We recommend Academy of Virtual Professionals (http://www.AcademyVP.com), which offers training and personal coaching based on this very book and a range of other courses, including a course on transitioning practices.

There are also a growing number of colleges adopting VA Certificate programs to their curriculums. Check out your local college, visit http://www.VA-TheSeries.com for a listing of colleges utilizing this book, and look online for distance learning opportunities.

For training in a broad range of subjects beneficial for the virtual assistant to further develop their skill set you'll want to check out places like http://www.vaclassroom.com or http://www.lynda.com. And, keep in mind that many software companies offer tutorials and videos on their websites. You can find lots of tips and tricks for specific software features on http://www.YouTube.com, as well.

Practice Pay Solutions (http://www.practicepaysolutions.com) offers training specifically for using their shopping cart system, which is actually a private label system also known as 1shoppingcart.com, kickstartcart.com and several other names.

When selecting a training program, we recommend that you check them out very carefully. Consider the following when seeking a qualified training instructor or program (and be sure to check the references of former students):

- Is the instructor a practicing VA?
- What is their background?
- How long have they been in business?
- Do they have prior experience in training?

For medical, legal, business basics, software, and other training, you can take classes at various adult education classes, online or at a very well-known school called At-Home Professions (http://www.at-homeprofessions.edu). It has an excellent reputation in the following specialties: Legal Transcription, Medical Transcription, Secretarial/Word Processing, Bookkeeping, Paralegal Training, and Computer Basics. They provide all the needed materials including books, lessons, and learning aids.

Coaching is an excellent means to obtain training. It enables the VA to get individual personalized attention and to get answers to questions as they arise. The personalized touch is very much appreciated by the VA as they are able to get specific help in targeting their market more effectively, generating a proposal for a client, identifying their niche, and much more. We both offer coaching and have found it very beneficial to the VA to jumpstart their business. To get the most out of working with a coach, it helps to be as honest as possible. Know that the training will come from them, but you will need to do the work. Also, be organized and consistent. Take great notes to implement what you learn as soon as you're able. To find out more about our individualized coaching, send an e-mail to authors@va-theseries.com.

While assessing your skills in the beginning is important, continuing education is equally important to your success. It's not enough to simply assess your skills for the purpose of starting your business. Technology is constantly changing and as a highly successful VA you'll want to be on the leading edge of technology. It's not necessary to be proficient at everything; nor, is it necessary to own every piece of software on the market, but knowing the right resources will prove valuable to your continued success as a business owner.

Continuing education can be in the form of taking classes online or offline, attending business conferences, attending industry conferences, participating in webinars, teleclasses, or reading a book.

In Their Own Words:

Tess Strand Alipour: None specific to administration. I did have a few years of retail management experience, so there was some office admin and bookkeeping in that.

Shane Bowlin: In 1997, I enrolled in the Virtual Training Program at AssistU.com. I earned their Certified Professional Virtual Assistant (CPVA) designation.

Jeannine Clontz: When I first started out in 1998, I took a refresher course in Secretarial Studies through "At Home Professions" to be sure that I was still at the top of my game, and in touch with new technological advances. I also took a class in Legal Transcription at our local community college. Since then, I have focused on VA certifications. I have my IVAA CVA (Certified Virtual Assistant through IVAA.org); MVA (Master Virtual Assistant through VACertification.com); EthicsChecked™ (through Staffcentrix, now being offered at IVAA.org); CRESS (Certified Real Estate Support Specialist through IVAA.org); PREVA (Professional Real Estate VA through REVANetwork.com); and CRVA (Certified Realtor.com Virtual Assistant through Realtor.com). I purchased a club membership at my local New Horizons Training Center, which has provided me with in-depth software training in many of my Microsoft and Adobe software packages.

Nora Rubinoff: I attended VAU, and I've taken a number of online courses and seminars through the years. Most VAs don't need education on how to use their computer, software, etc. – what they need is assistance on how to run an online or internet-based business. That's where education was important to me.

Donna Toothaker: No VA training, but consistently took business courses. For me, it was 'easy' to provide the VA services, so it was more important that I learn how to build/grow the business aspect effectively.

Susan Totman: By the time I became a full-time VA in 1999 after 12 years doing it part-time, in addition to developing and refining both general secretarial as well as office management and administrative skills, I was well-equipped to start and manage my own business.

Certification

Becoming certified in any profession indicates to others that you are held to a certain level of standards for your particular industry. The virtual assistant industry is no exception. By obtaining certification, you will receive the recognition and respect from clients and peers that you possess a higher level of experience in the industry. In addition, you will be telling clients that you take your business very seriously and that you are committed to upholding the standards of the VA industry. While certification offers a degree of distinction, it will not make or break your success as a VA. Don't let this trip you up and get in the way of getting your business started. We feel it's useful, but not absolutely necessary.

The biggest challenge in the VA industry for certification is that there is no real governing body to oversee the industry as a whole. There is no standardized testing or criteria for achieving the certification other than what the organization or groups of individuals offering a test or assessment of qualifications defines. A college certificate program is of course accredited per their state institution's requirements.

Susan Totman shares with us that she has received great value in obtaining her certification. "I became certified as a Master Virtual Assistant because I thought it would further my goal of becoming one of the best out there. Though there are many people out there that do not believe certification is necessary or even beneficial, I can tell you – it WAS. I have retained many clients because of that certification. The process at the time was rigorous and I had to provide evidence that I was worthy of the certification with strong references to back it up. It was not an easy process, but was well worth the effort."

Here are some groups who issue certification in the VA industry:

- International Virtual Assistant Association (IVAA) members can take an exam to become a Certified Virtual Assistant, or CVA. They also offer EthicsCheck certification and CRESS, Certified Real Estate Support Specialist. http://www.ivaa.org

- AssistU graduates can obtain one of two different designations based upon the level of training they receive through AssistU and the number of hours working in the industry. AssistU designations include that of a Certified Professional Virtual Assistant, or CPVA, and the Certified Master Virtual Assistant, or CMVA. http://www.assistu.com

- Accredited Secretaries Online - ASO with ACS is committed to promoting its accreditation process and its accredited members through government bodies, bureau, corporations, suppliers, general media and the industry at large. Such an approach enhances: (1) Credibility - Recognition as a professional in the industry will attract the respect of suppliers and buyers; (2) Awareness - The wide promotion of ASO accreditation will identify the individual as an achiever; (3) Career Path - ASO accreditation lies with the individual and is therefore portable as and when the individual changes jobs within the industry. It should be recognized as a mark of professionalism by clients, employers and potential clients and employers; (4) Self-Esteem - A sense of achievement contributes to self-esteem, confidence, high standards and ethical practice; and (5) Promotion - Status as an ASO will enhance promotional opportunities, which will help win business. http://www.asecretary.com.au/

- Certified Canadian Virtual Assistant, or CCVA, is offered to members of the Canadian Virtual Assistant Connection.

In the more traditional world of executive assistants and administrative assistants, there are certifications offered by the International Association of Administrative Professionals: CPS or Certified Professional Secretary and CAP or Certified Administration Professional. http://www/iaap-hq.org.

What Services Can You Offer?

When starting a VA business, one of your first considerations is what services you want to provide. What you want to do is match your skills and talents with the right clients who can best utilize them. Think about a year or so from now, who do you want your clientele to consist of? Who is your ideal client?

There is great debate over whether or not a VA should specialize or always remain general in their service offering. When first getting started it's hard to keep yourself from wanting to list every possible thing you know how to do as a service you provide, even if you don't particularly like to do that task. Remember, you're the one in control of your work, not your employer who hands you a job description. Only offer the things you like to do—first and foremost! Just because you state in your marketing materials that you offer this service or that service does not mean that the opportunity will not arise for you to cross sell your other talents as services. A visitor to your website may take a liking to you and still make contact to see if you offer something that's not listed as a service on your site. You'll want to target a particular industry with a set of services or a particular service to a wide range of industries.

So how do you choose? That's strictly up to you. Sometimes identifying what you don't like to do will help narrow the field. If you've just spent the last 10 years as an executive assistant to the president of a Fortune 500 company, you're more likely to offer general administrative tasks to any type of company. On the other hand, if you just spent 15 years as the office manager for a small insurance company, your expertise will lie in knowing the ins and outs of the insurance industry, making insurance agents ideal clients for you to be of service to. It could be that you spent 20 years working for attorneys, and you couldn't bear to spend another millisecond of your life involved in the legal world. Maybe you want to make a complete change, and build your skill set to complement your knowledge and expertise in another area. The key is to do what works for you and makes you happy in your business. You'll also find the SWOT Analysis later in the book can help you to focus in on a niche.

Keep in mind that nothing is set in stone. You can change your service offering at any point in time. Most likely, after a few years in business, you'll look back at your original service offering and see that major changes took place. You might even get a chuckle out of it and say, "What in the world was I thinking!"

Following is a sampling of services you may want to consider, along with a brief description of each. These services can be combined or specialized in any manner depending upon your skills. This is certainly not an all-inclusive list, these are merely some of the more noteworthy and common services offered.

- **Association Management:** Meeting minute transcription, meeting reminder cards or calls, database management, meeting agendas, meeting and convention planning, newsletters, mailing services, bookkeeping, and banking services.

- **Competitive Research**: Research clients' competitors and report findings.

- **Concierge Services**: Dinner recommendations and reservations, tickets, travel research and arrangements, transportation arrangements, directions, gift buying, car rentals, general errand running.

- **Contact Management:** Maintain client database of contacts using a variety of applications, both online and offline.

- **Desktop Publishing**: Design and layout of business cards, newsletters, flyers, catalogs, brochures, menus.

- **Digital Imaging**: Digital photography, graphic design, scanning of documents, photographs, etc.

- **Editing/Proofreading**: Editing and proofreading client documents.

- **Event Planning**: Organizing all or various aspects of an event. This might include arranging for a venue, food and beverage or catering, contract negotiations, special transportation, security, and entertainment.

- **Executive Personal Assistant**: Combination of duties with a high level of decision-making, coordination, purchase authority, on behalf of the company executive(s).

- **File Conversion**: Convert files from one format to the other. Example: Word to PDF format.

- **General bookkeeping**: Process and mail invoices and statements. Bill paying, checkbook balancing, collection calls, bookkeeping, etc.

- **Graphic Design**: Designing images for use on the web or in print.

- **Information Processing**: Combination of word processing, data processing, database management, spreadsheets, and resume preparation.

- **Internet Administration**: Administration of chat rooms, message boards, and online groups.

- **Internet Marketing:** Assist clients in marketing their products and services in the online world.

- **Internet Research**: Research and report findings on specific topics. You can do academic research, business and marketing research, locator services (alumni, family, military, etc.)

- **Interpreting**: Translate from one language to another.

- **Meeting Planning:** Organizing all or various aspects of a meeting. This might include arranging meeting space, A/V requirements, speakers, food and beverage, sleeping rooms, contract negotiations, and transportation.

- **Organizing Consultant:** Rearrange office space, plan and pack for relocation, develop procedures, set up filing systems, time management, and office automation.

- **Photocopying**: Black and white or color copies.

- **Presentations**: Preparing slide presentations in a program such as Microsoft PowerPoint. Requires knowledge of the application, as well as presentation techniques. Might also include preparation of handouts and transparencies. Slides can show birthdays, business/marketing, graduations, weddings, etc.

- **Public Relations**: Writing and submitting press releases. Arranging interviews with the media. Promote the general "image" of the company.

- **Realtor Support**: Includes desktop publishing, bulk mailings, database management, letter writing, thank-you card writing, and making phone calls. See also, Transaction Coordinator.

- **Reminder Service**: Remind clients of important dates and events.

- **Scheduling**: Arrange and manage schedule for meetings, deadlines, appointments, and possibly personal activities.

- **Shopping cart setup and maintenance:** Ecommerce solutions, affiliate programs, autoresponders, products, and other such items associated with purchasing products online.

- **Social Media Management**: Setup and maintenance of blogs, Facebook, Twitter, and LinkedIn profiles, event responses, and fan pages.

- **Systems Management**: Manage system network.

- **Technical Support**: Hardware and software installation, maintenance, troubleshooting, and tutoring.

- **Teleclass and Webinar Management:** Coordinate all aspects of teleclasses and webinars.

- **Transaction Coordinator**: Realtor listing management, marketing/mail-out program coordination and contract-to-close processing. Can involve use of online transaction management programs.

- **Transcription**: Transcribing standard and micro-cassette tapes as well as digital audio files. Medical, legal and general transcription.

- **Web Design, Development and Maintenance**: Design client websites. May include development of copy and ongoing maintenance.

- **Word Processing**: Many of the chapters in this book deal with this, including Legal Transcription, Medical Transcription, Targeting Writers, etc.

- **Writing**: Business, technical, academic, resume, and ghost writing. Includes formatting papers and manuscripts, as well as business plans and reports.

In Their Own Words:

Shane Bowlin: I work primarily with authors, speakers, and celebrities to offer a variety of Concierge Services. For example: coordinating all aspects of travel arrangements, detailed complete itineraries, accommodations, tracking frequent flyer and guest programs. I also work hand-in-hand with publishers, agents, and publicists doing the following: book tours, media promotion, follow up reimbursements, marketing, off-line and on-line print and broadcast media, books, tapes, misc. products, off-line and on-line distribute marketing materials, following up on leads and generating new ones, presentations, book signings, and speaking engagements.

Jeannine Clontz: I allow businesses and departments to develop, market and promote their business by providing "as needed" administrative support. I offer word processing, desktop publishing, transcription (trained for legal), manuscripts, database management, mailing services, resumes, general bookkeeping, Internet research and more!

Alyssa Gregory: Because of the team-based approach I take, I consider myself a full-service VA firm. With the support of my team members, we can tackle just about any need a client may have, and if we can't we know how to locate the resources we need.

Kathy Ritchie: Complete virtual office assistance to include: word processing, desktop publishing, graphic and heraldic designs, spreadsheets, Internet research/ investigations, crossword/wordsearch puzzle creation, manuscripts, manuals, newsletters and more.

Barbara Rowen: I provide administrative and secretarial services to small and home-based businesses, including business writing, word processing, editing and proofreading, desktop publishing, Internet research and contact management services.

Nora Rubinoff: We offer services to both Mac and PC-based users – we're bilingual! Our certified Master Virtual Assistant services include project management, customer relationship management, customized e-mail marketing campaigns, research and analysis, productivity enhancement, social media and new media support, WordPress blog creation and support, online reputation management, presentations and other virtual office services. Additionally, we offer affordable small business web design and web hosting including green and carbon neutral web hosting, website redesign and website maintenance.

Nancy Seeger: Customized website design for unique look, advanced level coding adhering to today's web standards, graphic layout for publications.

Susan Totman: Currently my services are project-based, including research, database development, web development, and small business consulting.

Services to Complement Your VA Practice

Paralegal: This is a perfect opportunity for a VA to expand her services. You can easily do most aspects of paralegal work via the Internet. You will want to emphasize this on your website. The attorneys at the offices that I work for simply e-mailed the information that needed to be compiled into a pleading; the paralegal composed it and e-mailed it back to the attorney's office. They have done this on numerous occasions.

You can be instrumental in doing their researching as well. You can research, then summarize your findings and e-mail it to the attorney's office. Many paralegals are responsible for complete pleading preparation. One thing that many do state though is that they often get weekend work and rush jobs. Given the nature of your business, you should decide if that would be an inconvenience.

Referral Services: Many virtual assistants have capitalized on this by offering referral services in addition to their business. If they can't do the job, then they refer it to someone who can. The person accepting the work then pays a small referral fee.

Nina Feldman, of Nina Feldman Connections, has been brokering to other word processors/desktop publishers since 1981. She is known to have "invented" this type of service. She states:

> "We all know how hard it is to turn down work. In order to avoid sending those extra customers into the 'wild blue yonder,' during my first few years in business I developed a small network of independent word processors with whom I could share the overflow. When clients call me with jobs for which I'm too busy or that require a software or skill I don't have, I find word processors in my network who fit the clients' needs."

She has set up her referral service to collect a percentage of the job from the VA once completed. She prefers this arrangement over subcontracting the work out because when you subcontract, the work that leaves your office must meet your own high standards. This requires proofing the work before giving it to the client. If the subcontractor is sick or does a bad job, you end up typing or correcting the assignment.

If you think you'd like to speak with Nina in reference to this, please contact her via e-mail at connections@ninafeldman.com or stop by her website at http://www.ninafeldman.com. She also markets the Brenner Pricing Guidelines.

Personalized Specialty Letters: Many VAs now spice up their businesses during the holidays. Personalized, specialty letters are not only a treat for children, but also a good source of revenue for VAs. Letters can come from Santa, the Easter Bunny, the Tooth Fairy, or whatever you can imagine.

Success and repeat orders for personalized specialty letters is achieved by one's ability to remember the age of 4 or 5. To produce a quality letter, one must be able to think like the child, and also be prepared for some diligent work. This is not something you can whip out in a few minutes. There is a lot to know and do in creating and marketing letters that will be taken to school to show off to peers. You must also remember that when marketing, you need to do your marketing well in advance so that the actual letters, etc. will be received at the appropriate time.

Newsletters and Other Publications: Many VAs also enhance their practice and share their expertise by creating newsletters. It's an excellent addition, especially for those who love the creativity. You can offer advertising and promote affiliate programs to generate another stream of revenue for your business.

Social Media Marketing: Social media is not just for celebrities! It's quickly becoming a necessary business tool for all. Many VAs specialize in providing social media marketing. This includes blogging for clients as well as posting to Facebook, updating LinkedIn profiles, maintaining wikis, and managing Twitter accounts.

Print Broker: Ideal source of additional revenue for those who offer desktop publishing or typesetting requiring the services of an outside printing company. Contact a couple of printers and set up an agreement with the printer for commission, or a discount on all jobs you source through their company.

Online Transaction Coordinator: Working with the realtors and becoming a transaction coordinator is an exciting field you can look into. The VA and the realtor work together by managing the many facets associated with buying or selling a home. Working with either the buying or selling agent, the VA maintains all the listing information, coordinates inspections and appraisals, gathers all the necessary documents to the transaction, provides necessary follow-up, and makes all responsible parties accountable for their tasks. (See Chapter on Real Estate Industry.)

Information Products: In the information age we live in, it's tough not to try to capitalize on your expertise by providing information products as a subject matter expert. This can include hosting teleseminars, creating e-books, writing books, and a host of other mediums for delivery print and digital content. Creating joint ventures with your clients and other colleagues can prove beneficial in creating information products.

SendOutCards.com: Many virtual assistants have added this service of sending out cards for clients and become SendOutCards representatives. With so many clients wanting to do follow up, it's a great way to capitalize on something that needs to be done regularly, while also adding to your income.

Getting Started!

Type Of Business Entity To Set Up

The very first thing you need to do when you finish reading this book is to go out and get Bernard Kamoroff's book *Small Time Operator: How To Start Your Own Business, Keep Your Books, Pay Your Tax and Stay Out of Trouble!"* He's just completed a new edition. I've used it for years and whenever a question arises I almost always can find the answer there. It greatly enabled me to understand the business side of my business.

With that said, let's move on to the legalities of starting your home business. Let's first start with which type of business entity to set up. There are several different legal structures from which you can choose to set up your business. These are the **sole proprietorship, the partnership, and the corporation**. Each has its own particular advantages and disadvantages, depending on your situation.

Bernard Kamoroff states is his book, *Small Time Operator,* "There are over 20 million small businesses in this country, and most of them are sole proprietorships." In researching for this book, I found that many VAs set up their business as a sole proprietorship. I believe that's because it's the easiest to set up and also the easiest to keep records for. With a sole proprietorship, you simply start doing business. This allows you the opportunity to make the decisions, run the business, keep the profits, and requires less legal requirements. As long as you run an honest business, keep good records, and pay your taxes, most VAs should be fine as a sole proprietorship. However, this is one business decision each individual VA should make for their VA business. In addition to the information provided here, go online to the message boards, attend chats, and talk with others. It will just provide the added confidence you might need to make the right choice.

The Sole Proprietorship

The sole proprietorship is a business structure where the business is owned and operated by only one person. LaDonna D. Vick states in her book, *A Self-Publisher's Guide to Publishing Your Own Book, E-Book, or Booklet,* "A sole proprietorship means you are running the business as the sole owner and any tax or legal actions of that business go directly to you as if you did everything as an individual. It is the simplest business to start and maintain."

To establish a sole proprietorship all you need to do is obtain whatever licenses are needed in your local area to begin operations. Some counties will combine your licensing and registrations. Laws vary from state to state, so we recommend obtaining information on how to get licensed for your particular area through your county clerk, occupational licenses department, or your Secretary of State. They will usually be able to guide you to the proper offices for the proper paperwork and registration. Often, they have a kit prepared and you just need to follow the instructions provided. Visit http://www.VA-TheSeries.com for links to state resources for starting a business.

It should also be noted that along with being your own boss there are responsibilities that go along with it. All business decisions, all business debt incurred, etc., belong to you alone. You and your business are one and the same, so make smart decisions. Be aware that any damages from any lawsuit can be brought against your personal assets.

Sole proprietorships don't require an EIN (Employer Identification Number) unless they have employees. You use your social security number for tax purposes.

ADVANTAGES OF THE SOLE PROPRIETORSHIP:
- Ease and speed of formation
- Complete control
- Relative freedom from government regulations and taxes

DISADVANTAGES OF THE SOLE PROPRIETORSHIP:
- Unlimited liability
- Total responsibility

If you set your business up as a sole proprietor you will deposit all your income into your business checking account. Then you withdraw as much money from the business as you choose for your salary by writing checks payable to yourself for the amount of money you wish. You don't have to pay payroll taxes because this money is not considered employee wages. You also cannot deduct it as a business expense.

The sole proprietorship itself does not file income tax returns. You will file a Schedule C "Profit or Loss from Business" with your 1040 return and pay personal income taxes on the profit. You may also pay self-employment tax in addition to income tax.

Partnerships

There are advantages to a partnership; however, you have to be careful here, as well. Among the advantages are that one VA might have more capital, more skills or specialties, to offer, etc. For example, one VA will excel in one area, while another VA in another area. We've encountered many situations where VAs have called stating they were going to start a business together. In their excitement to start a business, they had neglected to work out any of the details. They just assumed it would all work out in the end. It doesn't. Take the time initially to work out all the details and then, when situations arise, you will know how to handle them without the emotions that might be involved.

A partnership agreement is an absolute must. This is an agreement outlining how the partnership is to be run. However, a partnership agreement is not binding on third parties. Therefore, if one partner owes a debt, both partners are responsible for that debt.

Many states have adopted a uniform partnership act that defines a partnership as an association of two or more persons to carry on as co-owners of a business for profit. The contract or articles developed for use in your partnership may be very simple or require more detail. I highly recommend seeking an attorney's advice when setting one up.

PARTNERSHIP vs. SOLE PROPRIETORSHIP

Here are some areas where a partnership and proprietorship differ:
- Limited life of the partnership
- Share in management
- Share in profits

Corporations

The corporation is the most complex of the three business enterprises. The biggest difference between a corporation and the other two enterprises involves liability and tax laws. Personal assets are not at risk in a corporation, but there exists more taxation because corporations are taxed as corporate income and the shareholders' dividends are also taxed.

A corporation is a legal entity, which means that the business is legally separate from its owners. Thus, if the corporation were to not pay its bills, your personal assets would not be at risk.

Keep in mind that although your personal assets are less likely to be used to pay off a business debt, *you are personally responsible* for your own acts whether you are incorporated or not. Therefore, if you are responsible for a wrongful act, you will remain liable for that act.

S Corporations are used by some home-based businesses as they offer limited liability, without the additional taxation of a regular corporation. However, these require more in the way of legalities than setting up a sole proprietorship.

You can also set up a **Limited Liability Corporation, or LLC**. An LLC is kind of a cross between a partnership and a corporation whereby the business owner is protected from personal liability, but the taxation is passed directly to the owners and not the entity itself. Owners of an LLC are called members.

A Note on Taxes:

Since you are no longer working for someone, you are required to file your own taxes. Your business must file an annual income tax return. The majority of VAs elect to operate as a sole proprietor. As a sole proprietor, you will file a Schedule C "Profit or Loss From Business" and attach it to your own income tax return. LaDonna D. Vick states in her book, *A Self-Publishers Guide to Publishing Your Own Book, E-Book, or Booklet,* "The federal income tax is a pay-as-you-go tax. You must pay the tax as you earn or receive income during the year. If you are a sole proprietor, partnership, or an S corporation, you have to make estimated tax payments if you expect to owe tax of $1,000 or more when you file your return."

Also, one thing to note is that for some, if you file jointly with your spouse, you can work it so that the two of you work together so that your spouse deducts the least amount of deductions, therefore, getting less money each paycheck and paying more into the government. This can offset some of the payments you need to make into the government.

The key to successful tax filing is keeping accurate records. Whether or not you use accounting software, you must have some kind of system in place for tracking income and expenses. Don't be discouraged if your first year in business doesn't show a profit.

The best advice we can offer on the subject of taxes is to consult your accountant and your tax preparer. These professionals know your financial situation and can best guide you on what you need to do for your business. If you choose not to consult a professional, then we highly recommend you visit the federal and state websites and READ THE IRS GUIDELINES CAREFULLY.

Naming Your Business

"The name of your company is vital. You want to have a conversation with your customer, and your name is the first word in that conversation."
- David Placek, Lexicon Branding Inc.

Choosing a name for your business is an important business decision. Just think, every letter that goes out, every card that will be printed, every piece of letterhead that you utilize, will bear that name. Will it adequately describe you and your business?

The business name you choose should be able to enhance your business brand. Your brand is very important and your name is a big part of that branding effort. Your business name needs to clearly express what services you provide and not limit you if you choose to expand the business into other areas, which can hold you back from achieving your full potential in those areas.

You want your clients to remember your name easily and be able to repeat your name to their clients. You get not only repeat business, but word-of-mouth as well. If your name is troublesome to remember or too unprofessional, chances are people won't remember it. Some suggest that you might want to consider avoiding names that will begin with "The" or "An" if you plan to advertise in the Yellow Pages. Your name will then be put in an unspecific category "The" instead of the name of your company. I've found that this isn't that big of a problem, but something you should at least take into consideration.

When deciding on a name, think about the impression you are leaving with your clients, "Would you want to do business with that company?" Bernadette Davis brought up a good point when she stated, "My first unofficial name was IMH Secretarial Service (In My Home!) It sounded too homemade to me. I wanted something that didn't SAY that I had an office in my home."

In addition, it's very important to think of the professional image you create. I recently heard of a VA service—Lucky Fingers Virtual Assisting. To me, it really didn't have the professionalism that I feel a client would expect. Now others might feel differently, and again, that's a personal choice.

Here are some additional tips:

- Be creative—What best describes you and your business?
- What name is consistent with your business, yet allows for growth?
- What name isn't too cutesy or trendy?
- What name is simple and easy to remember?
- What name reflects the professional image you are seeking?
- What name doesn't limit your services if you plan to expand into other areas?
- What acronym does your company name spell and is it appropriate?

Some VAs can get stuck here. Don't be one of them. They feel that if their name isn't absolutely perfect they can't start their business. They focus solely on this and not on any other aspect of starting their business. Now you can't get your cards or anything, but you can create your business plan, set up your daily operational procedures, etc. Do some of this while thinking of a name. It will come to you. Just don't use the excuse that you can't decide on a business name as a reason to delay starting your business.

If you plan to have an Internet presence (which we know you do!) you will want to check available domain names. We recommend not having a name too similar to another. What if that company develops a bad reputation on the Internet? You don't want your name to be associated with it, unnecessarily.

If you are planning to be listed in the Yellow Pages and online directories where the listings are alphabetical, it is best to have a name that begins with one of the first letters of the alphabet. If you choose a name starting with "Virtual Assistant," for instance, you would be listed near the end of the category. This is a definite disadvantage. Most people start at the "A's" and work their way down. However, this isn't to say it has to be an "A." Just keep this in mind. On the other hand, the search engines do not list findings in alphabetical order so it's not as important.

You don't want to have the same name as another virtual assistant company, particularly in your local market. To avoid this, search your local phone book under Secretarial Services, Typing Services, and Word Processing Services to see if another company presently has this name. This won't guarantee that no one else has registered under that name, but you eliminate the obvious ones. Call directory assistance in your area and the surrounding areas and see if this name is in use. You can then do a records check with the Department of State, Division of Corporations, Fictitious Names Department or the County Clerk. Do your online research through search engines and VA directories to identify potential name conflicts in other parts of the world.

You would need to use your full real name in your business name in order to avoid filing for a Fictitious Name Statement (assumed business name or d.b.a. - doing business as). For example, Kathy Jones Virtual Assisting would work in most states. However, if you choose a fictitious name, you will have to register with your county or state and publicize it. It is a very simple process. Normally when you register to get your occupational license, they will provide a packet of information on how to register your business name. Some states require you to advertise in the local newspaper a fictitious name listing.

Trademark: Many corporations will get their name trademarked from the U.S. Patent & Trademark Office. A business with a federally trademarked name has the exclusive use of that name. To have national name protection, you might want to register your name as a trademark. To do this you will want to contact the U.S. Patent and Trademark Offices in Washington, D.C or their website at http://www.uspto.gov for further information. We have witnessed businesses that run into problems because their name was already trademarked. If you will do business internationally, you may also consider securing the trademark in other countries. While getting a trademark is great, if you don't plan to monitor its use and take action on infringements, there is no sense in going through the process to begin with. You can help to protect yourself by setting up Google Alerts for your name, company name and tag lines or slogans to see what's being published on the Internet. (Google Alerts are set up through a Google account to routinely scour the web for the specified search criteria. Then, you can have a report e-mailed to you regularly for monitoring.)

Here are some interesting quotes we gathered that really tell it how it is when naming your business.

"The right name is an advertisement in itself." – *Claude C. Hopkins*

"The most important thing is to use the correct words." – *Confucius*

"Products are created in the factory, but brands are created in the mind." – *Walter Landor*

"...today, almost 2 million brand names or trademarks are registered with the U.S. government. To be successful, it helps a great deal to have a good name." – *Jack Trout*

"Our biggest asset is four letters: SONY." – *Norio Ohga, Sony Corporation*

"Good names don't make products succeed so clearly as bad names make products fail." – *Ira Bachrac, NameLab*

In Their Own Words:

Tess Strand Alipour – Codehead, LLP: I have always called my husband a 'codehead' because he is a brilliant programmer, so it was a natural choice.

Jeannine Clontz - Accurate Business Services: With the help of a fabulous book I purchased when I first started my business, "*Words from Home*" by Diana Ennen. In that publication, it was suggested that you choose a name high up in the alphabet so that you will get higher rankings in the Yellow Pages, membership lists, etc...has worked flawlessly for me. I'm usually the first or second listing in directories, etc.

Alyssa Gregory – avertua, LLC: It's a made up word that is meant to be a play on "a virtual." And the domain was available!

Kathy Ritchie - Ritchie Secretarial Service: I chose this name to be all inclusive of what I provide my clients. Whether virtually or in the physical world, my services are still secretarial (+) in nature.

Barbara Rowen - Virtually Everything: I originally thought of and purchased the domain name when I became involved in a partnership with another VA. That venture never got off the ground, but I held onto the name. After becoming more dissatisfied with using my own name for my business, I decided to change my business name to Virtually Everything. Some of my clients have used it to describe what I do for them by saying, "Barbara does virtually everything," although I am the first one to point out that I do not do bookkeeping. The response I have received with the name has been very positive, and it is very powerful to say that I own "Virtually Everything."

Nora Rubinoff - *At Your Service Cincinnati, Ltd:* I am based in the Cincinnati area. AYS prides itself in providing a concierge-level of service to our clients. At Your Service helps convey that message.

Nancy Seeger – *Arts Assistance:* Part of my niche market is serving the needs of the music industry, specifically smaller ensembles and artists.

Patty Shannon - *The Wordstation:* The first registered business name was "The Workstation." It was my husband's idea—at the time, all of my work was done at my computer workstation! In January 2003 we decided to incorporate, and found that "Workstation" was taken as a corporate name. So we made a slight change to "The Wordstation" which works just as well with what we're doing here. But changing over everything (stationery, business cards, phone listing, awning, etc.) has been a nightmare.

Donna Toothaker – *1st VA:* My husband chose it, thinking it would show up higher in alpha lists. I was easy, so, I went with it.

Susan Totman – *Elite Office Support*: I decided on this name because "Elite" signifies "the best" and "Office Support" clearly defines my business, providing "elite office support" to client businesses and individuals worldwide.

Obtaining Licenses and Other Business Basics

We love how Bernard Kamoroff refers to obtaining a license in his book, *Small Time Operator.* He states, "When you open a new business, every government agency that can claim jurisdiction over you wants to get into the act. There are forms to file, permits and licenses to obtain, regulations and restrictions to understand and to heed. And, always, there are fees to pay."

Licensing requirements will vary from city to city. In my area of south Florida, we are required to have a city license and a county license. Here, you get the information by calling the City Occupational Department. They need to be renewed annually and it normally costs approximately $200.00 a year. Now where I'm originally from in Ohio, you contact the County Auditor's Office. There, they send you a free business start-up kit from the state, which explains everything. There are some areas where you contact the County Clerk's Office. In many cases, everything you need for filing can be found online. The department may change, but the procedure is basically the same. It's simple...I promise you! And it feels so good to do. Don't dread it as another thing to cross off the list to do to get your business started. Instead, think of it as one additional step on your journey to achieving your dream.

Check out the resources at http://www.VA-TheSeries.com. We've compiled a listing of links for all the states where you'll find information on starting a business.

I highly recommend getting your licenses as soon as possible. In order to get your business checking account, you will be required to have one. Each year, you will get your renewal notice a few months in advance of when it is due. Pay it promptly. It's worth it to be able to file it away, and not worry about it again until next year.

Insurance
You will want to make sure that you have insurance for your family, as well as for your business.

Let's first discuss insurance for your business. This is something you will want to discuss with your agent. In Bernard Kamoroff's book, *Small Time Operator*, he does warn that, "Some policies actually void coverage if the home is used as a business without the insurance company's knowledge and approval." It pays to contact your agent and get the facts.

The good news is that times have changed and home-based businesses are much more acceptable then they were years ago. If you have homeowners insurance, you could possibly get a special rider put on your insurance policy to cover your business. However, some companies require a separate policy. Your insurance agent is the best one to discuss exactly what your needs are.

Now for medical insurance; it's important if you are not covered by your spouse's insurance that you look into and obtain the necessary insurance for you and your family. You don't want to go without insurance. Even if you get something with a high deductible to protect you if you would need to be hospitalized, it would save you from huge debts that neither you nor your business could afford.

Many associations do offer insurance plans as part of their package. Just check thoroughly into what you are getting. The time to ask the questions is before you acquire the expense, not after. The hospital, doctor, etc., doesn't care that you thought that this charge was covered; they just want their money. And boy, can I tell you, sometimes they aren't too friendly, either. I'm very fortunate and have a great plan through my husband's insurance company. However, over the past couple of years I have had some major medical problems. What I have discovered, and have learned the hard way, is that I no longer just assume I know the answers and what I believe the policy says; I now ask. This way, you know that you and your family are protected just in case something were to happen.

Disaster Relief Plan

We thought it appropriate to fit this in. You may never need this, and hopefully you won't, but the smart business owner will prepare their business just in case of an unfortunate disaster. We're talking about not only planning for backing up your computer, but also backing up your business. Viruses are a real threat to your computer. You absolutely must have a good virus program installed on your computer, and you must have it set up to retrieve updated virus protection. Most will automatically, at a certain time of day, go retrieve the latest version and scan the computer. Also, stay updated with the news on what's out there. Yes, it's a hassle, but you need to know and protect yourself accordingly. When you see warning of a new virus threat, adhere to them and do whatever is necessary to protect your computer. I tend to go a little overboard, which drives my husband crazy, but makes me feel secure. And it's just like the old saying, "If mom's happy, everyone's happy."

Think now about ways you can prepare your business for something like this. Your insurance papers, your important company papers, backup disks, etc., should be kept in a fire-resistant, waterproof cabinet. Office supply stores sell them cheaply. In south Florida, with hurricane season, we are constantly reminded to do these things, but elsewhere around the country, you might not be.

Keeping backups of your software off-site is crucial should a disaster happen within your office that would ruin the backup devices. Can you imagine having to repurchase all of your software? You will also want to keep a backup of your important documents off-site, as well.

One time, a VA colleague of ours experienced the devastating effects of disaster when her home was hit by a tornado. She experienced personal injury and total destruction. It took time to get insurance to reimburse her to buy her new computer. Her files and equipment were destroyed. A number of industry colleagues did come through and help her out with some supplies and equipment, and that helped tremendously. But, when she shared with us the photos of her home and what occurred in just seconds, we were quickly reminded how important it is to take the necessary steps now. What can you do? Do it!

Also, let's say that tomorrow you end up in the hospital. Would checks bounce? Would clients' work get done? This can prove to be a real problem. I know, this happened to me, and talk about a panic among my clients. I learned that I needed to keep better records and keep everything labeled better. I used to love being the only one in charge who knew what was going on, but I learned that could easily backfire. I found it beneficial to tell my husband, my backup, or even have my files in the computer outlined in such a way that anyone could see what was what. Most importantly, I needed to tell my husband about my bankbooks and to also have him on my bank accounts. And, I had to have all my clients' names, phone numbers, and e-mail addresses where he could find them. When you're in the hospital, you don't want to be concentrating on contacting clients. If you have them all written out, it's a matter of telling someone where to look.

There is insurance for the self-employed if you become disabled for a short-term. Check with your insurance agent or consider becoming a member of the National Association of Self-Employed (http://www.nase.org). They offer a number of benefit packages for small business owners.

Another reason for a disaster recovery plan, which is critical to the success of your business, is that your clients are entrusting you with their work and, in turn, not only can you be financially affected, but they can, too. They need the peace of mind in knowing that you have taken the steps to keep their files, records, and everything else concerning their business safe. They need to know that if something were to happen that you would have someone you have entrusted to contact them and let them know what is happening.

When completing your plan, write down all aspects of your business so that someone could walk right in and take over. Take the time to write down your corporate structure, clients and contact information, subcontractors, website information and web hosting information

We have included a simple example of a Disaster Recovery Plan in the Appendix. And be sure to check out the book *Home Office Recovery Plan* by Patty Gale and Diana Ennen. (http://www.VA-TheSeries.com)

No one knows my ability the way I do.
I am pushing against it all the time.
–John Steinbeck

Business Planning 101

Creating A Business Plan

Creating a business plan is the most important aspect of starting a business. It is defined as a document that establishes the mission, goals and objectives of your enterprise. In detail, it explains how you intend to accomplish your goals and objectives. Essentially, the plan will become your road map to success. We want to thank Steve Windhaus for helping us with this chapter. His expertise is sure to guide you in the right direction in preparing your plan.

Anyone that has approached me about starting a business or being "stuck" in their business knows that one of the first questions I ask VAs at any level (i.e., aspiring, new, or veteran) is, "Have you done a business plan?" It amazes me the number of times I've heard the answer, "No, do I need one?" You most certainly do! You wouldn't start out on a family trip across the country without a map of how to get there, would you? Your business is no different. How can you know how you're going to achieve your business goals and objectives if you haven't established them? How can you know how to reach potential clients, what your operation truly requires and how much cash is required if you haven't established who those potential clients are? To be successful in any business you have to know what you want to do, how you're going to do it, and how you're going to get there. It is not a secret that more than half the businesses today fail due to the lack of a business plan—don't become a statistic! Remember, poor planning produces poor results.

There seems to be a common misconception that because it's a "small business," and you're not looking for financing, you don't need a business plan. I talk to VAs regularly who are struggling to get clients, are trying to figure out what services to offer, and who are trying to figure out how to market to clients. These VAs have been in business for several months (sometimes years). They have their name, their website, a vision, and a huge desire to succeed—all key components of a business, but all missing one important factor—a solid business plan. We get carried away with getting that first client when it only takes a short time to put a plan together that will save you a great deal of time down the road. The amount of time required to develop the plan depends on the depth of research you want to invest in it. Regardless of the time required, put a plan together that is sure to get you good results. When you do, it will be much easier to find clients, keep them, and continually grow your business.

The lack of a plan can leave you feeling unorganized and unsettled. We highly recommend taking this step. Some may choose just to write a very informal plan, which includes just the basics, while others will be more elaborate. Either one is fine. Just be sure to do one, including the marketing, operations and financial elements of your business. You will see how motivating it is to write down all your hopes and dreams for your business. When we keep them in our heads, we have a hard time trying to keep track. On paper they have substance, and become better to evaluate.

Visit your plan often. I recall wondering why my previous employer would prepare a three-year strategic plan annually. I thought, "It's a three-year plan, shouldn't it be good for three years?" It didn't take me long to realize that's because business changes. We must regularly account for changes in the economy, competition, strategies, and market conditions while adjusting current strategies. I recommend reviewing your business plan in the following timelines:

- **Comprehensive Review & Evaluation: Yearly**—Do this once a year. Previous reviews and adjustments to marketing, operations and finances will make the yearly process much easier to conduct.

- **Cash Flow Projections: Monthly**—Cash is truly king for small business. You need to compare cash flow projections to real-time cash flow. Pay attention to how well receipts are being collected. Pay your bills only when they are due unless the creditor offers a discount for early payment. No one is going to give you better credit ratings just because the bill was paid 10 or 15 days earlier than the due date. On the other hand, don't wait too late. Late payment fees can be exorbitant.

- **Profit & Loss Statements and Balance Sheets: Quarterly**—If you are like most small, self-employed businesses, there are self-employment taxes to pay every quarter, and profit and loss statements are the foundation of income tax returns. You begin developing a vision of what to anticipate at the end of the tax year—will there be taxes to pay and how much? A quarterly review of the P&L also gives you a clear picture of how assets are being used to generate sales. The use of those assets is reflected in the expenses on the P&L sheet. The balance sheet is your static picture of the financial well being of the company. How does the net worth appear compared to earlier points in time?

- **Marketing: As Needed**—When things are going well, with sales and revenues consistently improving, you know the marketing element of your business plan is well-developed. When sales are declining, customers don't return for repeat business, or when you are simply not satisfied that sales are not growing, that is the time to review your market research, advertising and promotional strategies. At the very least, you want to make a monthly comparison of projected and actual sales dollars, types of services offered, average sales per customer number and type of customers by business sector.

This timetable addresses marketing when needed, and operations and finances as needed.

What Goes Into a Business Plan?

The following information is provided to help you get started. Hopefully, it should provide you with the basics that should be developed and found in any business plan. The main components of a business plan are:

1. Cover Sheet
This is the first page of the plan and should contain the following:
- Company name, address, phone number, fax number, and web address.
- Company logo, if available.
- Your name and title.
- Date the document was drafted or revised.

Why put so much into a cover sheet? You never can tell when the day may come when your plan becomes a document for formal review if seeking a partner or funding.

2. Table of Contents
Every business plan should have a table of contents, especially when reviewing a hard copy, or when submitting it for review by another individual.

3. Company Overview
Write three or four paragraphs briefly describing the nature of your company and services. Include the legal business structure, location, general geographic area served, a general description of services offered, and something outstanding about your business—what makes it stand out from the competition.

4. Mission Statement
The mission statement describes the nature and philosophy of your business. It summarizes what you want your business to become. Keep the statement short and concise to 50 words or less.

5. Goals
Goals expand on your mission statement. I think it's extremely important to write down the goals for your business—where you want to be six months from now, two years from now, etc. Expand on the mission statement to better define the marketing, operational and financial goals of your company. Some examples include:

- Offer a menu of virtual assistant services directed to an underserved geographic market.
- Incorporate partners within one year to meet the increasing demands for your services.
- Maintain fiscal oversight of cash flow and cash investments in the marketing and operations of the business.

Set goals to shape your future. The Internet has opened up this huge new market for us and it's all for the taking.

I'm a real goal setter. I love setting goals and then striving to achieve them. In fact, that's one of the reasons I try to set a goal each day. I love the good feeling that comes along once done. It doesn't have to be anything major, just something that I know, once accomplished, will make my business or me, better.

6. Objectives

You now expand on those goals with achievable and measurable objectives. You are setting quantified standards of success for this business. Examples include:

- Have all home-based operations and the office fully operational in three months from start-up.
- Achieve consistent, positive cash flow within eight months of start-up.
- Establish a portfolio of 10 existing clients by the end of the 12th month.
- Achieve annual net profit by the end of 14 months.
- Penetrate the geographic target market with the advertising and promotional strategies by the end of June 2011.

When you achieve an objective in the business, reward yourself for a job well done. Go out for a dinner with your significant other or business partners.

7. Financial Requirements

This section should be mandatory for anyone "starting from scratch" or a VA firm that has not yet achieved positive cash flow. Every business venture requires the investment of capital. Without exception, money needs to be in the operating account at all times. Ultimately, you want to be able to provide a matrix that lists the sources and uses of funds:

Sources		
Cash	$20,000	
Uses		**$20,000**
Operating Overhead - 6 months	10,000	
Office Leasehold Improvements	4,000	
Advertising	5,000	
Business Plan - Market Research	1,000	**$20,000**

In the example above, the VA has determined the need for $20,000 cash for the first six months of operation. An existing VA needs to project monthly cash requirements to the point in time when the company achieves positive cash flow.

The next seven elements of your business plan relate specifically to marketing. These are the most critical sections of that document. Marketing involves everything you have to do in determining a need for your service, creating awareness of your service to potential clients, making those potential clients want your service, and then selling your service. This determines from where the money will come, so pay close attention. The effort, research, and answers you get will ultimately determine the answer to a very important question—*why solicit my services when there are other VAs and other sources of similar and like services out there?*

8. Marketing—Services Offered

Be specific here and provide detailed descriptions for each of your services. For example, don't simply state that you offer word processing. Elaborate on the media used. Do you provide insertion of charts, graphs and images? Do you perform word processing in Microsoft Office, Corel, Smart Suite or Open Office?

Delivery of the finished product can also be an important service. Do you provide hard copies, e-mail attachments, CD ROM or zip files of the finished product?

By the way, make note of the expenses you will incur for each of the services provided. They are not operating expenses that occur whether or not you are making sales; they happen when you perform a specific service. Examples of these types of costs include registering a URL, "burning" documents to a CD and mailing it to the client, subcontracting website development, contracting ISP or website hosting services for the client, and producing and conducting a mass mailing to a client's customers. These are called "costs of sales."

9. Marketing—Your Customers

To whom do you intend to sell your services—people, companies, or both? You really need to do some research. Who are the typical VA customers? Examine your competition. Are there types of businesses that could use your services, but are not targeted by the competition? Do you want to concentrate on start-ups (in business for one year or less) or existing businesses?

10. Marketing—Geographic Target Market

Some VAs may want to focus on face-to-face contact when selling their services. They will likely concentrate their efforts in local markets encompassing cities, counties or major metropolitan areas. Others may want to open up to whatever market offers opportunity. They want to rely on a website and promoting the business on the Internet, as well as locally, in face-to-face networking. Do make note of the expenses involved in promoting your business in the local and grander markets. For example, a website is useful to all VAs. However, local geographic target markets will not place as great a demand on advertising and promotional dollars as a VA focusing on the national level.

11. Marketing—Pricing

Try to learn as much as possible about the pricing offered by the competition. You may think that is very hard to do, but not so. For example, I just read a column in a local newspaper about a VA firm located in the same city. The article included the prices it offers for three general categories of services. Go on the Internet. You will find VA fees are easy to view at several competitors' websites. Make only a temporary decision. You have a vision of what are the expenses for each service, and what kind of profit is desired. On that basis, set a fee structure for each of your services, including retainer fees. They can be the most lucrative, consistent source of income.

12. Marketing—SWOT

In the market research phase, we uncover the truths about our business and the market. With our own business we perform what is called a SWOT analysis. SWOT stands for *Strengths, Weaknesses, Opportunities, and Threats.* This analysis is the most critical part of your marketing plan. Everything else in your marketing strategy is determined by the SWOT analysis.

Most likely you will have just completed a thorough review of your business in preparing the business plan. That means you have already determined your company's philosophy, as well as the vision and mission statements. This is the first step in preparing the SWOT analysis—a business review. A SWOT analysis is very subjective, but should be based on objective market research. You can produce better quality results by being objective and not overanalyzing. Look at where your business is now and where you want it to be in the future.

Secondly, make a list of your company's strengths and weaknesses. Maintain a separate list for each. Strengths and weaknesses are driven by internal factors, based on comparisons to the competition, and include aspects of your business that add value to your service. For example, strengths may include a unique service offering, business location, or quality processes and procedures. Your weaknesses might include lack of marketing expertise or length of time in business compared to the competition. Think about things like image, communication, direction, efficiency, responsiveness, job knowledge, planning, flexibility, etc.

Next, make a list of opportunities and threats. Opportunities and threats are external forces. Like strengths and weaknesses, they are based on comparisons to the competition, but also include an examination of general market trends impacting your particular business sector. A sample opportunity might be creating strategic alliances with other companies. A sample threat might be competitor pricing. Opportunities and threats can also be determined by the general economic conditions in your geographic target market. A sample opportunity can be the growth of the types of businesses that would seek your services. A sample threat might be a recession resulting in the closure of the types of businesses that would seek your services.

After a thorough review of all your lists, you can then determine in what areas you can use your strengths to identify opportunities in the market—opportunities that give you a competitive edge. Then identify what weaknesses could pose potential threats. Try creating a matrix like this:

	Strength	Weaknesses
Opportunities	S-O	W-O
Threats	S-T	W-T

S-O: identifies opportunities that are a good fit for your strengths.
W-O: identifies weaknesses to be overcome to pursue opportunities.
S-T: identifies ways to use your strengths to reduce risk of threats.
W-T: identifies weaknesses, which pose a threat to external forces.

After completing the exercise above, take the results and give them substance by ranking them in order of importance based upon your business goals and objectives. The SWOT analysis can be beneficial in determining your niche in the marketplace. The thought process alone can prove beneficial for you.

13. Marketing—Advertising & Promotional Strategy

Okay, you decided on a geographic target market. You have done your research to determine, more or less (this is not rocket science), what kind of clients are out there and how easy or difficult they will be to capture as clients. So how is your competition advertising to this market? Do they have websites, brochures, participate in local trade shows with exhibits, and advertise in the local Yellow Pages? What kinds of promotional strategies are they using to create awareness of the company? Do they sponsor a local youth sports team, participate as a member of the local chamber of commerce, and retain membership in the IVAA? Pay close attention to what successful VAs do. There's a reason why they succeed. They don't spend advertising dollars and participate in promotional types of activities if sales are not to be gained from those investments.

Now you want to develop a matrix of advertising and promotional expenses for the next three years. You examined the service, target customer, the geographic market, pricing and SWOT.

Media	Year 1	Year 2	Year 3
Website Development	$500		
Website Hosting	240	$280	$300
Yellow Pages	1000	1100	1200
IVAA Membership	75	65	65
Chamber of Commerce Dues	250	260	300
Brochure	500		300
Business Cards	50	50	50
Total	$2,615	$1,755	$2,215

Remember, you will want to develop these costs by month for the first year. Cash flow is critical, and there are several of these expenses that must be timed to coincide with the availability of cash funds, as well as when the target customer is most likely to be exposed to the advertising.

You've come so far—congratulations! Now that you know how you're going to get on the road to success, you need to implement your plan of action. Establish a detailed plan of advertising and promotions. See Marketing Strategies for more information.

14. Marketing—Sales Projections

It's now "crunch time," especially for the startup. It's easier for the existing VA firms with a track record to project sales for the next three years than it is for the startup, but this should be done. How else are you going to be able to determine what will likely be required, in cash, to achieve positive cash flow?

The next two sections of the plan relate to the expenses of operating your venture. They will describe how you wish to run the business, and the expenses involved with each.

15. Operations—Ownership & Management

This may or may not be an important section. If you are only self-employed, this section is not necessary unless you plan to enter into a partnership or hire employees at a later date in the next three years. You want to note job duties and responsibilities if more than one person is a part of this VA firm. In any case, you want to list expected costs associated with compensation, benefits expenses and any other cost associated with personnel.

16. Operations—Operating Expenses

Make a line-item listing of all the expenses that you will incur, whether or not the sales are being made and revenues collected. Typically, these include utilities, office supplies, travel, equipment maintenance and purchases. Don't ignore any of these expenses simply because you are home-based. At income tax time, a home-based business can deduct a portion of the residence expenses if you own the home. Typically, a portion of real estate taxes, home insurance, electricity, gas, water and certain home repairs qualify as deductions against the home-based company's expenses on the profit and loss statement. You will want to review IRS publication 587 on the Business Use of the Home. For those located outside the home, your expenses are easily recognized and itemized.

17. Financial Plan

Your financial plan provides an account of your financial needs, sources of funding, and a basic outline of what will be required to succeed. Every business plan should project into the next three years. No, that does not mean you should expect the income and expenses to be exactly like that, but we all like financial planning. We all want to see what can potentially occur, financially, if our plans come to fruition. However, for most entrepreneurs, VAs alike, developing financial projections can be a headache. On the other hand, there are VAs who provide bookkeeping and accounting functions to their clients. This process, for them, will be relatively easy, whereas market research could be their Achilles heel. Given the importance of these projections, we have devoted an entire section on understanding and developing them. Read on!

Thoughts About Market Research and Writing the Plan

As noted above, market research and strategies are the most important sections of a business plan. They determine the feasibility of your business. They determine how you will spend money to make money. Here is where you get creative while putting yourself in the position of your potential clients. Consider drawing upon other resources such as family, friends, or business associates to help you identify ways in which you can attack the market. Hold a brainstorming session and capture as many ideas as possible.

What makes those clients tick? Are they driven by price? How are you going to position your services? Will it be based on price or customer service? How can you reach the market in a way that no one else does? How will you reach your targeted audience? Use a mix of strategies and establish your USP or Unique Selling Position. A USP is the position you place your company in the eyes of your market by adding value that is perceived to be better than any other.

Finally, here are some very important things, at the risk of being somewhat repetitive, you must never forget:

- Seek reliable sources of market research data. For example, the most reliable and comprehensive source of demographic data is the U.S. Census Bureau. http://www.census.gov.
- Be objective. Don't commit to finding only that data that supports your vision. Be open to learning if some of your services may not be profitable.
- Pay close attention to successful VAs; there is nothing wrong in doing some of what makes them successful. Just be certain it will work in your market.
- Pay close attention to unsuccessful VAs. You don't want to make their mistakes.
- Advertise and promote your business where the customer is likely to find you. Don't spend dollars on advertising that won't be seen or read by your target customer. I don't expect VAs will advertise in the Sports section of a newspaper. On the other hand, given the nature of the profession, it is apparent a website is appropriate, especially in larger geographic markets.
- Put systems in place for tracking and measuring your performance and results. Do you have a system in place for tracking leads? How often will you follow-up? When do you implement secondary strategies?
- Be careful when deciding the geographic target market. Typically, you spend more advertising dollars in a larger geographic market. You want to ensure advertising dollars result in sales that cover that expense, a portion of operating expenses and leave you a profit.

Regardless of the size of your business plan, these matters must be taken seriously, whether you invest $10,000 or $100,000. You are in business to make a profit. How well you develop the marketing of your company will likely determine how likely you are to make that profit.

I have given you a list of sections to include in your business plan. That is the chronological order in which you should develop the plan. However, it will not be the order in which you will complete the plan. The first draft (oh, did I forget to tell you the plan should be drafted and then finalized?) will provide the greatest challenges. Simply develop your research, operations, costs and sales projections. When developing your financial projections, most likely, the first draft will indicate you are over-optimistic in sales, costs are too high or sales are not enough to cover the costs. Usually, the first draft contains a combination of all these symptoms.

The idea is to craft a plan that is realistic. You need to balance expenses to income. You want to be conservative. It is better to overestimate expenses and underestimate sales. If expenses are less than expected and sales are greater than expected, you won't find yourself in crisis management.

You will find yourself revisiting past sections of the plan to fine tune the total package. If sincere and objective, you will realize when that magic moment has arrived—I have a good business plan that has substance, includes all of my costs and is conservative in its sales projections

Wow! You did it. Doesn't it feel great? And don't forget to go back and revise sections 5, 6 and 7 of the plan. When completing the marketing, operating and financial sections of the plan, you will notice there are some changes in those goals, objectives and funding requirements. It is a natural part of the business planning process. You have a vision, but now it is tempered with the reality of your potential market.

Financial Statements

Understanding and developing the Financial Plan for your business plan is an extremely important step in building and succeeding in business. These financial statements provide answers to questions such as, what money is needed to open the business, cover operating expenses and pay back a business loan.

It is unfortunate that many business owners steer away from writing their business plan due to their fear of these statements. Once you have an understanding of these statements and how they work, you will find out they are not as bad as you thought. As with all financial matters, though, you should always contact your accountant for specialized advice.

It is always a good idea to update your financial statements on a quarterly basis. This not only gives you a feel for how well your business has been doing, but also what you need to do to increase revenue during the next quarter.

The following financial statements are an essential part of writing a business plan: Projected Cash Flow, Cash Flow Assumptions, Projected Income Statement, Projected Balance Sheet, Break-Even Analysis, and if you decide to seek financing, the Financing Plan. New business owners should also include a Start-Up Costs worksheet to give them a place to start with their financials.

1. Start-Up Costs

This is an excellent tool for new businesses. New business owners should look at what you already have versus what you will need to purchase to get your business off to a good start. It is a very good idea to include items already purchased, as this gives you and your audience an overall view of what assets your company has.

This worksheet should include categories for advertising, professional fees, postage and any other expenses your company will be expected to pay for. The following is just a few of the categories that could be considered:

Equipment	Deposits Paid
Rent / Lease	Legal & Professional Services
Office Supplies	Phone
Promotional & Advertising	Postage
Licenses & Permits	Association Fees
Insurance	

2. Projected Cash Flow

The Projected Cash Flow statement provides a snapshot of your company's financial picture. It tells you how much cash you will bring in and how much will be outgoing at any given time of the year. This can prepare you when planning your personal budget, especially if you will be drawing money from your business to live on. Your Projected Cash Flow statement does not have to be a calendar year, it can also reflect a fiscal year, or even, if you prefer, a year that begins in February or October. Please keep in mind the audience of your business plan. Bankers may not care, but a prospective partner may get confused.

This statement is a forecast of your company's net worth and is not intended to be set in stone. There can be any number of reasons why you do not meet the revenue, or the expenses you expected during a specific month. Obstacles will pop up unexpectedly; you didn't plan for a slow season, or your computer dies and you need to purchase a new one. Understand that this statement is intended to give you an idea of where you want to be, and then develop strategies to get you to your goals for the next quarter.

One of the biggest obstacles in creating a realistic projected cash flow statement is determining the company's revenue a year in advance. For new VAs, this can be a harrowing experience. How can they know what they will make a month from now, much less a whole year? I have found that the best way to determine what you will earn is to determine your cost per hour, then going back to your marketing plan strategies to determine what your goals are in terms of acquiring clients and multiply the number of hours you plan to work for those clients by your hourly rate. You will want to keep in mind the number of hours per month you are willing to work, as well as the number of billable hours you will have left. Some of those hours you are willing to work will have to be dedicated to marketing your business, and should be accounted for when projecting your sales. It wouldn't be realistic to say you are expecting revenue for 40 hours a week when a portion of those hours are to be designated for the administrative tasks of your own company.

The following is an example of what your Projected Cash Flow statement might look like:

PROJECTED CASH FLOW
FOR THE PERIOD JANUARY 1, 2003 TO DECEMBER 31, 2003

	as of 12/31/2002	Jan	Feb	Mar	April	May	June	July	Aug	Sep	Oct	Nov	Dec	Yearly Totals
CASH INFLOWS														
BEGINNING CASH														
Plus: Cash Sales (Services)														
Owner's Contribution														
Less: Equipment Purchased														
TOTAL AVAILABLE CASH														
CASH OUTFLOWS														
OPERATING EXPENSES:														
Telephone														
Office Supplies														
Advertising														
Professional Fees														
Automobile Expenses														
Repairs/Maintenance														
Non-Depreciable Equipment														
Association Fees														
Website Development														
TOTAL EXPENSES														
Available Cash - Total Exp.														
Less: Owners Draw														
ENDING CASH														

3. Cash Flow Assumptions

The Cash Flow Assumptions should reflect your own reasons as to why you believe you will generate the revenue and incur the expenses during a particular month. Remember to be very reasonable with your assumptions. Make sure to include seasonal or expected downtimes. For example, if you believe that business slows down around Christmas, your expected income may be less than other times of the year. The same principle works for expenses, as well. Your expenses may take into account an increase in advertising expenses in September due to an ad in the Yellow Pages.

The Cash Flow Assumptions can be on a separate sheet or on the same page as your Projected Cash Flow Statement, but it is very important to come up with a system that you, or your audience, can refer back and forth between the two statements. When I completed my business plan, I allocated Column A of the worksheet program I used to input the assumption number next to the line item it was referring to. It is better to give the reader an easy reference to your assumption.

In the same vein, while it is not necessary to explain every instance, you should make every effort to explain your assumptions of important issues. Three months from now when you review your statements, will you remember why you had allocated $300 for advertising during the month of March?

Also, try to determine what others may ask when looking at your assumptions. Many times you will find that something may not be as realistic as you originally thought. And you may even think of an obstacle as you write your assumptions, giving you time to prepare for it.

4. Projected Income Statement

The Income Statement is another important document that must be included in your business plan. This statement documents the revenues and expenses of your business and determines if your company has incurred a profit or a loss. Once you have been in business for a while, you may want to include a factual income statement versus a projected one.

Make sure that the expenses in this statement match the expenses in your Projected Cash Flow statement. This is the first place depreciation will show up in your financial statements. Depreciation does not go in the Projected Cash Flow worksheet. Depreciation normally is determined by taking 1/7th of the total cost per year (U.S. residents). To get accurate depreciation rates, it is important that you check with your accountant. Generally, if the equipment lasts longer than a year, depreciate. If the depreciable equipment is less than $250, take the expense now instead of over a period of years. It is also a good idea to keep track of your equipment list for government purposes.

The percentages in the column on the right give the business owner an idea of how much the expenses are compared to income.

INCOME		
Fees and Services	$0.00	0.00%
TOTAL INCOME	$0.00	0.00%
GROSS PROFIT	$0.00	0.00%
OPERATING EXPENSES		
Telephone	$0.00	0.00%
Office Supplies	$0.00	0.00%
Advertising	$0.00	0.00%
Professional Fees	$0.00	0.00%
Automobile Expenses	$0.00	0.00%
Repairs/Maintenance	$0.00	0.00%
Depreciation	$0.00	0.00%
Non-Depreciable Equipment	$0.00	0.00%
Association Fees	$0.00	0.00%
Website development	$0.00	0.00%
TOTAL OPERATING EXPENSES	$0.00	0.00%
NET PROFIT (LOSS)	$0.00	0.00%

5. Projected Balance Sheet

The Balance Sheet must balance! Forcing the bottom line to balance by putting the same number at the bottom of each side will not give an accurate assessment of your company's financials, and will raise a red flag if sending to a banker or investor. Take the extra effort to find out why it doesn't balance.

A really good way to get the Balance Sheet to balance is to work backward. Most people want to start from the top left and work their way to the bottom right. Try working from the bottom right up to the top left to figure out what is wrong.

You may want to include Business Ratios on the Balance Sheet. These ratios will help determine the company's worth and impress your banker, if you choose to seek financing.

The Current Ratio measures the ability of the business to pay for its current liabilities from its current assets.

The Debt Ratio measures the percent of assets financed by someone other than the owner(s). This is a nice way of saying how much of the company you own outright, and how much is owned by your investors.

Equity Ratio is the amount of money the owner(s) has invested in the business.

Return on Equity (or Investment) is the percentage of return the owner/investor makes in the business.

While these ratios are not mandatory for your business plan, they are essential when seeking financing. And, as every business owner should know where their company stands financially, these ratios are important. The *Virtual Assistant – The Series: Financial Statements CD* add-on template, developed by Sheryl Michilli of Kaisana Administrative Support, includes these ratios in the Balance Sheet and is formulated to automatically calculate them.

6. Break-Even Analysis

The Break-Even Analysis determines what income your company needs to make in order to cover all expenses, but still operate without a profit.

To complete this statement, you will need to know the average price per hour; your company's fixed costs and your variable costs (if any). To get the revised break-even point, you will also need to know the total amount designated as Owner's Draw.

Fixed costs are defined as anything you spend regardless of whether you have a client or not. These are expenses you must pay in order to keep your business running, such as telephone, advertising, etc.

Variable costs are defined as monies spent to create your product, such as the cost of wax and wicks to create candles. This would also include the cost of labor to produce the product, such as the wages of the employee hired to create the candles. Companies that provide services normally would not have variable costs due to the fact that there are no great costs to producing a finalized project.

In order to determine the break-even point for you company, take your fixed costs and divide by your hourly rate. To get the revised break-even cost, simply take the total of the fixed costs plus the amount withdrawn from the company for your personal use (Owner's Draw) and divide by your hourly rate. To determine the total sales needed to break-even, divide the revised break-even point by your hourly rate.

7. Financing Plan

This document should only be included if you plan to acquire money from a banker or investor. It should include the amount of money you are requesting, how you plan to use the money and how you will pay the money back. Be as specific as possible and as in the assumptions, try to determine what questions your audience may ask.

As mentioned earlier, the *Virtual Assistant – The Series* add-on template is a tool that includes the first six statements mentioned in this section and is formulated to calculate your Income Statement, Business Plan and Break-Even Analysis using the figures you input for revenue and expenses in the Projected Cash Flow statement. The template includes instructions, and is a stress-free system to eliminate the hassles and fear of developing the Financial Statements for your business plan.

Marketing Strategies

One of the greatest challenges for any business is finding the perfect client; even more important is keeping that perfect client. Using the proper channels to create an interest in your service and secure paying clients is key to success. Completing your marketing plan will get you on your way. In this chapter, we've included some tools and recommendations for preparing or enhancing your strategic marketing plan. Use a mix of marketing strategies and determine what works for you. Always be sure to ask clients how they heard about your company so you can track and measure your marketing efforts. The proper marketing tactics can truly be the determining factor between success and failure. That's why we have spent such a great deal of effort in trying to provide you with all the tools you will need to succeed.

Marketing doesn't always require a lot of money. Many VAs feel that they need to immediately spend the money and place an ad. This simply isn't always true. As Liz Folger states in her book, *The Stay-At-Home Mom's Guide to Making Money From Home*, "The first thing that comes into many peoples' minds is, 'I've got to place an ad somewhere.' If you learn just one thing, learn this: Pay for an ad only as a last resort. Most home-business owners spend way too much money on advertising their businesses."

Advertising is a means used to defend your company product or service. Promotion is a means of creating awareness of your product or service. How can you advertise to defend your market share if you haven't created a market presence? Sharing information about your business with everyone you meet is a form of creating what I call "mind share." By creating mind share, you increase your chances of getting a referral down the road from the people who know about your business.

You may feel that everyone you come in contact with is a potential client. This might be true if you haven't yet defined your market niche. If you're still unsure of what you will specialize in, then it's time to revisit your mission statement and SWOT analysis. Working with a small, targeted audience can prove more profitable in the long run.

You should have a good understanding of exactly whom you plan to target, as well as how you plan to target them. Here are some ways that we recommend.

Online Marketing
Online marketing is an exciting advertising and marketing tool fueled by the steadily growing number of people connecting to online services. The key is to get your business recognized not only on your site, but throughout the internet. Jackie Ulmer of Street Smart Wealth (http://www.streetsmartwealth.com) has mastered this. In doing my research for this book, she was absolutely everywhere. Best yet, she gained immediate recognition by providing her photo to various sites she was linked to. You were able to connect her immediately to her business and to her website. (Read more about her in the Maximizing The Internet chapter.)

Here are some examples of this type of promotion:

<u>Free Website Promotion</u> comes in the form of: banner, text or button exchanges; responding to blog posts; answering questions in group forums, and Web awards. Many VAs report great results through their "free" and "pay-per-click" advertising efforts. Find places that allow advertising and place an ad. Although the ad might be free, be sure to stay within your targeted audience. When responding to blog posts and answering questions, always include a link back to your website. The same with article marketing - include your URL in your resource box whenever possible.

<u>Viral Marketing</u> is basically a form of word-of-mouth where the marketing message is passed along through electronic means. For example, forwarding an e-mail message to an associate about a new service you heard about. Twitter is an excellent example of the power of viral marketing. One post can be passed along to thousands and thousands of people in a matter of seconds.

<u>Link Popularity</u> is like getting people to vote for your site by linking to it on their own site. It's trying to get your website in the available search engines. You can improve your site's link popularity since some of the search engines figure that into the ranking process. Link popularity is the measure of the quality and quantity of sites that link to your site. This can go hand-in-hand with reciprocal links, whereby two people agree to exchange links on one another's site. It's kind of like trying to stay popular in school. Popular kids attract many friends—popular sites attract many links. Shy, quiet kids have difficulty attracting friends—unpopular sites have difficulty attracting links.

<u>Search Engine Optimization</u> includes the process of maximizing your site content, getting the most out of your keywords, elements of site design and structure. Everyone wants to be at the top of the search engines. The best advice we can offer is to stay abreast of the ever-changing search engine submission guidelines. If you aren't able to do this, then seek the help of a professional. Search engine rankings are a critical part of your business if you rely on the traffic from your website to gain clients.

<u>E-mail marketing</u> requires knowledge of permission marketing. Permission marketing, as the term indicates, is when the receiver of the e-mail has granted permission to receive the information you are sending. Opt-in e-mail would be an example of permission marketing, since there is an explicit interest in receiving certain type of e-mail. Other examples include e-zines and electronic newsletters.

Networking Online
Participation in forums, message boards, social media, and other online communities is a form of online networking. What potential you have today to reach thousands of prospective clients. Spend the time to learn about Internet marketing and how you can reach those prospects. It's well worth the time. When participating in online networking groups, you'll want to be sure to adhere to the participation guidelines in regard to advertising. You will want to limit your participation to those groups with members of your targeted audience. When a topic comes across where you can offer your expertise, jump on it!

Online networking is an extremely effective way to network. The biggest advantage is that it's done in the comfort of your own office. Many VAs recommended this approach as an effective way to spread the word about your services, and to get advice on operating your business successfully. Not only can it provide you with a wealth of information, but also access to other professionals and home-based businesses. You will discover that there are hundreds of other VAs who are eager to help you get your business started and keep it running successfully. You can network through associations such as the IVAA, Virtual Assistant Forums, and HBWM, etc. We won't list all the VA sites again, but throughout the book, we have included them.

We'd be remiss if we didn't mention the increasing popularity of social networking sites like Facebook and LinkedIn, as well as the power of Twitter. While you may still be hesitant to get involved in this kind of social media activity, you can't ignore them. Social networking can be a great avenue for connecting with potential clients, staying in touch with current clients, and a means of communication with industry colleagues. They can also be a huge resource for up-to-the-minute information about anything under the sun. Most importantly, social networking is known to result in getting more business.

At minimum, we recommend you set up a professional profile on LinkedIn and consider creating a fan page for your business on Facebook. We consider LinkedIn to be the ultimate professional network. Facebook can be a mix of a personal profile page to connect with family and friends, or you can set up your business fan page to connect on a more professional level. Each have a variety of special interest groups you can join for increasing your connection with potential and current clients.

For more information on understanding Social Media as a whole, check out *The Social Media Bible* (http://www.socialmediabible.com). To find success on LinkedIn consider *42 Rules for Success on Linked In* by Chris Muccio, David Burns, and Peggy Murrah. And for everything you want to know about success on Facebook, you'll want to see what's happening at http://www.MariSmith.com.

Face-to-Face Networking
Networking allows you to let your potential clients know who you are and that you have a business that's ready to help them. It can be an integral part of your business and a wonderful tool to use to get clients. Plus, it offers the camaraderie often needed for those home-based workers who miss the workplace atmosphere.

Making your name familiar to prospective customers is a way to gain mind share. People are more willing to work with a new service if they have heard about you or have had the opportunity to meet you. They gain confidence that you can help their business.

One way to network is to contact other VAs in your area. See if there is a local or regional VA group that meets regularly. Check the listing at http://www.va-theseries.com or the IVAA VA Connection listing at http://www.ivaa.org or do an online search. You might be able to work out an arrangement where you send each other work. For example, often times I get too busy to take on a new client. I will then send new clients over to another business in the area. She will do the same for me when she gets too busy. So far, it's been an ideal situation for both of us. Plus, we are finding solutions for our clients. It's good to be able to send clients to someone who can get the job done for them.

You can also network through speaking engagements in your community. Many VAs have found this to be a great way to obtain recognition and respect. You could present a class on how to start a business through your local university, Chamber of Commerce or other business organization. Contact them and obtain the person's name you should speak with to obtain additional information.

Nora Rubinoff shares this about marketing locally: "I learned to market by participating in a lot of local chamber events and networking. While a portion of our business comes from my local area, the majority is across the US. Starting locally allowed me to gain practice and comfort in things such as my elevator speech, unique selling proposition, networking at events and prospect meetings. That confidence helped me then as I branched out and began to market more online."

Here are some tips to make your networking experience better:

- Dress professionally and always check your appearance once you arrive, just to make sure everything is fine. Arrive early for any necessary setup.
- Even though you are dressing professionally, make sure you are comfortable. Shoes that hurt your feet, and that you tend to have to slip off regularly don't create a positive appearance.
- Leave your cell phone off or on vibrate. Everyone has cell phones today, and it doesn't create the appearance of success to be constantly receiving calls. Plus, you don't want to have your kids keep calling to ask where you put their skates.
- Try not to spend all the time with the people you already know. Try to meet new contacts. What sometimes helps though is to use your "old contacts" to your advantage. For example, when a new person stops by your group you can introduce yourself and then say, "Oh, have you met…," and then introduce your friend as well. This can be a great icebreaker for everyone.
- Always have your short elevator speech prepared introducing your services, as well as business cards handy, and don't forget that pen. And make it a nice pen, too! You can get one for $4.00 or $5.00 at office supply stores. For holidays, I always ask for a personalized pen as a gift. I feel good with a nice pen in my hand. I know when I see others with a good pen I think, "Gee, they must be successful." No one needs to know that is your only good pen and you've had Mac and Cheese for dinner for days, and are struggling to get started. It will be our little secret.
- Be a good listener. People can tell when you aren't interested in their conversation. If you want their business, you should be interested in their business. Pay attention to what is being said as if there were going to be a test later, because there just might be when asked if you recall something that was said just a bit ago. And remember to make eye contact.
- Collect as many business cards as possible. Be sure to make any special notes on the back of a contact's card that will help you remember them and why you need to make contact.
- Immediately following the networking event, send a thank-you note expressing that it was nice meeting them. You can design your own to make it a little more personal. Make sure you sign your own name—don't have it typed.

- Follow-up with those contacts you identified as hot prospects. Refer to the notes you took on the back of their business card and let them know how you can benefit their company.

Yellow Pages

You might want to consider placing an ad in the Yellow Pages. Even if you only get a one-line ad, which states your name and address (and is usually free with a business line), it can produce results. Listings in the Yellow Pages are in alphabetical order. Keep this in mind when naming your business if you do plan to advertise here. To obtain this free listing, install a separate business telephone line. This costs slightly more than a regular residential line; however, you get a free listing under the section of your choice. This ad includes your company name, address, and telephone number. For a larger monthly fee, you can obtain a display ad as well as an online listing. Check what is currently listed and make your ad stand out and be recognized. Include specific information and any additional specialties such as medical or legal transcription, desktop publishing, editing, web hosting, bookkeeping, etc. A client will first call those ads that list the services he is seeking.

E-mails to Potential Clients

This is a cheaper alternative to sending a letter. I'm still not convinced that it replaces a nice professional letter sent, but I do know that it works. I've spoken to several VAs who have gained regular clients this way. The advice that they gave me was to make sure that the e-mail is short, to the point, outlines the benefits you can provide, and then leads them to your website where the client can obtain additional information. Be sure to abide by the rules of unsolicited e-mail so that your e-mail is not considered spam.

Former Employers

Call your former employers and tell them about your new venture. They already know you and your work, so this could be a great opportunity for both of you. Also, if you have a good relationship with them, ask them to spread the news. A little mention from them to their friends and business associates at lunch can bring you clients. Of course, in return you will want to show your appreciation by giving them a discount on their first services or by some other means.

Consider Other Local Businesses in Your Field

Your next contact should be any other businesses that do the same sort of thing as your former employer. Since you're already familiar with the company and what's required, you would be one step ahead of the game.

Specialty Items

Don't you just love getting those little giveaway items when you go to the local expo? I know I do. I also know that most of them get thrown away or tucked away in the junk drawer never to be seen again. Every now and then I'll come across a really cool gadget that I can really put to good use. I'm always open to receiving a nice golf shirt or sweatshirt from a vendor, or even a client. I remember my old boss asking me if I even owned a shirt that didn't have someone's logo on it. Better yet, he wondered if I'd ever paid for a shirt.

Make your ad specialty items count. Do your research and select items that are going to get you the most bang for your buck. Select items that are going to give you a great deal of mileage with your marketing message—something that the recipient is not likely to toss in the junk drawer. The object of the game here is to keep your message out there for everyone to see—particularly your company logo. If I were wearing just any old shirt when passing by my boss, he wouldn't have paid any attention to it. But he was sure to notice when I was wearing someone's logo. Get the picture?

Nowadays, I mainly wear shirts containing my own company logo rather than someone else's. When I attend networking events and business expos I'm sure to be wearing Another 8 Hours logo apparel. My kids even have polo shirts with my logo embroidered on them.

Advertising in Newsletters and E-Zines

Many associations, online communities, and even other VAs offer inexpensive advertising in their newsletters. Take advantage of this opportunity for marketing. It's a cost-effective means for getting your name out there. And sometimes you get a free ad once you join an association. Remember, the more exposure you give your business, the better. The key is to advertise where the readership is your target audience and spend your dollars wisely. Develop an ad and keep it the same or similar in repeat listings. That way, there will be immediate recognition when they see you advertised again. You can split test your ads to see which gets the best response rate. Remember that recognition is key to success!!! You never want to hear the phrase, "Gee, I didn't know you existed." Everyone should know about you!

I'm a big fan of going to the library and getting the newsletters there. Which ones can I get into? There are often ones for real estate agents, doctors, etc. Our community has a newsletter and also a book that comes out quarterly with events for the kids that accepts advertising.

Magazines

This will depend on your target market. One market that is good to target through magazine ads is authors. You can advertise in the *Writer's Digest Magazine*. With authors, you can type their work from any location. They merely send you their manuscript, and once complete you mail it back or e-mail it to them. We go further into detail in the "Targeting Authors" section. Focus on industry-related magazines that cater to your target market.

Web Decals and Vehicle Signage

Many VAs have found using web decals, magnetic signs, license plate holders, and vinyl lettering on their vehicle to be effective. It can merely state their web address or their domain name, or you can include a list of services with your logo and contact number. Check the search engines and your local sign company to find something right for you.

Client Relationship Building

Making your clients feel special is key to relationship building. Take the time to send your clients a token of your appreciation. Whether it is in the form of ad specialty items or something a bit more personal, take the time to get them something useful. Whenever possible, include your company logo. Kick it up a notch and send the client an item containing your logo and theirs to signify the partnership you have created. If the client has kids, you might even consider sending a gift for the kids instead of the client—or both, for that matter. The key is relationship building and making them feel important.

Budgets don't always allow for spending money on ad specialty items and other gift items. For Christmas one year, I sent all my clients, past and present, a holiday postcard that included a $10 off gift certificate in lieu of holiday gifts. I figured money is tight everywhere so what better way to say thanks than to save them some money. Plus, it didn't really affect my cash flow. I received over 90% of my postcards back in three months time.

I've even ordered pizzas for one of my online client's staff. I found out from the office manager that every payday Friday they order out. I sent the money in advance to the office manager and she placed the order. Boy, were they surprised. They loved it. (Next time I might need a favor; I bet they remember this, too!)

For local clients, take the time to stop by and see them throughout the year. Take them to lunch, get them tickets to a local sporting event, or drop off goodies. Diana is known to drop in on local clients around the holidays with her daughters. We also, out of the blue, will stop by and drop off bagels and cream cheese or donuts for the office staff. It is important that they get to know the personal side of you, as well as the professional side.

Direct Mail
I have always had great success with direct mail as a tool for marketing. ALWAYS!! Many of the VAs that I have mentored have tried it and met with good success as well. However, for some, it proves not to be the case. So my recommendation is this—TRY IT! And then try it again! You can follow-up with another mailing, too. I know that's how I got many of my clients. I got them because I sent them the second letter or postcard. The clients that I did get were professionals who I still work for today. These are regular businesses that need work on an ongoing basis. They can become the bread and butter of your business, where you know each week you will receive a check. But again, this is one of those things where you just see if it works for your business. As with all advertising, just because it doesn't work at one point, doesn't mean that it won't work at another time.

A follow-up call on your mailing can be the key to your success. Here's a sample script:

> Good morning Mr. Jones. This is Diana Ennen with Virtual Word Publishing. I was just following up on the letter that I sent you last week about my virtual assistant business. I was wondering if you had any questions or would like to receive additional information.
>
> #1 - If they say they don't have a copy of it – fax or e-mail them a copy.
> #2 - If they request additional information – offer to schedule an appointment to stop by with your portfolio. If not, forward them your portfolio via Overnight or Priority Mail, e-mail, or send a link to your online portfolio. It will appear as though you really want their business!
>
> Thank you for your time. I look forward to working with you.

What you could do is send a professional letter with your business card, and/or brochure, to your targeted market. The biggest advantage to direct mail is you specifically target the market you wish to specialize in. Start out with a small, manageable, targeted group. Take the time to compose a letter that effectively conveys what your business can do for them. The first sentence has to be POWERFUL AND INVITING. Spell out how the client will *benefit* from your services. Keep your letter short and get to the point quickly. Use no more than three or four short paragraphs. Bold or bullet the features that you want to stand out. In the letter, let them know exactly how your business is going to make their business better. Make absolutely sure the letter is letter-perfect—no typos and grammatically correct. Nothing can lose a potential client quicker than a typo in an introductory letter. It just looks bad, real bad!

It's also helpful to create the desire to contact you immediately. You want them to respond when they receive the letter, not weeks later. We recommend including a bonus offer in your letter, such as 20% discount off their work if they respond within a two-week time period.

Following is a list of the companies you can target with letters:

- Attorneys' offices
- Major corporations such as Microsoft, IBM, etc.
- For medical transcription work, target individual medical practices, medical groups and hospitals. (Don't forget chiropractors, therapists, etc.)
- Secretarial/personnel agencies—Emphasize in the letters that you specialize in resumes and computer tutoring (if you choose to).
- New businesses. Their addresses can be found under Legal Notices in newspapers and online.
- Grade schools, high schools, colleges and universities
- Court reporting agencies
- Churches/Christian organizations
- Mortgage companies
- Real estate/insurance agents
- Printers
- Hotels/motels
- Publishers/literary agents/online bookstores
- Internet companies
- Newsgroups and work-at-home groups
- Florists/restaurants/movie rentals
- Construction companies and builders

Now, just because you're sending a letter doesn't mean you are targeting local clients. I believe this is one of the things that many VAs misinterpret. You can send letters anywhere; a stamp is a stamp. You can send letters to publishers, major corporations, dot-com companies, media companies, newspapers, etc. One of Kelly's favorite sayings is, "Think outside the box." Be creative. We are not limited by anything!!

It is always good to follow-up with a postcard. Many of the specialty paper supply companies or office supply stores have special cards that are just perfect for this type of campaign. Wait a couple of weeks or so before making additional contact. Consider sending a series of postcards to create the name recognition you need. Remember, mind share can be very effective. It can take as many as 8-10 times for a prospect to see your name before they will actually remember you. Making these periodic "touches" with the postcards, or maybe a newsletter will increase your chances of gaining that mind share. One of the final touches might include a phone call to secure the relationship.

Local Businesses

Visit local businesses where your potential clients might frequent. Places like the computer supply store, the printer's, office supply stores, and any parcel post and mail handling businesses such as PostNet. Even local restaurants and gyms will have a place for cards. Ask if you can place your business cards or brochure on their counter. Some places will allow you to put your card in cardholders. We recommend taking along a holder just to have in case they do. Your card will get much more recognition in a nice business card holder.

Government Agencies and Non-Profit Associations

Contact government and city official agencies and non-profit associations. These are usually found at the beginning of your phone book or under the name of your city as well as online. Often times they can use your help. And best of all, they are in contact with other businesses in your area so if you do a real good job for them (which I know you will!), they can spread the word to the business community.

Cold Calling

I've been in business now for over 20 years and cold calling still sends shivers down my spine. But some people have found it a successful marketing tool. When I found this article from Jim McCormick, I knew immediately we needed it for our book. He was kind enough to let us use it. Send some business his way and thank him for me, would you!

Cold Calling
From Cowardly to Courageous - How to Succeed at Cold Calling
By Jim McCormick[1] - www.TakeRisks.com or 1.650.726.2900
(Printed with Permission Jim McCormick)

There it is. That darn phone. And you have to pick it up and call someone you don't know. You need to make some cold calls.

The first thing to know is this - the longer you put off picking up the phone and making that first call, the heavier that phone gets. Give it enough time and you'll swear the phone weighs 500 pounds when you try to lift it.

I've been skydiving for years. In thousands of jumps, I've learned some valuable lessons that apply to lots of things ... including cold calling. So, let me share some insights with you I've reaped from all those skydives that will make you more successful at cold calling.

So, how do you get started? How do you overcome the understandable fear of cold calling? Here are a few simple steps.

---

[1] Jim McCormick is a professional skydiver and motivational speaker. As a skydiver, he regularly deals with performance-threatening fear. As a speaker, he regularly encounters the challenge of cold calling. In both roles, he draws on his experiences as a World Record and North Pole skydiver to prevail. More information on Jim and his presentations is available at www.TakeRisks.com or +1.650.726.2900.

Step 1 - You Have to Believe in What You're Offering

You have to believe in the product or service you are offering. You have to know you are selling something of value - something that will assist the person or organization you are calling.

If you are not sure of the benefits you are offering your prospect, you need to sit down and think about it. Ask yourself, "How will this person or their organization be better off if they buy what I am selling?" How will they sell more, operate better, be happier - whatever the benefits are they will enjoy.

This is vital! Do not bother going on to the next steps until you have this really clear in your mind. You will be wasting your time. You have to be absolutely convinced, deep down, of the value of your product or service.

Now if you are stumped on this one, get some help. Ask some colleagues or friends for their thoughts on the value you are offering. If you do all this and conclude there really is not much value in what you are offering ... move on! You will never be a success at selling something you don't believe in. And life is too short to spend your time doing it.

It's similar to skydiving. If you do not believe in yourself and your equipment, you have no business being in the plane. You owe it to yourself, and your prospects, to only sell something you in which you truly believe.

Step 2 - See It From the Buyer's Viewpoint

When I was getting certified to take people for their first skydive, I was required to put on the student harness and ride on the front of an experienced instructor - just like my students do now. This was required because it is critical that I understand my student's viewpoint. Experiencing a jump from the student's perspective has definitely made me a better instructor.

It is the same for cold calling. You have to put yourself in the buyer's shoes. In your mind, trade places with your prospect. Ask yourself, "What would make me say, 'yes'?" And also ask yourself, "What would make me say, 'no'?" You have to appreciate the buyer's perspective to effectively sell to them.

It may help to ask people you have already sold to why they said, "yes." What made the difference to them? You'll gain valuable insights that will help you better understand you prospects' perspective - and make you more effective.

Step 3 - Separate Yourself from the Inevitable Rejection

When you are cold calling, you will experience rejection. It is unavoidable. Here is the important thing to keep in mind: It is not about you! Your prospect is not rejecting you. They are rejecting the product or service you are offering. They may just not need it right now. Or they may be so overwhelmed with challenges they just cannot focus on what you are offering and have to say. They are not rejecting you! They do not even know you.

Rejection is a part of life. So is occasional sub-par performance. I have walked away from many skydives very disappointed with my performance. But you have to shake it off and keep going. If I allowed my disappointment to get to me, I would eventually stop jumping. And that would deprive me of something I truly love.

It is similar with cold calling. If you allow the rejection to get to you, it will profoundly impact your effectiveness. When you get the "no's," the terse responses, or even the hang ups, you have to be able to say to yourself, "Oh well, their loss. I'm sorry they're not able to take advantage of the wonderful product or service I am offering right now. But I am going to keep calling to find people who can" - and mean it.

Step 4 - Accept the Fear - Then Move Through It

No one likes being rejected or hearing "no." That is normal and okay. It is easy to allow the desire to succeed lapse into a desire not to fail, which can then lapse into fear.

Don't worry. Being fearful of rejection or failure is common and appropriate. What is important is that you not play games with yourself. If the fear is there, don't try to fool yourself into thinking otherwise. Don't deny it.

Until you accept the presence of the fear, it is in charge. When you accept its presence and the fact that it is likely affecting you, you take a great deal of the power away from the fear.

I have had to learn this lesson thoroughly in order to succeed as a Professional Exhibition Skydiver. If I had not learned to acknowledge and accept my fears, there is no way I could have successfully jumped into small landing areas on the middle of large cities or into sporting events with audiences of over 100,000. (If you would like more information in this method of fear management, see the article called Risking to Win at www.TakeRisks.com.) So, accept that the fear is there and you are experiencing it. Not doing so will hold you back.

Step 5 - Keep Dialing

You build momentum with each call. When you stop dialing, you lose it. Set things up so you have plenty of prospects to call before you get started. Do your research in advance. When it comes time to call, do it with a vengeance! The sooner you make the next call, regardless of whether it is a sale or not, the better. You build momentum. One sale will lead to another.

If the last call was not a success, it is even more important to pick up the phone right away. The longer you wait, the more likely it is to get to you.

Cold calling will always be challenging. But you can make it more pleasant and be more successful at it by following these steps. Now get started. The sooner the better! It's time to leave the plane!

Newspaper/Job Bank

Search a local newspaper, online newspaper or Job Bank. Pay specific attention to the companies that advertise for the skills you possess. You will want to sell yourself well. Let them see how utilizing your services will help make their business more successful. As always, emphasize the benefits they will receive. Let them know, however, that you are not looking for a job that you will be going to their office.

Newsletters

Want to become an expert in your field—start sending newsletters. Newsletters are a great way to spread the word about your business and show others that you know your business well. Not only does it keep you in touch with your clients on a regular basis, but it also allows them to see some of your creativity. No black and white, plain-Jane stuff. Design it to be colorful, creative, and best of all, your very own creation. Be sure to research the most effective medium to use for your newsletter based upon your target audience and subscribers. Also consider whether or not your newsletter is best received in HTML or plain text format.

Classified Advertising

If you choose classified advertising, then you want to do your research before you spend any money. Check to see if those advertising in the classifieds are frequent advertisers. For example, most people will advertise in a paper if it's producing results. If it's not, they aren't going to waste their money. Look at a history of the publication to see who the repeat advertisers are. If you see a trend of one or two time only ads that never return, it probably means they are not getting results.

Check what is out there. Yes, you have your daily paper, but what else? Find out. Get them all. Now, get them for the next few weeks. Are there repeat advertisers in there? See what I'm getting at here. Call in the meantime and find out the advertising requirements and rates. Keep a chart so you can log this information. Now you will want to revisit this as your business progresses.

I have found advertising in local weekly newspapers can be productive. These are generally cheaper so you can keep your ad in there longer. It's very important for clients to see your ad repeatedly. When they need work done, they will already be familiar with your services.

Your Local Chamber of Commerce

So many people have stated that joining the Chamber of Commerce has been a great marketing tool for them. Wanda relayed the following information.

> I joined the Hoover Chamber of Commerce. Hoover is a fairly large town in Birmingham, and has a good-sized business community. They have over

1,000 members, many of which I am told are small to medium-sized businesses – which is one of my targets.

This particular chamber had many things to offer that I could benefit from:

- They have three networking functions per month. The first one is in the morning (Coffee and Contacts), the second one is lunch, and the third one is from 5:30 – 7:00p.m. (I think they call it Business After Hours or something like that). The only one that there is a charge for is lunch – and the cost is $10.
- I was able to put flyers and business cards in their office. I was also told that at the next luncheon (when I will be "presented" as a new member), I could print up flyers and put one in each chair.
- I will be included in the "Welcome to Hoover" guide for newcomers to the city, as well as new members to the Chamber. The middle of the book has a "Yellow Pages" of sorts, divided into categories and listing all members.
- They have a conference room available with a calendar hanging on the door. I can stop by and write my reservation in, or I can call and have them check availability. While utilizing the conference room, I am also able to use their copier, fax, telephone, etc. Soft drinks are even included in the refrigerator. For me, Hoover is a good halfway point between where I am located and Birmingham, so the conference room benefit was a huge one for me.
- Their web page is still under construction, but once complete, I will get a free hot link from their website to mine.
- They have a monthly newsletter. I was told that I could write an industry-related article with a by-line and my picture (if I wanted) and have it included in the next issue. They also offer advertising in their newsletter, and the rates are VERY reasonable.
- I can get free membership listing updates sent to me via fax – to utilize for mail-outs.
- I know that there was more, but these are the main points that "sold" me. I'm hoping that I'll be able to pick up some business from this investment. Oh yeah, it is tax-deductible too!

Can you see the potential? We sure can.

Always wear a nametag when networking

When networking, always wear a nametag. It provides a visual reminder of your name associated with your company name. If you have room to include your logo, that's all the better for building your brand. Your nametag should always be worn on the right side so that when you shake hands with people they are drawn to the right and can clearly identify you by name. (Naturally, if no one else is wearing one, I'd forego it. But many networking events encourage you to wear your nametag.)

Establish your elevator speech

An elevator speech is a canned message about your business. The message should be short enough, but descriptive enough that someone riding in an elevator with you would have an accurate picture of what you do in the time it takes to get from the first floor to the third floor—roughly 7 to 10 seconds. Your elevator speech should be designed to promote continued conversation; it is not meant to be a sales pitch. The speech is not meant to be a complete listing of all your services. It should describe the benefits and value that you bring to your clients. You can adjust the speech to fit the audience. In some cases offering a small case study with a personal touch can have great impact. Here are some examples:

Example 1: I allow sales professionals to spend more time in front of their clients and less time behind their desk.

Example 2: I help busy people get more mileage out of their day. Along the way, I help them save time and money.

Example 3: I come to the rescue when small business owners are spending more time on administrative tasks than they are growing their own business.

Example 4: I help others with the PR and marketing so they can focus more time on their business growth.

Write Articles

When you are reading an article in the newspaper or a local newsletter, aren't you impressed with the person writing it and often think of them as an expert in their field? We do. You can be THAT expert.

We highly recommend you create an article marketing campaign and submit articles regularly. The Internet has paved the way to getting your business on the front page of Google every time. Always submit to the top-ranking sites. Check http://www.VA-TheSeries.com resources for a listing.

You can add your articles to your website, blog, newsletter, and send it out to industry websites. Make sure to use effective Social Bookmarking through places like http://www.digg.com or http://www.stumpleupon.com to get more mileage out of your article. Sharing links to your articles on the social networks will trigger that viral marketing we spoke about earlier. Be sure to include a share button on your article page or blog post to make it easy for your readers to share through their networks, feeds, and so on.

One of the most important criteria is to make your articles informative and interesting. Liz Folger in *The Stay-At-Home Mom's Guide to Making Money From Home* states, "Be sure you include a small bio that tells what you do and a way that interested readers (that is, prospective clients) can get in touch with you."

In all articles, include a link back to your website for more information or for a free gift. Also be sure to include a bio and a reprint statement like "You are free to reprint this article as long as BIO is included."

Offer your services as a prize

Offer blocks of time for your services to be given away in contests, at networking events, in gift baskets, etc. Also, contact schools, businesses, political parties, etc. You'd be amazed how quickly your business recognition will spread when you give away some freebies. How about home-based business associations or welcoming centers in your area? How about your city council? See what I mean?

Business Expo

These can be a great way to promote your business. Your local Chamber of Commerce can provide you with a list of expos in your area. Also check online at Trade Show News Network (http://www.tsnn.com). The great advantage of participating in these expos is that you meet people face-to-face. Also, these are often advertised in your newspaper with the section on community events. You'd be amazed how successful these can prove to be for you. If you can't afford to exhibit, at least plan to attend. Don't forget to take plenty of business cards and network with not only those who stop by your exhibit, but also other exhibitors at the event as well.

Create a Mailing List

You should create a mailing list of all your clients and potential clients. Your repeat clients are going to be your main bread and butter, so you will want to keep your name in front of them. Therefore, occasionally send them updates on your business, any new services you perform, a newsletter, a holiday greeting, etc. Let them see that you really value them as a client. With holiday greetings, it's important to sign the card personally. It shows them you care enough to take the time. Consider including a personal note, a joke about a hard assignment you survived, a mention of a success of theirs, or something.

Referral Marketing

It takes a bit of work, but you can really drive the sales home by creating a referral network. Not long ago, I was doing some research for a mortgage consultant client of mine. Along the way, I came across a site called "By Referral Only." It was here that I found a statement by Joe Stumpf, founder and CEO of By Referral Only®, which really sums it up when it comes to referral marketing. "A referral is sending someone you like to someone you respect." Pretty powerful, huh? I thought so. Think about it. Think about those people you would refer to your family and friends; do you like them? Do you have faith in them and trust that your family and friends would be satisfied with their product or services as well?

In order to get your clients to send you referrals, you have to provide them with a positive experience in working with your company. Next, you can't be afraid to seize the moment and ask for referrals from everyone. Everyone could include satisfied clients, not-so-satisfied clients, family, and friends. For those you choose to include within your referral network, have you educated them on your company mission statement? Do they have a clear understanding of what your business is about in the event they should have to explain it? Could you do the same for their company if faced with a potential referral?

Many virtual assistants will also send referrals to other virtual assistants, particularly if they can't do the work requested by the client. This type of referral arrangement may or may not be tied to a financial incentive. If a more formal arrangement is needed then be sure to get the proper agreement in place. Otherwise, a token gift or flat fee can suffice—it's not required but rather a courtesy.

Use your business cards
Your business card is your calling card, the most important marketing tool you can leave behind. Don't skimp on its design. Give your cards out freely and in multiple quantities. I rarely ever give out just one card. Be sure to include all contact numbers, your logo, tag line, and your URL. Some are now adding their Twitter name and Facebook profile page, too. Don't forget that you can send your business card electronically so recipients can add your business card to their database or contact program.

My business card is like a mini-brochure. It's a fold over style so I have lots of room to list a sampling of services provided. Because of the style, I'm able to use my card as a kind of "clip" when mailing documents to a client. Instead of a paperclip, I slip my card either over the top of all the documents I'm sending or I place it right at the fold. Either way, when they open the envelope they pull out everything at once with my card being the first thing they touch and see.

Use a signature line
A signature line is like the closing of a letter, only it's for e-mail and you can also add information about the benefits of your business. This is like a miniature ad.

Voice Mail
Use your outgoing mail message to your advantage. You've already got the callers attention; why not offer them some information on your company. At a minimum you should include your company name, tag line, and URL.

Advertise your URL
Let people know how to find you and your website. Put your URL on everything that goes out of your office, including all stationery, letters, business cards, catalogs, brochures, etc. Invest in a car decal, magnetic sign or a license plate holder. Also, do an aggressive marketing campaign so your website is visible and drives traffic to your site.

Develop a Tag Line
Your tag line, or slogan, is a short impact statement that drives the message home about what you do. Have you ever played the game where you get a list of company slogans and you had to match them with the right company? I used to love that game. Your slogan helps to create your brand and build that all important mind share. A great resource to help you design your tag line is http://www.yudkin.com/generate.htm.

Respond to RFPs
Many organizations offer an RFP, Request for Proposal, system whereby clients submit their virtual assistant needs through an online form and that information is then passed along to the members or posted in a member area. If your company is interested and qualified, then you would respond accordingly to the client. Your response would include: a brief intro, information about your services as they pertain to the needs outlined in the RFP, benefits of partnering with you, an invitation to visit your website for more information, and a call to action – suggest a time to talk by phone. Don't forget your contact info!

Press Release

What a wonderful way to spread the news about your business and get your name out there. Not only does your company gain credibility, you can be considered an expert in your field when written correctly. With online press release sites and the use of Google Alerts you can increase your speed to market when potential clients are tracking certain keywords.

A good press release is to the point and contains all the information necessary to print a story without having to contact you. You will want to begin the release with a headline at the top in bold print. The first paragraph should contain the most important information.

As Liz Folger states in her book, *The Stay-At-Home Mom's Guide to Making Money From Home,* "Make yourself newsworthy and not sound like an advertisement. Have you just started your business, just received an award, or added a new product to your line? Don't be afraid to toot your own horn. If you don't, no one else will."

To become newsworthy, have something unique or different to say that would benefit the readers of that particular newspaper.

Liz Folger's book also provides the following tips for a successful press release:

- Become familiar with the publications you would like to send your press release to.
- Use a cover letter only if you're announcing an event you want the editor to attend.
- Get the writing and photo guidelines for each publication you want to send to.
- Include an upbeat and clear photo of your product or service in use. The paper is more likely to run your story if you include a picture.
- Know the editor you need to send the press release to and spell his or her name correctly.
- To announce the opening of your new business, send your release to the editor of the business section.

Here are some additional tips:

- In the first paragraph answer who, what, why, when, and how and give a quick summary of the story.
- Write in the present tense and use short sentences and paragraphs.
- Include all contact information.
- For a press release that can be used anytime, write FOR IMMEDIATE RELEASE.
- Think of a good angle, one that would gain recognition and is newsworthy.
- Write the release on your company letterhead if sending by mail.
- Keep it to one page in length; 300-650 words.
- Include your important keywords and your URL in the release.

In the release, don't write about yourself. The mere fact that you opened a business isn't newsworthy, yet. However, the fact that you opened a business and are now *filling a need* is. Emphasize in your release how more businesses are choosing virtual assistants to help them with their work overload – VAs are solving a problem and how.

The appearance of your press release is important to get it noticed. Because editors receive hundreds of press releases, you want yours to impress them enough to make it through the first cut. Above all else, it has to be newsworthy. If it sounds too much like advertising, it won't make it. Keep it professional and in third person as much as possible, avoid "I" usage.

Barbara Brabec suggests in *Homemade Money: How to Select, Start, Manage, Market and Multiply the Profits of a Business At Home:*

> A press release must look 'crisp' and be easy to read with ample margins all around. Releases can be printed on plain white paper, on your business letterhead, or on a special news release letterhead you may wish to design.

Elements Of A Release

Following are typical items in most releases:

- The name and number of someone to contact are standard inclusions. It will aid the editor when and if he has questions. Many releases are thrown out because a contact person is not included.

- The second item is the headline. Make it attention grabbing to create interest, and use your keywords as much as possible to improve search engine rankings.

- Next is your copy. After your copy is the following symbol, centered on the page.

###

- The first line of your copy should begin with your city, state and the date and in bold.

- The last paragraph should include your call to action by summarizing your press release and including how they are going to get in touch with you or respond appropriately to the release.

- While it's not recommended to go beyond one page, if there are additional pages, the bottom of the first page would include the word "More" in lieu of "###".

Online press releases can be submitted to http://www.PRWeb.com and numerous other free press release places. See http://www.VA-TheSeries.com for a more extensive list of places to submit.

In Their Own Words:

Tess Strand Alipour: When I started my practice, I was living and traveling in various countries including: India, Nepal, Turkey and Iran, so there wasn't much local networking or marketing I could do, and at that time, Twitter and Facebook didn't even exist. I had a website, of course, and a business blog, but the leads I received from the website were not always an ideal match.

I have always found that my best source for new, ideal clients comes through referrals from current clients. The new potential clients come to me already evangelized about what I do, how I work, etc. Of course, with rave references from the existing client - nine times out of ten, in my experience - a referral from an existing client is a match made in heaven and because they know what to expect to some degree, the intake and initiation process is much quicker and smoother for both of us.

Simply asking for referrals, and thanking clients graciously for any new contracts you've gained through their connections can work wonders to build a practice to capacity.

Alyssa Gregory: The majority of my marketing activities are focused on word-of-mouth, client referrals, and online marketing through social media. I have not had much success with offline/local marketing.

Andrea Pixley: I do not market locally. Instead, I rely highly on search engines, online networking groups, and word-of-mouth. Since I move every two to three years, I feel traditional marketing methods are a waste of my time and money.

Kathy Ritchie: My marketing is mainly online. I've tried placing advertising in newspapers which has little or no return. Most successful marketing has been by word-of-mouth, and online advertising, submitting my site to search engines and so on.

Barbara Rowen: Face-to-face networking and word-of-mouth has worked the best for my business. I prefer to work within the local market, and networking organizations such as Business Networking International (BNI) and the local Chamber of Commerce have worked well for me. Both organizations have helped me with my marketing skills, from standing up in front of groups to introduce my business (without the shaking and stuttering) to working on several elevator speeches for various audiences. The exposure I receive through these two organizations have actually "put me on the map" as a viable online business service company in my community.

Nancy Seeger: Networking, social media and some volunteering. Portfolio examples are important and keeping a reference in designed sites of business name help increase awareness.

Donna Toothaker: I market online. I publish a weekly e-zine, I submit my articles to directories weekly, I blog (not as often as I should), I utilize social media. My weekly e-zine has brought in a lot of business, as has social media.

I spent a lot of time, money, and effort having a table at a tradeshow, which was very unsuccessful. I didn't make one dime, as people in my area don't understand virtual assistance. So local marketing has not worked for my business.

Susan Totman: Initially I did mailings, newspaper ads, yellow pages, my website, handing out business cards and word-of-mouth. Yellow pages and direct mailings. I got very little business using these. A few resumes and general clerical jobs, but no long-term clients, which is what I was looking for.

My most successful marketing tool has definitely been my website. I constantly update it by adding new content. I put the URL on my business cards and told people to go there to read more about VAs.

Jeannine Clontz
Accurate Business Services
E-mail: Jeannine@Accbizsvcs.com
www.Accbizsvcs.com

When I first started my business in 1998, we were considered secretarial services, or providers of business support services. The virtual assistant designation was just taking shape on the Internet. I never dreamed that I could market to clients outside of my metropolitan area, but I have.

I sort of started my business by accident. I was actually researching a business opportunity for my husband who was very unhappy with his career path. I was the main breadwinner, so it certainly was a huge leap for me to start my own VA practice. Thankfully, my husband was not only extremely supportive of my venture, but even left a job he enjoyed to go somewhere that offered health insurance and benefits that we now lacked because of my self-employed status.

I decided on becoming a VA because that's where I felt most comfortable with my talents and experience. Although I had spent 15 years in outside sales and purchasing, I was always heavily involved with the daily administration and customer service aspects for these organizations. I feel that you need to really LOVE what you do, and you have to be the best at doing it. That's how I feel about my skills as a VA. I also think that outsourcing is the wave of the future. I have found that outsourcing has become an affordable option to businesses of all sizes that have a need and desire to work with trained entrepreneurial people who can provide the skills needed, when they need them. I think that in its truest form, this is what a VA does.

I found that the best way to dive in was to get involved in the community, which I soon realized I truly loved. I joined my local Chamber (actually, I now belong to two), networking groups like BNI, and non-profit groups like Kiwanis, and Optimists. It put me out in front of a lot of businesspeople who could potentially become clients. It also allowed me the opportunity to donate my time to speak on business and customer service issues to these groups, which has helped them gain confidence in my experience and abilities.

Volunteering your time to be involved in the VA industry is a wonderful way to get to know other entrepreneurs that really care about the industry and want to give back and assist in promoting and supporting the industry, while helping potential clients feel comfortable working in a "virtual" environment.

My volunteer spirit got me involved with assisting a VA site with the business ethics portion of their certification program. Since researching the subject, I have become quite passionate about educating organizations and individuals on the importance of having a strong sense of ethics, and how it can be incorporated into their everyday lives.

I now volunteer some time to two of what I consider to be the TOP VA sites on the Web, the International Virtual Assistant's Association (ivaa.org), and the Real Estate VA

Network (REVANetwork.com). I've spoken at a conference on business ethics, helped create and implement codes of ethics, bylaws, and web content, as well as being a volunteer columnist on the subject of business ethics. I find it extremely rewarding, and the incredible relationships I've built will continue and grow for many years to come.

I have been amazed to find how willing VAs are to share, support, and mentor each other. If I ever have a question about a client situation, software problem, or just looking to get tips on marketing and promotion, there are always multiple responses to help me make the most informed decisions about the running of my VA practice.

If you're reading this book, you've taken your first step in finding out how to join our ranks and start a successful and profitable VA practice. So come on in, the water's fine!

Determining Your Rates

Determining what to charge for your services can be one of the most challenging tasks you will encounter. Do your homework; take the time to research competitors in your area. You might consider searching for various positions in the target area on Salary.com (http://www.salary.com). You can also consult the Industry Production Standards publication distributed by OBCAI (http://www.officebusinesscenters.com).

Connie Champagne states, "I have chosen to use different rates for different services, reasoning that clients should expect to pay more for tasks requiring higher level of skills and experience." However, an interesting analysis of this subject can be found at: http://desktoppub.about.com/library/inkspot/bl_price_001.htm.

Don't sell yourself short. Be confident in your pricing. Nothing can shout "**AMATEUR**" more than talking with a potential client and being unsure of your rates. Don't be timid either, as you are providing a valuable service. It's up to you to convince your client that you feel strongly that you can help make their business better and you deserve top dollar for doing so. In addition, support your claims by showing the client a comparison of partnering with a VA versus hiring an employee.

Determine the price you want to be paid based upon your own skills and experience. Our research shows most pricing is centered on a base price of $35 per hour and can be as high as $100 or more for more specialized services. However, the rate does depend on the services you provide and also how long you've been in business. Premium services deem a premium price. Another consideration is the area in which you live. You will receive more in some areas than in others.

There are different ways in which you can charge for services: by the hour, by the project, by the page, and even packaged services. For something like meeting planning, you could charge a certain percentage of the total event cost. Many VAs offer reduced rates for a monthly retainer option. With a monthly retainer, your client commits to a certain number of hours per month at a predetermined rate. If you work less than the committed number of hours, you are still paid the same. If you work over the committed number of hours, then you would bill the client for the additional hours at that same rate or whatever is agreed upon. Following the philosophy of partnering with clients, the retainer agreement can prove to be the most beneficial for all parties. Your client benefits from knowing that they are guaranteed a set amount of your time each month while enjoying the cost savings. You benefit from the guarantee of monthly income and can better manage your time based upon your various client needs.

Clients who hire you for a specific service are easy to bill. Those clients who use several of your services that might have different rates are a different story. In those instances, I take a look at the different services and come up with an average to do them all. There will also be times that clients ask you to perform a task that you have never priced out. Don't be too quick to quote a price when you are not sure what the job entails and how long it will take you to complete it. Ask the right questions and even get a sampling of the work to be performed. You don't want to get in a situation where you have under-priced your services.

Remember, you are running this business and can charge whatever you want for services. It's also important to remember that you want to earn an income from this business. Not pricing your services correctly will make a huge impact on your bottom line. When doing the market research for your business plan, you should check out other VAs, as well as local businesses with similar services. By checking local businesses, you can determine what the market will bear in your area of the country. You may also find various pricing studies that have been conducted on a particular service, as well as established industry production standards.

We consulted Robert Brenner[1] of Brenner Information Group who shared this information with us on pricing.

© 2003 Robert Brenner, Brenner Information Group

What should a VA watch for when determining price?

Pricing is one of the most challenging things that a business owner faces. It's part art and part science. And most small business owners do not do a very good job at pricing their work. They typically try to set rates below that of their competitors. But what if each competitor entering the market is doing the same thing? Prices consistently get lower until owners begin to realize that they are losing money each time they do a job.

Here's what VAs need to do to establish their price. First determine your cost basis for each task that you do. The budgeted hourly cost concept is a good model to follow. Once you know what it costs to do each job, adding a percent profit to the number lets you generate a baseline price that you can charge. At least then you know that you are covering your costs and making some money for your efforts.

The second thing that you need to do is determine what price the market will bear. Collecting prices or buying an hourly price listing is how you start. Make a chart showing how many competitors have rates at each price point. This price distribution chart will show you the lowest price, highest price, and how prices are grouped. These groupings define a market, and you need to decide which market you want to sell to. This determines the top and bottom price you can charge.

Lastly, see where your baseline price fits on this chart. This may show you which market segment you must enter. It also shows you how much flexibility you have in setting the price that you quote.

---

[1] Professor Robert Brenner, president of Brenner Information Group, lecturer, teacher, and author of over 75 books. You can reach him through his website at http://www.brennerbooks.com or by telephone at (858) 538-0093.

So you analyze cost and you analyze the market. And then you set your final price based on sound business principles. And this is how it should be.

Is it best to use a flat hourly basis or price according to the task?

Pricing by the hour or pricing by the task depends on the uncertainty in the work and how many times you've done the task before. If you simply aren't sure how long it will take to do a job, or if your client often changes the scope of the work, or alters the time schedule, you may want to charge by the hour.

If you've done this job many times before, and you know how long it will likely take, then you can price by the task or by the complete job. For example, suppose you can proofread between 4 and 20 pages an hour (about 10 pages an hour typical). If your hourly rate is $20 an hour, then you should be charging about $2 a page to proofread documents. Do you?

Likewise if you can typically scan and color correct about 4 full page scans an hour, you could charge $5 per scan based on a time and rate basis.

For those who charge $15 an hour, what are they REALLY earning?

If you earned $15 working for someone else, you cannot charge $15 an hour and run a viable business. Here's why. When a company pays you, they are actually billing out your work at a much higher rate. This is because they must pay taxes, insurance, benefits, and other overhead out of what they charge. For example, when I worked as an engineer, I was paid about $30 an hour, but my work was being billed out at $100 an hour. The company needed to make a profit on everything that I did for our client.

In addition, productivity plays a major role in how much net income you can earn for your company. Let's say you can work 2,080 hours a year. But if you are a sole proprietor, one-person company, you can't work all the time. Part of the time you must be looking for more jobs, and part of your time you will be doing the company paperwork and invoicing and trying to get paid. It's called the "30-60-10" rule. Thirty percent of the time you are performing billable work; 60% of the time you are marketing for more work, and 10% of the time you are trying to get paid. A small business owner typically works 100% of the time, but charges for only 30% of the time.

There's an interesting chart that I put in my pricing guidebooks showing how much you really earn. For example, at $10 an hour, the maximum possible revenue you can earn is $20,800 a year. This is for working 100% of the 2,080 hours each year. But if you're only 30% productive, you actually earn just $6,240 a year. And this is BEFORE taxes. Remember, if you're a sole proprietor, and if you are married, both of your incomes are combined for taxes so your tax bite can be huge. Deduct expenses and taxes from your gross revenue and your earnings could be only $4,000 a year! This is like paying yourself $1.92 an hour! You could make more money flipping burgers down the street!

Let's say you have one really stable client, and you can work 70% of the time. Your possible earnings are $14,560 a year. After expenses and taxes you could realize $11,000 each year. This is equivalent to $5.29 an hour. Now how do you feel about charging just $10 an hour?

Now do the calculations at a billing rate of $15 an hour. At 100% productivity, you can earn $31,200 a year. Get realistic and analyze this at 30% productivity, and you are now pulling in $9,360 a year. After expenses and taxes are deducted, you could have $5,990 to keep. You're actually paying yourself $2.88 an hour. At 70% productivity, you can earn $21,840. After expenses and taxes are removed, you could have $13,978 left for you. This is equivalent to $6.72 an hour. This is much better and certainly more realistic.

There are a number of ways to improve on this bottom line picture. You can increase your rates. You can increase your productivity. And you can hire lower-paid, part-time support.

We recently conducted a VA industry survey to find out what is real in earnings and pricing. The results are an eye-opener. For information, contact the Brenner Information Group offices at brenner@brennerbooks.com.

How can VAs use industry production standards when most VAs are not performing task-oriented services?

The two most likely questions that you'll get from prospective clients are "How much will it cost?" and "How long will it take?" If you can't give a quick estimated response to these questions, you'll lose your sale before you even get to your pitch.

Pricing tables and hourly rates books can help you understand what your competitors are charging. And industry production time standards enable you to give a quick ballpark estimate as to how long a job will take.

Naturally the number of hours a job will take depend on many factors: your current workload, the value of the job, the number of interruptions you experience, the resources that will be required, your skills, and how motivated you are to work today. This is why being able to tell a client (or prospective client) that it typically takes between XX and YY hours to do this type of job is useful. It sets the bounds of expectation in the mind of the buyer. They can mentally budget the job and be more receptive when you give them the price.

Another good use for industry production standards is in generating a flat rate so you can bid on any project. If you know how long, and you know how much, you can estimate any job. And you will know how much money you'll make, or how much room you have to negotiate. A "standard" performance time is critical in this model. And it works.

How would industry production standards come into play with VAs who have long-term relationships with clients?

If you have few clients, one or more of whom have been clients for a long time, you can develop a historical record of how long each of their jobs have taken. Breaking each job out into tasks and recording how long each task takes lets you develop a good basis for future estimates. This makes it easier to estimate the time you should allocate to each job when it is repeated.

In the book, *Desktop Production Time Standards,* there is a method that shows how to determine the number of times you must complete a task before you can define a "time standard." The more times you perform a task, the better you get at estimating how long it will take.

Industry production standards play a key role in establishing baseline prices and estimating what flat rate price to quote on new projects.

In Their Own Words:

Tess Strand Alipour: For non-specialty services [general administrative assistance] I charge $35 hourly. For my specialty services [SEO, content development, web development, graphic design, press releases, consulting, etc.] the rate varies from $55 - $150 hourly.

Jeannine Clontz: Most word processing and general secretarial tasks are invoiced at $28-30/hour. Desktop publishing is at $45-55/hour, and general bookkeeping is at $40-50/hour. Faxes are $1.15-1.30/page, and phone calls range from $.50-.75/each (based on a 5-minute call). I arrived at my prices through market research, industry publications (like Brenner Books), experience within the industry, and by networking with other VA business owners.

Alyssa Gregory: $50-100/hour, depending on the service.

Kathy Ritchie: I arrived at my pricing by acting on my own comfort level. When I raised prices the last time, it was actually to slow the growth of my business. I was surprised when each client accepted the raise and I have not stopped growing. I use my own comfort level when pricing. For extras, I charge for long distance, postage, labels and envelopes, and the check paper used for taking payments for clients. I don't have rush pricing, but I do charge more for after hours or weekends. I try to keep all evenings and weekends strictly non-business.

Barbara Rowen: After researching several VA sites, and paying attention to discussions on the boards, I had an idea of what I should be charging for my services. I then checked into various temp and employment agencies in my area to find out two things: what they were willing to pay me and what they charged their client for me. I was shocked at the results. Just knowing what they would be charging a company for me to do secretarial and administrative work caused me to increase my rates, because I was undercutting myself. I believe I am worth every penny I charge my clients, and they are getting an excellent value for their money.

Donna Toothaker: My last hourly rate was set at $70/hr, or $65/hr for retainers. However, since then, I've moved my services into monthly packages, which range from $325/month up to $1495/month, depending on the type of package/service. I arrived at these based on how many hours we determined it took to provide certain groups of services. Then I added a cushion for time and cost. I also determined the value of the result that these packages gave to the client.

Susan Totman: I currently charge $55 per hour. In 1987, I started my business charging $12/hour. That was taking into consideration my expenses, taxes, and other overhead at the time, plus it was affordable to my clients. At the time, I had health insurance through my husband's employer. Over the years, the rate has increased as my skill level increased and developed, and what the market would bear, as well as my own increased costs and expenses of running my business. I strive to make 50% of my hourly rate my take-home pay at minimum. It would cost clients considerably more than what they pay me if they had to support the overhead of an in-house employee of the same skill level.

Working with Subcontractors

A growing number of virtual assistants expand their business with the help of qualified subcontractors. It's a way for them to build their business without working 24/7. What happens in business is once you start getting clients, you personally can only handle so much work and then you have to start turning work away. However, when you hire subcontractors to help you, you can continue to expand and grow your business while also making a profit on the subcontracted work. We highly recommend it.

Subcontractors are typically other virtual assistants, but that's not absolutely the case. You can hire them for everything from helping with administrative tasks to taking over your bookkeeping, article and press release submission, to web work and social media marketing and everything in between. Consider what you need to free up your time to work on your business and then contract it out, just like you tell your clients.

I know one of the main tasks that my VA does is to help me with my social book marketing efforts. When I get interviewed in the media, I can quickly send over my link and she can make sure it gets all the exposure we need. She also assists with sending out articles and press releases, updating my blog, etc.

Here are a few tips for working effectively with a subcontractor.

1) Hire someone who is qualified and above all else dependable. Get references and check those references.
2) Hire someone that is very familiar with the work that you need done or at least is willing to be trained on it.
3) Have a contract that outlines the working relationship.
4) Be clear on your instructions and deadlines. Write everything down. Remember that it can cost you more if you are unclear and work needs to be redone.
5) Give yourself some leeway with client deadlines. Make sure you have some extra time before the client expects the work so you can review it or even if you don't need to review it, so you can have extra time in case you don't get the work back in time from your subcontractor.
6) Communication is key. When things come up, discuss them promptly; don't let them brew. You'll discover that it's so much easier to resolve problems this way.
7) Be good to your subcontractor and reward them well. You want them to stay with you for a long time so make sure you treat them well.
8) Be prepared to pay the subcontractor whether you collect from a client or not. It's not their fault if your client pays late or doesn't pay at all. They still did the work.

Creating a multi-VA business is an upward trend in the industry. Under this type of business model, you take on more of a managerial role while the VA team members handle the client work. In some cases, there is another level of a Project Manager that manages the entire workload across the team.

There are pros and cons to both business models. Check out all the options and do what works best for you. And by all means, it's perfectly acceptable to remain solo.

Software Used

The type of software you use will depend greatly on what services you offer. Don't feel intimidated if you don't possess knowledge of all the software mentioned below. The longer you are in business, the more knowledge you will gain. You will, however, want to be proficient at the programs required to perform the services offered. For example, if you plan on offering word processing, you will want to be familiar with Microsoft Word or WordPerfect.

If a client approaches you about working in a program you do not know, be honest and let them know. It's possible that you can quickly learn the program or subcontract the associated tasks. Don't misrepresent yourself by accepting work that you cannot perform. I've often taken on assignments and then was able to teach myself what was required to do a specific job. However, if you feel that you will have problems, offer to find another VA who can assist with this particular project.

There are a great number of software packages available today. It can be a challenge to keep up with the latest and greatest. Do your best to stay abreast of technology and, at minimum, be aware of what's available even if you don't purchase the latest version, or the latest piece of software. For the software you do purchase, be sure to keep the necessary backup copy (off-site) in the event you have to reload the software. In addition, make frequent checks for online updates to keep the program running smoothly. Take advantage of free and low cost trial versions to familiarize yourself with it before investing.

Software can really put a dent in your finances, too. Take advantage of obtaining software programs through Ebay auctions or places like Amazon. Often times, purchasing an older version through alternate sources and then purchasing an upgrade from the software manufacturer can minimize your expenses. Whatever means you use for obtaining the software, be sure to keep it legal and act according to the licensing agreement. All purchased software should be eligible for registration with the vendor. Most vendors have trial versions available; use these trials whenever you are unsure whether the program will work for you before investing your money.

I briefly mentioned keeping an off-site copy of the original software. Most software these days is downloadable directly from the Internet or you purchase it on CD Rom. Any software that you download should be copied onto CD, or some type of medium, that can be maintained off-site in case you ever have to reload. Keeping backups of your software off-site is crucial should a disaster happen within your office that would ruin the backup devices.

I recommend getting a CD binder and keeping all your original software together in the binder. Be sure to include all the necessary serial numbers, registration numbers, unlock codes, etc. Your insurance agent and your accountant will be very proud of you for doing this!

When discussing software with clients, be sure to compare versions for compatibility. When preparing documents for printing, be sure to confirm the type of files they can accept. You will also want to confirm whether your client and printer, or other file recipients are on a PC or Mac computer.

Following is a list of different software and online services you might encounter or consider purchasing. We have omitted the use of versions as we recommend the latest version whenever possible. This list is not meant to be all-inclusive; it's simply a sampling of various programs.

- E-mail Clients
    - Outlook
    - Outlook Express
    - Thunderbird
    - Eudora
    - Google and Yahoo E-mail
    - Zimbra

- Calendars
    - Outlook
    - Sunbird
    - iCal
    - BusyCal
    - Zimbra
    - Google and Yahoo Calendar

- Information Processing
    - Microsoft Office including Word, Excel, PowerPoint and Access
    - WordPerfect

- Web Design, Blogs, and Content Management Systems (CMS)
    - Dreamweaver
    - WordPress
    - Typepad
    - Drupal
    - Joomla

- Desktop Publishing
    - Adobe Pagemaker, InDesign, or Framemaker
    - Microsoft Publisher
    - Quark Xpress
    - Corel Draw

- Illustration, Photo, Layout and Graphics
    - Adobe Illustrator
    - Adobe Photoshop
    - Paint Shop Pro
    - CorelDRAW Graphics
    - Freehand
    - Xara X
    - Fireworks

- Project Management and Collaboration
  - Microsoft Project
  - Basecamp
  - Central Desktop
  - Google Docs
  - Zoho Projects

- Accounting
  - Peachtree
  - Quickbooks, Quickbooks Pro
  - Quicken
  - Freshbooks

- Time Tracking
  - Quickbooks
  - TraxTime
  - Office Time

- Online Meetings
  - Skype
  - GoToMeeting
  - GoToWebinar
  - WebEx

- FTP
  - Transmit
  - CyberDuck
  - Filezilla
  - Cute FTP

- Anti-Virus
  - McAfee
  - Norton
  - AVG

- Web Browsers
  - Internet
  - Firefox
  - AOL
  - Google Chrome
  - Safari

- Presentation and Multimedia
  - Microsoft Powerpoint
  - Adobe Director
  - Keynote
  - Flash

- Specialty Software
  - Adobe Acrobat (PDF file creation)
  - Audacity (audio)
  - Camtasia (screen capture studio)
  - WinZip (file compress/uncompress)
  - 1ShoppingCart.com, PracticePaySolutions.com (shopping carts)
  - Mozy, Carbonite, JungleDisk (online backup)
  - DropBox (online storage with desktop access)

- Remote access
  - pcAnywhere
  - LogMeIn
  - GoToMyPC

- Conference calls
  - FreeConference.com
  - NoCostConference.com
  - FreeConferenceCall.com

In Their Own Words:

Tess Strand Alipour: The software I use most often and on a regular basis is: Adobe CS suite, Cute FTP, Microsoft Office Suite, Audacity, Screenhunter, Skype, EchoSign [this is not really software, but is such an awesome online resource it has to be included in my arsenal].

Alyssa Gregory: All standard office tools, plus design apps like Photoshop, Illustrator, Dreamweaver, etc.

Jeannine Clontz: I have the complete Microsoft Office Professional XP package that includes: Word, Excel, Publisher, PowerPoint, Access, Outlook and Outlook Express. I have QuickBooks 2002, and Quicken Basic 2002. I have the complete package of Adobe products which includes: PageMaker, Illustrator, Acrobat, and Distiller. I also have the complete Word Perfect Suite, but all of my clients have switched over to using Microsoft products, so it's no longer loaded onto my hard drive. I am always looking to increase my marketability by providing the most up-to-date software available, which also gives me the ability to be compatible with any potential client.

Nora Rubinoff: We use and support all popular Mac and PC-based applications.

Nancy Seeger: Adobe Design Suite CS4, Macintosh applications, ScreenFlow, Skype, Transmit, Acrobat Professional, BusyCal, Quark, OfficeTime, BaseCamp, Central Desktop.

Susan Totman: Microsoft Office; Open Office; Quickbooks; Skype; Desktop; Winzip Professional; Twhirl; Kaspersky Antivirus and Internet Protection; Filezilla; Macromedia (now Adobe) Studio – Dreamweaver, Flash, Fireworks, Homesite, Flashpaper; Adobe Acrobat Professional.

Equipment And Office Setup

This chapter is one where we're going to prefix it with two words—no three words, THINK, THINK, THINK!! You'll thank us when you're done.

When deciding on your equipment, write everything down. You want a solid game plan. I've seen too many decide to start a business and then go shopping. ***WRONG!!!*** This is an extremely costly mistake. You need to refer to your business and marketing plans for your short-term and long-term operational needs. Do your research to find out what's out there, and you need to know exactly what you need. Salesmen get paid to sell you. That's why when you go shopping, you should have written down exactly what you want, where you can get the best price, and how long it will take to get it delivered and installed. If you don't think you will ever use the extras that the vendor will try to sell you, don't buy them. However, if in fact they give you a discount on something that six months down the road you will be utilizing, then buy it now at the discount if you can afford it. Also, keep in mind that down time is critical to your business. Clients won't understand it, they need their work when it's due. If you don't have someone who can provide assistance with your hardware, make sure that you make the appropriate provisions to keep your business up and running.

Publications and websites such as *PC Magazine*, *Cnet*, and *ZDNet* offer reviews and product ratings on almost any kind of equipment you could imagine. Do your homework and be sure to purchase the right equipment for getting the job done. Having the biggest, the best, and the most expensive equipment does not always mean your office will operate effectively and efficiently. Be a smart shopper.

You can't be in this business without a fast, reliable computer. This is a great starting point to review your equipment needs. Your computer is a prime example of not purchasing the most powerful machine on the market. Purchase what you need now and in the immediate future, consulting your budget for when the next computer purchase is planned. Why? Because what you buy today that you might not need, will be better and most likely less expensive in the not too distant future. Plus, with the constant changes in technology, your computer is often considered "old" the day after you buy it. Relying once again on your business operational plans, you can quickly identify exactly what programs you will need, what kind of graphics card you will need, whether or not you need modem capabilities, ample storage space, and the right amount of RAM and memory to run the programs you require. It is highly recommended to purchase the fastest computer you can afford. In regard to speed, you have to also consider things like RAM and cache. If you know someone who knows a great deal more about computers than you do, or if you can afford to hire an IT consultant, we recommend asking them to assist you with your purchase. This is an investment in your business and should be taken very seriously. Again, do your homework and don't be afraid to contact the technical support people of the computer manufacturer if you need assistance.

Other computer-related considerations are:

- Writable CD Rom
- CD Rom

- Monitor (recommend no smaller than 17")
- Ergonomic mouse and keyboard
- External hard drive for backup
- USB ports
- Networking and router capabilities
- Surge protectors (protect your investments!)
- UPS backup power protection
- Cables and connectors

I'll let you in on a little secret—I purchased both my laptop and my desktop through Dell in the refurbished store on their website. Each came with software and components that I selected based on my criteria. Each came with the same warranty as a new machine, with the option to purchase additional coverage. Check it out, you just might find what you need. Dell is not the only one who offers refurbished machines. Check your preferred manufacturer's site or give them a call to see if they have refurbished machines at discounted prices. Make sure that you have access to someone who can fix your computer or a warranty that will go with your refurbished system.

The Internet and e-mail will become the lifeline of your business and you need to stay connected. Now that you have the right computer, you need a good ISP, DSL, or cable service provider to access the Internet. Select the right provider at the right price for your area. If you can avoid dial-up, you will be better off in the long run. DSL or cable will not tie up phones lines that could be better utilized for client calls. You might even eliminate the need for an additional phone line by choosing DSL or cable. If you are charged by the minute for your phone service, dial-up can quickly run up your phone expense unless the ISP has a toll-free dial-up number. Consult your operational plan and budget to see what you can afford while still operating efficiently. Remember, you are in the business of selling time and your time, as well as your client's time, is valuable. The less time you spend waiting for downloads and uploads from the Internet, the more productive you can be. Your Internet connection speed plays a major role in managing your time effectively. Most DSL companies will provide a backup dial-up number to allow you access should their service ever go down. Be sure to ask if they offer this feature. I'm not aware of the cable companies having dial-up backup. If you find this to be true with your cable company, then I highly recommend securing an ISP for dial-up should your cable communications be interrupted.

I don't know about you, but if I can't get on the Internet to at least check my e-mail, I feel totally lost. It's like removing one of my limbs or something. The interruption to your business is difficult to deal with and you have to know that the interruption will occur in the middle of a tight deadline. Be prepared! You'll be glad that you are. I have DSL in the office and cable in the home office. My DSL provider offers a dial-up backup number. The dial-up number proved very useful when I moved offices. When I was done moving and ready to get back to business, the DSL service was not yet functional so I used the dial-up number. It also came in handy when the DSL provider experienced a power outage that shut down all their servers for several hours. My experience with the cable provider is, whenever it storms, the cable is the first thing to go out. I'm prepared for that outage! I also have a broadband from my cell phone carrier that I can also utilize when my business, or family life, takes me out of the office or on the road. This might sound like a lot of trouble and a huge expense, but in reality the costs are minimal when I look at the revenue lost by not being able to service clients in every situation that involves Internet access.

Next on the list are your office space, desk, and chair. Be sure to delineate your office space. If possible, have an area that can be shut off from the rest of the family. This area should be off limits to others, if at all possible. The space should be comfortable and clutter-free. Your office, whether you choose to have clients visit or not, should be maintained as though a client could walk through the door at any given moment. A desk positioned properly in conjunction with other office equipment and filing cabinets should be at the right height with the appropriate amount of work surface—a key component to operating effectively. Select a chair that is ergonomically correct for you.

One of the driving forces to moving Kelly's office outside the home was that she was slowly becoming less productive. The space she had at home was small and it was in an open area in the family room of their house—no privacy at all. She spent way too time shuffling stacks around her desktop and the floor. Since her family couldn't give up any more of their living space for the business, she chose to move the business outside of her home. She still maintains an office at home and logs in remotely to the office computer or uses a laptop that still allows the flexibility in where and when she can work.

A great deal of your work will most likely require a printer—quite possibly a fax machine and a scanner, too. You can get all of these things in one machine, or you can get separate machines. Will you produce everything in black and white or will you also require color? Should you go with a laser, an inkjet, or both? The combination fax, copier, scanner, printer (a/k/a all-in-one or multi-function) machines are nice, but remember if anything goes wrong with one function, you're usually out of luck on all of them. I have an Epson Color Inkjet printer that also prints on CD/DVDs and a multi-function color laser jet with a flatbed scanner/copier. In addition, I have a Brother multi-function fax/PC-fax/copier/scanner/laser printer that I use mainly for faxing and some copying. I also have an online fax program should I be away from the office or if I ever experience fax machine problems. Pay close attention to the price of replacement toner, ink, and drums when purchasing printers. Some times the replacements can cost you more than a new less expensive printer.

You will find that a fax machine is a necessity. Will you need an actual fax machine or will an online fax program suffice? Maybe a PC to fax will work? I tend to lean toward having a stand-alone fax. I've used the faxes that go with your computer, and my clients hated it. They disliked having to call me whenever they wanted to fax me. Also, I wasn't able to fax documents for them because I couldn't utilize their letterhead. Therefore, I'd suggest getting a stand-alone fax as soon as possible. Online fax capabilities are also a consideration. If utilizing an online fax service, be sure to check whether you can attach documents from your computer to be included in the body of the fax. Some forego the fax and scan to e-mail their documents or post to online file sharing sites.

A good office phone is important, too. I went through the process of buying all the cheap cordless phones that have less than desirable reception. Invest in a good phone from the start and you'll save yourself money in the long run. In the beginning, I think you can get by without a separate phone line. However, as things get rolling you will want to have your own number. I also have a toll-free number to minimize expenses for my customers. If you plan to offer phone-answering services for your clients you might also consider getting a two-line phone for extra numbers. Be sure that your office is equipped with the proper jacks and wiring.

Be careful with your use of phone numbers. While it might not seem affordable at the start of business to get your own dedicated line, consider what it costs to reprint all your business cards, stationery, advertisements, or brochures when you change your number. You would also have to notify all current and potential customers, as well as change your listing in the million directories you are listed in on the Internet. Can you tell I learned this from experience? So, my advice would be to invest in a dedicated business number from the beginning. You don't have to go whole hog on this, just get another line installed with an additional number; they call it multi-ring in my area, for use as a fax number. Even though you are a "business," this doesn't mean that you have to have a "business" plan from the phone company.

Along the lines of the phone is the need for an answering machine or voice mail. Unless you can afford to contract with an answering service, it is imperative that callers can communicate with you through an alternate means if you are unreachable by phone. Effective voice mail communication is key. Give your callers the option of leaving you a detailed message. Return the call at the next opportune moment. Take advantage of your outgoing message to lead callers to your website for additional information about your company. You can also offer your e-mail address as another means of contacting you. If you follow strict business hours, which is recommended, announce your hours in your outgoing message.

One of the more popular solutions for phone, fax, toll-free number and voice mail is to utilize a unified messaging system such as FreedomVoice, Grasshopper, or RingCentral. This allows you a single toll-free number to use as both your phone and your fax. It allows for routing of calls to different numbers throughout the day based on a schedule you define. You can have voice mails delivered as audio files to your inbox as well as faxes delivered as graphic files. Some even translate your voice mail to text and include it in the e-mail.

The options for telecommunications are countless. The key is to think big picture without overextending and spending half your budget on staying connected. Find solutions you can grow into over time. And for the most part, you can always take a phone number with you in the event you need to make a change in service providers. Be sure to investigate standard VoIP as well as Skype for keeping connected at an affordable price—quality is key when considering these options.

For those offering transcription, you will need a transcriber. A micro and a standard cassette are the most common. Digital dictation is growing in popularity. It allows clients the freedom to dictate and not have to drop off tapes. Your client(s) will need a computer and digital recorder for this type of dictation. These files can be recorded in a number of formats depending on the recorder. Examples include: .wav, .dss, .mp3, .iaf. You will need a WAV foot pedal that plugs into your computer's serial or USB port. You will need special software, such as Express Scribe, for managing the audio dictation file on your computer. When you receive the digital voice files via e-mail from your client you can convert it to any of many formats. Once the file arrives, the software installed interprets the file and you transcribe it the same as you do a normal tape. Essentially, you are replacing the transcribing machine with the computer and WAV pedal, the audio tape with the audio file.

Additional equipment will depend upon the services your offer, your budget, and your desire or ability to use other technology. Some other equipment I find useful includes: multiple thumb or flash drives, a CD and DVD writer, a graphics tablet, digital camera, and an external hard drive for backups. I have a Plantronics headset, which I use for online meetings at places such as GoToMeeting. And I don't know what I would do without my mobile phone - this is a necessity. When I'm out of the office, I can forward my business line to my cell phone and never miss a call.

Of course, you will need an abundance of office supplies. It is imperative to have enough paperclips, file folders, tape, toner, postage, paper, and whatever other supplies necessary to operate on a daily basis. Nothing can interrupt your day more than having to stop a project to run to the office supply store.

Don't forget the need for ample filing and storage space and be good to your eyes by having the proper lighting! Utilize both overhead and task lighting to help eliminate eyestrain.

In Their Own Words:

Tess Strand Alipour: The only equipment I have ever needed is a good laptop, an excellent wireless Internet router, and a reliable external hard drive. When I was abroad, it was all I could handle traveling with from country to country. Now that I have been back in the States, I have added a printer but rarely use it, if ever.

Jeannine Clontz: To stay competitive, I think that it's necessary to have a decent copier (I have a Canon C180 II) that can handle 11x17 (for client newsletters), and a laserjet and inkjet printers. I have two standard sized transcribers and 1 micro sized transcriber, all of which I believe to be necessary to an active VA practice. I would LOVE to have a PDA, a color laser printer, and a color copier.

Alyssa Gregory: I use both a Mac and a PC – both are invaluable to me.

Kathy Ritchie: A computer with Internet access (a dedicated line for the modem is best, if possible); a telephone with voice mail or an answering machine; a fax machine or computer-based fax capability; basic software applications (Microsoft, Corel, and Lotus are sound investments for most). Individuals providing specialty services will know which tools of the trade are necessary.

Barbara Rowen: A high-speed computer with CD-RW, DVD, and Zip drives; Laptop; DSL line; color Inkjet All-In-One; color Laser printer with 12"X18" media capability; answering machine; transcription machines; and paper shredder for sensitive documents.

Nora Rubinoff: An iMac desktop computer, a ScanSnap scanner, a MacBook laptop, a high-quality headset, great black and white and color laser printers that are network printers, a Dymo printer for online postage.

Nancy Seeger: A Mac computer that is 2 years or younger, mid-to-high range (iMac 24" and MacBook Pro 3 Ghz), ScanSnap, Printer, Logitech Clear Chat Wireless, Phone with hands free headset (VOIP), external hard disk, Apple Base station.

Susan Totman: Good, recent computer; laptop is a bonus for meetings with clients and flexibility in work areas; laser printer; color laser printer (brochures, color presentations, printing books); good quality inkjet printer if you need to print photos; color lasers are not as good at printing images; scanner; staplers (long arm and standard); hole punches (2 and 3); binding machine if you will do any sort of publishing; paper cutter.

Establishing A Web Presence

Domain Name

Choose wisely! Selecting the right domain name can affect your business more than you might expect. It could actually cost you money in lost revenue and useless domain names—so be patient and don't just grab the first one that comes to mind because it sounds cute. Remember that your domain name provides exclusivity and credibility; plus, you can take it with you anywhere. When marketed correctly, your domain name becomes your brand and your identity as it relates to the online world. For that reason, and many others, it is important to use your domain name everywhere, including business cards, flyers, stationery, catalogs, signature files, and even your voice mail message.

It is important to have a name that conveys what you do best and follows the general theme and purpose of your website while still allowing for diversity, should you offer a variety of services. The name should be easy to remember, easy to convey in any format, not easily misspelled, or confusing; otherwise, you stand to lose traffic.

Remember that most people will be visiting your site through word-of-mouth by the most obvious relation to your business name. Try to avoid the use of hyphens and numbers in the name. For example, if someone referred you to Trees4Sale.com, they are most likely going to enter it as TreesForSale.com. In this instance, it might be to your benefit to reserve both domains as some might not try the number "4" when looking for you.

A common misconception about domain names is that they are case sensitive. Actually they are not. By writing out your name in both upper and lower case letters it makes it easier for the reader to follow and doesn't look like a string of letters. For example, the domain another8hours.com and theplannerpeople.com are more easily read as http://www.Another8Hours.com and http://www.ThePlannerPeople.com. Before you get really excited about a domain name, you will want to see if it's available. I have found the easiest site to check domain names is at http://www.Another8Hours.net or http://www.GoDaddy.com

Another 8 Hours was not my original choice for a company name. I went through a whole list of names that related to being a virtual assistant. It can be really rough to find a good domain name these days related to being a VA because everyone is using them up. I would often think to myself that I wished I had more hours in my day or that time would actually stand still so I could get caught up. Hence, the name Another 8 Hours was born. I get more comments on the creativity of my business name and people remember it. The downside is that people understand the concept, but they don't relate it to being a virtual assistant—that will come in time, however, as I continue to educate everyone I can on the whole industry.

Registering Your Domain Name
Once you have decided on a domain name and have determined its availability, you will then need to reserve the name through a registrar. You may want to consider purchasing all the extensions associated with the domain name such as the .com, .net, .us, .biz, .info, and .org. Once you register, you immediately get that license for that site name.

Domain names are purchased for a minimum of one year. There are numerous sites where you can purchase your domain name, all of which carry a fee ranging from $6.95 per year to $35.00 per year. Some sites may even offer free domain names, but you have to be sure you actually own the name. Be careful in your choice of a domain name registrar. For a full list of registrars, log onto ICANN.com. This is the Internet Corporation for Assigned Names and Numbers. Before making that final purchase, be sure to visit http://www.uspto.gov and check to see if the domain name you've selected is trademarked. You'd be surprised at the number of people who don't own their trademarked name, but are quick to come after you if you use it.

When registering your domain name, select a domain registrar that allows you to manage your domain through their website. Some registrars give the look and feel that you are actually purchasing your domain name along with web hosting, when in fact, they own the domain. Investigate the company and ask specific questions if you can't find the answers in their literature or on their site. Trying to stake claim to a domain name or change the ownership can be a monumental task.

In Their Own Words:

Tess Strand Alipour: http://www.virtualassistantforums.com

Alyssa Gregory: http://www.avertua.com

Kathy Ritchie: http://www.thebestva.com

Barbara Rowen: http://www.VirtuallyEverything.net

Nora Rubinoff: I own a few hundred domain names. My primary domain is http://www.aysweb.com. However, I use others to help me market through the use of landing pages, etc.

Nancy Seeger: http://www.artsassistance.com

Donna Toothaker: http://www.1stVA.com

Susan Totman: http://www.eliteofficesupport.com

Website

Your website allows customers to access information about your company and your services, and it also provides your clients with easy access to reaching you and purchasing your services. According to an SBA study, 65% of small businesses with an Internet presence make a profit or cover their website costs. The smallest firms benefit the most, with 35% relying on 10- to 99% of their sales coming from their website.

Many organizations, such as the IVAA, offer their members the option of hosting their websites at no cost or a minimal fee to get you started. This is a great opportunity for many, and one that we highly recommend. Let someone else help you out, until you get your feet wet. That way the pressure is off of you. Your website is set up and professionally done, and you can relax and concentrate and more important things—like getting clients.

Kim Haas, owner of KimHaas.com, offers the following advice: "Your website MUST present a professional appearance. Many sites appear to have been thrown together quickly or use 'pretty backgrounds.' Although this is acceptable for personal websites, it does not impress someone who's looking for a business product or service. If you must, link to your personal site where you can show off your talents with backgrounds, animation, etc., but keep your business site simple, clean and crisp for the ultimate results."

One thing that is recommended is to put your photo on your site. That way, the same with a press release, people feel a more personalized connection to you. It also enables you to add your photo to other links you have on other sites, which will allow immediate recognition for your company.

If you do decide to design your own website, you'll want to get very familiar with programs such as Adobe Dreamweaver. Some VAs are very knowledgeable in the area of HTML code and write their sites strictly from code. These days, blog-style websites are very attractive, utilizing programs such as WordPress, TypePad, Joomla, and other CMS or content management systems. Whatever you choose, be sure to take your time, check all your links, choose appropriate color schemes, and make sure that your content targets your audience.

You want your site to be easy to navigate, pleasing to the eye, and by all means avoid an unpleasant background as that can distract from the site and render the text unreadable. Update your site frequently, making sure all the appropriate links are in working order. As with brochures, one thing to avoid is lengthy paragraphs. You can easily lose your potential clients' interest. Consider bulleted lists that allow for easy scanning.

One of our biggest pet peeves is going to a site and having to search high and low in order to find the person and their contact information. This not only is an inconvenience, but, to many, it shouts SCAM as that's a trademark of SCAM companies - you can't find contact information anywhere on the site.

With your site, you can exchange advertising banners and website links with other virtual assistants or businesses to increase your link popularity. Link popularity can be beneficial in search engine rankings.

Susan Totman shares these features that are most beneficial with respect to attracting potential clients to your website:

1. Clearly identify the services offered.
2. Very clearly explain the process in which you work.
3. Identify exactly what hours you are willing to work and be available for your clients. *(If you don't do this, TRUST ME, you will regret it at some point, such as one of my clients who contacted me at 10PM one Easter evening because he could not access his e-mail.)*
4. The ability to pay from your website. *(PayPal button or other method to process a credit card directly from your website.)*
5. A submission form to allow clients to submit a general inquiry. This is often your first point of contact. Make fields for general information required so that the form cannot be submitted without entering some details. Make sure you have a CAPTCHA or other method of form protection to help weed out spammers.
6. Project management. Either software directly installed on your site or a hosted solution somewhere else like (ActivCollab or Basecamp). This will allow you to manage multiple projects and allow your clients to have an overview of their open projects at their fingertips. Clients love this.
7. Testimonials from a few clients. If you don't have clients yet, get general testimonials from previous employers or others who know your skills well.
8. A bookmark link so that people can bookmark the site easily and come back.
9. Social networking links to your Facebook and LinkedIn profiles, as well as your blog, if you have one.
10. A blog, if at all possible. Blogs have constantly changing and additional content, which is good.

Key activities to promote your website include:

1. Make sure your site is user-friendly and SEO-friendly (i.e., easily navigated, good colors that are easy on the eyes and pleasing to look at, neatly laid out and coded well so that the search engines will make the most of your content).
2. Submit to Google. (http://www.google.com/addurl)
3. Submit to Dmoz. (http://www.dmoz.org/add.html)
4. Submit to any pertinent business listing site you can find. There are tons of small business sites that allow you to enter all of your company information, including URL. The more links back to your site you can make, the better. Avoid sites that are questionable, have completely different subject matter from yours or are just link farms. A link farm is a group of web sites that all hyperlink to every other site in the group and is considered a form of spamming in the search engines.
5. Hand out business cards to anyone and everyone with your website address on them. Tell people to go there.
6. Create a Facebook fan page and place a fan box on your site. Put updates on your Facebook page as to what you're up to in your business. Keep it business

– not personal. Discuss new software; new equipment or new business experiences, like great places to advertise or tools that will make your clients' lives easier or ways to promote their own businesses.

7. Add a blog and blog regularly, at least once a week. Link to your main site and services regularly and make sure you submit your blog to the world. Here is a good guide to the best places to submit: http://www.searchenginejournal.com/20-essential-blog-directories-to-submit-your-blog-to/5998/

Selecting a Web Hosting Company

Your web hosting company should not be confused with your ISP (Internet Service Provider.) An ISP provides Internet access, whereas a web hosting company hosts websites on their servers. Choosing the right web hosting company is very important. We recommend you pay for web hosting rather than go with one of the free hosting sites. Free services tend to have annoying pop-ups and banners that detract from your site. Some free services will allow these banners to be removed, although you typically have to pay a fee for doing so. There are plenty of affordable web hosting companies out there to help you maintain that professional image you've been working toward.

When selecting a web hosting company, here are a few things to consider:

- Amount of space
- Access to CGI Bin (for custom scripts)
- Autoresponders
- E-mail forwarding or POP3 accounts (how many do you get)
- FTP access limitations (ideally you want unlimited 24/7)
- Statistics
- Control Panel access
- Technical Support (24 hours)
- Percentage of up time
- Monthly fee
- Backup utility

We've had great success with hosting plans through:
http://www.Another8Hours.net
http://www.ICDSoft
http://www.BlueHost.com
http://www.GoDaddy.com

Whether your hosting company provides statistics or not, you'll want to consider adding Google Analytics code to your site to monitor visitor traffic and activity.

Driving Traffic to Your Site

You cannot expect to put up a website and have people find you if they don't even know that you're there. Submitting your site to the search engines will improve your chances for better rankings. Getting your site listed in the DMOZ directory is one of the best things you can do. When writing your content, make it keyword rich and relevant to your audience. Other things that will help you achieve high rankings are optimization of images with relevant ALT tags, the number of sites that are linked to yours (link popularity), the relevance of your keywords to the content on your pages, the load time of your pages, the frequency of your keywords on your page (the higher up the better) and the list goes on.

Successful search engine optimization is a real art. The search engines are constantly changing their requirements for submission. If you are not able to keep up with current search engine optimization guidelines, then you will want to seek the assistance of a professional.

In Their Own Words:

Alyssa Gregory: Yes, I designed it. I recently added a free download for e-mail capture and this has been useful. My contact form is also used quite a bit by potential clients.

I do most of my promotion online through sites like Twitter, Facebook and LinkedIn. I also do a lot of freelance writing for highly-trafficked sites, so a lot of visitors are driven to my site that way.

Nora Rubinoff: Yes. I designed my site. Most beneficial are probably providing a good overview regarding services offered, the opportunity for prospects to get to know me a bit, and clear information about how I work and how to reach our business.

My site is a WordPress-based site. Utilizing great plugins that WordPress offers, such as Google Analytics and Google XML Site Maps helps with promotion of our site with search engines.

Nancy Seeger: I'm a web designer, designed my own website. The look and feel is targeted to what the music industry is most comfortable with, including colors and patterns.

Fundamental semantic coding is important to ensure it is search-engine friendly. Improperly coded websites cannot be read well by search engines because they lack prioritization of text. Also use Meta tags, links in footers of designed sites (makes for good SEO), reference the site in social media listings and active in social media.

Susan Totman: Yes. I designed all of my sites. I began teaching myself web development, including programming, in the late 1990s, so I have the benefit of being able to design and develop my own sites.

7 Reasons Why WordPress is the Right Choice for Modern Web Sites

by Nora Rubinoff
At Your Service Cincinnati Ltd.
http://www.aysweb.com

1. **Scalability.** WordPress is infinitely expandable. As your business grows, the structure and size of your site can grow, with no more than a few clicks of a mouse.

2. **Open source.** WordPress self-hosted sites are based on the open source WordPress application. WordPress's open source community is strong and diverse. There are many members of the community who are willing to help with questions you may have. Because open source code is freely available, developers are creating fantastic and innovative additions to WordPress all the time.

3. **Extendability.** WordPress is infinitely extendable by the wide variety of plugins that are available to integrate into your installation. There are plugins that help you with SEO, plugins that help with social media integration, and plugins that help you with your back-end interaction with the application.

4. **Great for management by diversely-located teams.** WordPress allows you to create users with different access levels to the installation. Diverse sets of teams can be collaborating at the same time without stepping on each other's toes — critical for the online world in which we work.

5. **Easy to implement.** WordPress self-hosted sites are best known for their incredibly quick installation. With a little back-end interaction at your host's control panel, you really can be off and running in hours.

6. **Not just for web sites.** WordPress is great for a web site, but it's also great for those who want to blog, vlog or podcast. Because of its scalability, it is easy to start small, and then implement a blog later on — or start with a blog and then later add static web content.

7. **Budget-friendly.** WordPress self-hosted sites are very inexpensive to implement. The WordPress software is free, as are many plugins and themes. Depending upon specialty plugins or themes you may choose to integrate into your site, there may be small costs associated with them. You pay for your hosting, and any specialty plugins or themes that have fees associated with them, and that's all. You really can implement a WordPress site for free (other than hosting costs).

Whether you are a small business owner on a budget or a large, established business ready to take your web presence to the next level, WordPress is a great solution.

Maximize the Internet

There is so much to be said about the Internet. We all utilize its power in a different manner and with a different purpose in mind. Do you even remember what it was like to not have Internet access? Can you imagine that your children would ever have to actually spend time in the library instead of doing their homework in the comfort of their own bedroom, with their own computer, with their own Internet access? Amazing! In this day of modern technology, we have become so reliant on computers and Internet access that we—the virtual assistant industry—are staking our claim. We're maximizing the Internet to introduce the world to a whole new concept of working smarter. We're maximizing the Internet and using it to our advantage to create a life-long career and generate revenue sufficient to support our families. Would you ever have imagined it was possible to live in a small town of Illinois and service a client in Hong Kong?

As Priscilla Y. Huff, author of *101 Best Home-Based Businesses for Women, 3rd.rev.ed.** and *The Self-Employed Woman's Guide to Launching a Home-Based Business,* states, "The women I interviewed in my book, *HerVenture.com,* said the Internet has been a powerful communications tool that has enabled them to make connections, spread the word, gain support and explore a myriad of avenues to contribute to the successes of their businesses. The Internet has presented them a vast array of affordable opportunities for self-employment, entrepreneurship and finding employment or employees that did not previously exist. The possibilities are endless!!"

Yes, the Internet is an amazing tool, but are you using it to your advantage? Have you gained sufficient knowledge on all of the ins and outs of the Internet, and your computer? If you haven't, we highly recommend doing so. We recommend obtaining the proper education through online classes, reading books, or attending classes at a local college. Learn all that you can about viruses, how to protect yourself from hackers, how to search the search engines properly, and so on. The Internet gives the feeling of power and that knowledge IS power.

From message boards to chat rooms, social networking to webinars, it's all there. Learn, explore. Start doing searches and record your findings. Don't think you'll remember? Capture your findings. Utilize the bookmarking feature of your browser to categorize your searches. Using social bookmarking sites like Digg.com and StumpleUpon.com allows you to share with others what you find. Become active and have fun.

The Internet is full of chats, teleclasses, webinars, and online summits that allow for increasing your knowledge and expanding your networking opportunities. Take advantage of all that you can, but be careful to manage your time wisely. If you get involved in the social networking arena, allocate only certain times a day that you will participate. You can easily become addicted, and before you know it, the day is gone and you haven't done any billable work—we speak from experience on this one!

10 Keys To Successful Online Marketing

By: Jackie Ulmer, The Street Smart Wealth Group, Walnut Hills, Box 1955, Blue Jay, CA 92317 • 909-337-3521 • http://www.streetsmartwealth.com

The Internet is definitely the wave of the future. Dot-com fever is everywhere, and it seems that there is no cure. Fortunes are being made online and you want to stake your claim. Here are a few key points to keep in mind as you develop and build your business:

1) Focus on the knowledge that you already have. Every website, newsletter and online venture needs to have a Unique Selling Proposition or USP. This is something that sets you apart from the rest. Everyone has knowledge between their ears that is different and unique. Use it. Be willing to go the extra mile to make your product stand out. To further develop this, find other websites and newsletters that are similar to yours. Study these and brainstorm about what appeals to you, and what you can do that is different.

2) Make sure your site is not another copycat website. Nothing is worse than seeing the same information over and over again on many websites. If you are offering affiliate programs, that's great. But, develop your own sales letter and testimonials. Don't just slap up a banner and hope it will make you millions. For more information on doing this effectively, go to: http://www.streetsmartwealth.com/sitesell.htm

3) Avoid constantly comparing yourself to others. Everyone comes to the table with different experiences, education, ideas, etc. If you are just getting started, you must realize that it will take time and many fine-tunings before you get your site, newsletter and product line just the way you want it. This is just part of the process.

4) View everything you do through the eyes of your potential customer. Make it about THEM, and not about you. Use the word "you" at least three times more than the word "I". Sorry, but people don't really care about YOU and what YOU have done. Turn your knowledge and experience into information that relates to them.

5) Tell people who you are, provide them with contact information and don't be anonymous. Your picture should be on your website, as well as where you are located, a phone number and valid e-mail address. You don't need to list your home address, but give them an idea of where you live. There is nothing worse than a website promising you overnight riches with no contact information. I don't know about you, but to me, this screams "SCAM" very loudly.

6) Automate your business as much as possible from the very beginning. Use autoresponders to provide highly-requested information about your product or service. Autoresponders are also a great way to follow-up and stay current with people that have expressed an interest in your offer. Most people do not buy on the first visit. Studies show that it takes 7 to 9 exposures before most people buy. If you give up too early, you'll miss the pot of gold at the end of the web!

7) Use common business etiquette and manners. Avoid the use of slang. Remember, the World Wide Web is just that - worldwide. You will never alienate an audience by using a

professional tone, but you might if you get too casual. Other than blatant spam, answer e-mails, even if it is a brief acknowledgment. You never know when you will interact with someone again, so treat each person as your most valued customer. They might be!

8) Ask questions of others! Successful people love to offer help and advice. There are bulletin boards all over the Internet where you can post messages looking for help on topics such as how to design something into your site, where to get a merchant account or anything else. If you don't ask, you'll never know. I learned through my first business venture that people are successful for a reason. One reason is that they didn't try to re-invent the wheel. If I can't find the answer on my own, I'm the first one to post a message or send an e-mail to someone that I think might have the answer. Try it! The responses and offers of help I have received from Internet millionaires are amazing.

9) Online marketing is great, but don't forget to market your business offline as well. Every time you give someone cash, write a check or give your credit card, include a business card with it. Tell people about your online business and ask them to spread the word. Word-of-mouth advertising is better than any other form. Press releases, offline classifieds and traditional methods of advertising are important to your online business.

10) Build relationships and use networking skills online. Visit bulletin boards and newsgroups and offer real help and assistance. Don't spam these places, but use a signature line promoting your business, if it is acceptable. If you are legitimate, people will remember you and it could be worth gold to you in the future. I hope these tips will help you. The most important thing is to just get started. Don't wait until you feel everything is perfect. It won't be. It never is. You will probably make thousands of changes. Everyone does! When you are changing, you are growing and your business will, too!

The tragedy in life doesn't lie
in not reaching your goal.
The tragedy lies
in having no goal to reach.
–Benjamin Mays

Specialty Services

Investigations/Researching

If you are good at finding things online and obtaining specific backgrounds on companies or people, you just might want to offer this service. I was amazed that there was such a market for this out there. I've always loved playing on the Internet finding things. Now my playtime is making me a profit. Investigations/Researching is a good profit-making avenue to pursue for a VA.

One of the main ways that I've incorporated investigations in my practice is with the attorneys I work with. I got my paralegal degree a couple of years ago and this enables me to do research for clients on pending court cases. It is great to track downs cites and records that help my clients win cases. The attorneys I work for have paralegals in their office, but even their paralegals are often too overworked to take on some research assignments. That's when they give me a call.

Another way that to incorporate research into your business is working with some author clients. Quite frequently, they will need fact checking done about a particular topic. Authors can also use research assistance in identifying where to submit their articles and press releases that will most effectively reach their target audience.

Kathy Ritchie of Ritchie Secretarial Service does a lot of investigation work. Kathy is a professional virtual assistant with over 20 years experience in office assistance and the successful operation of a virtual assistant practice since June 1996. Kathy granted us permission to utilize the following information to help you learn more about this aspect of the business. You can contact Kathy at kritchie@thebestva.com.

> I was good at finding things online, and obtaining specific background on companies or people. I'm nosy by nature so adding these services seemed natural. I especially like to research or investigate a company I have questions about before ordering their "perfect" product or service.
>
> Characteristics of a successful researcher or investigator include honesty, open-mindedness, curiosity, patience, skepticism, perception, persistence, caution, motivation, creativity, and in my case, just plain nosiness. Combine all these traits and the researcher/investigator is born. More important than any of these are good old-fashioned intuition and persistence. In my experience, intuition is the most valuable tool available to any researcher or investigator. Very often as adults our intuition is turned off or placed on the back burner. As a researcher or investigator you'll find you retrieve your intuition, dust it off and begin to trust it like an old friend. Intuition is invaluable!
>
> To truly research you must have a plan of attack. Decide where you want to go with the research and what you need to accomplish. Write down any questions, and endeavor to answer them before your research is complete.

When you research, you are either a) adding to a general body of knowledge; or b) solving a problem. Good research is clear, precise, accurate, reliable, valid, verifiable, objective and useful!

Investigation is different, but uses many of the same thought procedures. When investigating people, places, or things, I bookmark relevant website pages in a folder designated just for that case. This makes relocating the information quick and efficient. Reports should be detailed and formatted in an easy-to-follow method. Finally, whether it's research or investigation, to be accurate and believable, you must document or cite your sources. When you send a report of your findings to your client, include where you found the information. Cite sources you used in the background investigation of a person or company. And ALWAYS maintain an extremely high level of confidentiality with your research and investigation clients. This one step will ensure repeat business.

Examples of Research/Investigation

One client needed me to find her aunt who had been missing for more than 40 years! This was somewhat disconcerting due to the lack of information they had. All I was given to work on was the name at birth, the date of birth, last known address, and what they thought was the social security number. After searching through my genealogy links, along with verification of the social security number, I located her aunt. Unfortunately, the story didn't end happily. The aunt had died only two years before the search for her was started!

Another client needed me to locate her ex-husband and quickly! I was given a last known address, date of birth and name. Within 24 hours the most current address was located and from there the ex-husband was located as well. My client later told me the search for this person had been going on for nearly a year by the local police. I was very happy to have produced such quick results.

One client asked me to locate the wiring schematic for a 1978 Volvo Station Wagon's radio. From start to finish, the search took 8 minutes. This was a prime example of using search engines to their full potential!

One of my favorite assignments was researching the surname of my husband's best friend. This friend wasn't sure what information might be available. He sat behind me as I investigated the surname and was astonished by the vast amount of information I found within 30 minutes. He also learned the original clan name and is now a member! To further surprise him, I located his clan's tartan and coat of arms as well.

Meeting Planning

If you have ever been involved in planning a meeting, then you know from personal experience that it is not as easy as everyone thinks. There are a lot of details to tend to, all of which attendees take for granted. Sure, maybe anyone can plan a meeting, but can you plan a successful one?

I asked Joan Eisenstodt[1] of Eisenstodt Associates, LLC, Conference Consulting, Facilitation & Training, what are the key characteristics of a successful meeting planner: "Curiosity—an ability to ask lots of questions and see things, and see them in different ways. Sense of humor—keep it in perspective."

The key to a successful meeting is planning and careful attention to every detail. As Connie Corodimas, a personal trainer for a well-known fitness center states, "Pre-work is essential in planning a successful meeting. It is important to consider every detail, to eliminate unexpected challenges that might hamper the effectiveness of your message."

According to Joan Eisenstodt, "Every meeting planner should know their audience. Not just the surface information; dig deeper, know percentages of male/female, age ranges, nationalities, ethnicity, religions, specific needs, etc. Once known, plan your meeting (site, design, content, F&B, activities, outcomes) with the audience in mind."

The attendees determine the success of a meeting. The following information covers meeting basics and is not meant to be all-inclusive.

There are many types and sizes of meetings. No matter how big or how small the meeting, here are some key elements that need to be considered. Each of these areas needs to be discussed with your client so there is no question you are both working toward the same goal.

---

[1] *Joan L. Eisenstodt*, whose expertise is in facilitation and training, and for meetings: program planning, facilities contracts, negotiations, meeting management training, and general meeting management, brings more than 30 years of experience to her work. She founded Eisenstodt Associates, a Washington, DC-based meetings management and consulting company, in 1981. Since 1995, Joan Eisenstodt has continually been named "*One of the 25 Most Influential People in the Meetings Industry*" by *Meeting News* magazine. *Successful Meetings* magazine named *Joan* one of the "Power Players" ("10 Women Who are Changing the Industry") in their May 2000 issue. She was named "2001 e.communicator" by meetingmed.com. In August 2001, *Corporate Meetings & Incentives* magazine featured *Joan* on the cover as one of "The 'A' List 10 Women Meeting Industry Leaders." In May 2002, the Wisconsin Chapter of MPI honored *Joan* with their first "Award of Education Excellence" for presentations she had made to the Chapter.

Joan Eisenstodt can be reached at Eisenstodt Associates, LLC, 216 5th St., S.E., Washington, DC 20003-1103 USA; phone 202.543.7971 ext. 11; fax 202.543.4619; e-mail is eisenstodt@aol.com.

Determine Goals and Objectives
- What is the purpose of the meeting?
- What is to be accomplished at the meeting?
- What message is to be communicated?
- How is the message to be communicated?
- What challenges might you expect?

As an independent meeting planner, you may not feel it is your business to know these things. Actually it's quite the opposite. You, and your client, must understand the importance of identifying and communicating the goals and objectives. This part of the planning process is essential and could very well determine the overall success of the meeting.

For example, if you were holding a sales meeting to tell everyone that budgets will be cut next year, some jobs may be eliminated, and limited spending is crucial, you would not want to select an elaborate private resort facility to convey this message. This type of facility and frivolous spending would not give the impression that money is tight, or, that management does not fall under these new budget cuts.

Budget
- What is the budget for the meeting?
- Will guests be responsible for their own rooms, meals, or incidentals?
- What other expenses might be incurred for transportation, gifts, entertainment, and other related events?

Determining the budget up front will save you a great deal of time. There is nothing worse than going through the whole planning process and presenting your ideas to the client just to find that, although it's a great plan, it is not within the client's budget. Find out up front what the company will be picking up on behalf of the attendees, if group travel is appropriate, the expected room rate, and any other special items associated with the theme of the meeting. Don't forget to include taxes and tips in your budget—overlooking this can make for a big surprise when you get the final bill.

Pre-Planning
- Who needs to attend?
- Are guests/spouses invited?
- What is the total number of participants?
- How will expenses be covered?
- What is the extent of pre-meeting promotion?
- What is the appropriate length and time of the meeting?
- What are the dates of the meeting?
- Are these dates flexible?

When considering guest attendance, it's necessary to determine if the company will pick up all of their expenses or if the guests are simply welcome to attend at their own expense. Keep in mind that guest attendance can also lead to child attendance. Will you need to set up a special program for guests or are they on their own?

You will find in dealing with hotels, the more flexible your dates the easier it can be to find the facility you want. Additionally, you may be able to negotiate a better rate if you can fill an unexpected vacancy or plan to hold your meeting during the off-season.

Once these key elements have been determined, you are then better prepared to make decisions on where the meeting should be held and the type of meeting facility to be used. When choosing a site, there are many things to consider:

Site Selection
- Facility type (resort, hotel or conference center, convention center)
- Geographic location
- Audience demographics
- Appeal
- Accessibility
- Tax considerations (outside the United States)
- Site inspection
- Disability accessible
- Size of the property (number of rooms, meeting capacity)
- Concurrent events

Hotel Selection
- Cost
- Availability
- Number of other groups
- Check a number of hotels

Logistics
- Final decision maker
- Individual/Department responsibilities
- Scenario of events
- Airport arrival/departure/transportation
- Hotel arrival/departure/registration

Meeting Facilities
- Contract
- Billing arrangements
- Room size
- Number of rooms
- Food and beverage
- A/V requirements
- Entertainment
- Room setup

There are a lot of resources available on the Internet today. Rather than list them all here and take the risk that they will change, I recommend visiting Corbin Ball's website and look at his list of favorites. Corbin, a 20+-year veteran meeting planner and speaker, has over 3,000 links on his site for everything under the sun concerning meeting planning. You can find the list here: http://www.corbinball.com.

Another site that offers tremendous tools for meeting planning is http://www.mpoint.com. The following has been used with permission:

> mpoint.com is the premiere website for planners, featuring hundreds of resources to help plan better meetings, more quickly, and at the best possible price. Planners can search a global directory of more than 70,000 meeting facilities and suppliers. This site contains a set of tools that allows planners to find the information and ideas they need in an instant:
>
> - Fast search tools for facilities, suppliers, CVBs, and more
> - More multimedia facility descriptions
> - A direct facility comparison feature
> - An easy online RFP for facilities
> - Large archives of articles, checklists, and links
> - Lively planner communities
> - Industry-leading career resources
> - Online purchasing of executive gifts, booth giveaways, etc.

Meeting Alternatives: Instant messaging, Web collaboration, and Online groups
In light of today's technology, the heightened security, fuel costs, and budget concerns, many companies have elected to utilize alternative resources for holding meetings. Other considerations for not meeting face-to-face include less wasted time, less expense, and less time out of the office. More and more meetings are taking place on the Internet, via satellite, telephone, and video conferencing. The need for face-to-face meetings is quickly becoming less important to some companies. As a virtual assistant, you should be ready to suggest alternatives to meeting with your own clients from afar, as well as suggesting alternatives for your client's meetings. Take the time to research and learn the many tools that are available today for the virtual office environment. Programs such as GoToMeeting (http://www.gotomeeting.com), GoToWebinar (http://www.gotowebinar.com), and WebEx (http://www.webex.com) offer great tools for holding online meetings. Skype is another alternative that allows for video conferencing right over your computer with folks located all over the world. Whether you have the need for using such tools is not as important as knowing that they exist and having a general knowledge of their features. You never know when that client might come along that requires you to be available for an online meeting, or needs your direction in setting up such a meeting—show them you know your stuff by having the latest technology at your fingertips.

Working with Coaches and Speakers

Working with coaches and speakers is a niche market where many virtual assistants have experienced huge success. After all, the industry was born within the coaching world! One of the primary reasons is the demand. The services that virtual assistants provide are perfect for coaches and speakers. They realize that they can make more money and be more successful when they get the assistance they need and don't try to do everything themselves. It's a perfect match.

The range of services provided is countless. Many VAs are managing entire businesses for their coaching clients. The more popular services provided to coaches and speakers are listed below. Don't let the list scare you. This is when working with subcontractors and multi-VA teams can come in handy so you can provide the more specialized services.

- Teleseminars – scheduling, promoting, recording, transcribing.
- Shopping carts – maintenance, product additions, autoresponders, broadcasts, affiliate programs.
- Websites design and maintenance, blogs, membership sites.
- PR – article and press release marketing, building a brand, promoting events, list building.
- Developing courses, homework assignments, e-books, presentations.
- SEO / web analysis.
- Social networking – Facebook, Twitter, LinkedIn groups.
- Research – target audience, information for teleseminars, statistics.
- Brainstorming ideas – products, markets, alliances, JV partners.

There are so many ways to get clients. Just being active online works. Implement a press release and article campaign to get your name out there. Don't forget to be active on Facebook and Twitter. Follow those coaches you respect and interact with them frequently. See who they are following and follow some of them as well. Set up a "search" for coaching. Often times, the coaches will announce they are looking for assistance.

You can also attend events for speakers. Try and set up a booth there if possible. This is a perfect way to be front and center in front of your target audience. Most speakers have their event schedule listed on their website. See if they will be coming to your area and sign up to attend.

Scott Stratten, President of Un-Marketing shares this insight:

> The field of coaching parallels the field of virtual assistance in many ways. We both know what we do, but the rest of the world is in the dark. We must both market our services, and increase awareness about our fields in general. If we don't, coaches are stuck being asked "What team do you coach for?" and VAs are asked, "Does VA mean you live in Virginia?"

Targeting Writers and Authors

Writers are an excellent source of work for VAs. Normally, all work can be handled via mail or the Internet, it is easy to type, enjoyable to read, and it allows greater flexibility in your schedule. When working with other businesses, it often requires a 24- or 48-hour turnaround. There is a tremendous sense of accomplishment when you finish typing a manuscript, especially if it gets published. You will know that you had a part in its success.

How do you target your market for writers? Easy...starting with your website you can promote that you do manuscript typing. Also, there are magazines targeted for writers that you can advertise in. Go to your local bookstore and see. One such magazine is *Poets & Writers* (http://www.pw.org,). Another is *The Writer*. Authors read these, and often will look to these when it's time to get their manuscript typed, so it's worth checking into. You can also advertise in the *Writers' Digest Magazine*. They have a section that features word processors by state. This is the magazine that most writers subscribe to. In fact, in researching for this book I wanted to make sure that the *Writer's Digest* was producing results, so I contacted those who advertised there.

There are several other places that target authors in which you can advertise. The *Writer's Market* has a section entitled "Organizations of Interest" and "Publications of Interest" in the back of the book. Listed in these sections are the organizations and magazines that publish newsletters, magazines, and trade journals specifically for writers and others in the field. You can also find them online at http://www.writersmarket.com

The *Writer's Market* is a book that comes out yearly, which contains information on book and periodical publishers. Most writers use this book in looking for someone to publish their work. It provides useful information on how to prepare manuscripts, query letters, and other pertinent documents. I recommend obtaining the current year's book at the bookstore. Many VAs send letters to the publishers listed here offering their services and have met with success.

Another way to advertise your VA services to authors is to locate writer's groups in your area. Your daily newspaper should list these in their activities calendar. Often they allow you to hand out your business cards. Keep in mind you are offering a service to their authors. They need your assistance. Also, your local Barnes and Noble or other bookstores may have weekly or monthly get-togethers. I've found them to be beneficial. Check online for author and writer forums and other sites that target writers to see what promotional opportunities exist.

Seek out clients through many of the online avenues like Facebook, Twitter, and various blogs. A number of authors now have podcasts and radio shows. Look to connect with them there. And don't forget services such as HelpAReporter.com and Profnet to get listings from sources looking for experts. Attending writer's groups and writing seminars is another great way to connect with authors who may need assistant getting their book written or getting more PR once their book is done.

I've typed several manuscripts since I've been in business, and I used to believe that manuscript work was something that could be done after all the main projects were completed for the day. I have since discovered that the best way to type a manuscript is during your peak work times when you are at your best. The reason being is that it will take half the time to proof your work. I would type a manuscript at the end of the day when I was tired and once finished I would proof it. It works out so much better to do it while you are feeling your best, as it takes a lot less time to proof and you can feel more confident that there are fewer errors.

Once the author receives the work, if minor changes need to be made, the author can fax you the pages and then you can mail or e-mail the revised changes. If the work requires major rewriting and editing, have them mail you the changes. If the corrections and changes are additions or revisions that the *author* has made, then charge your hourly rate.

When I asked Patty Shannon, a VA who has been doing manuscript typing for many years, how gets her work, she stated, "About a third of my work comes handwritten, another third on tape, and the last third rough-typed on either a typewriter, computer or word processor. Only my proofreading work comes by e-mail."

Patsy LaFave has been able to provide us with excellent tips for targeting authors as well. She states that most of her work comes draft-typed with changes and corrections marked into the manuscript. She doesn't mind that because all the years as a secretary trained her to decipher the handwritten changes and how to insert them. She states, "It is nice, though, if the draft-typed manuscript comes double-spaced. I have done some from tape also. That is harder, more time-consuming, and more expensive. I charge by the hour for tape transcription."

Vivian Vican has owned her business since 1994. She types for several small magazines and handles outsourcing (scanning and proofreading) for several small publishers. She types directly for authors, lawyers, therapists and other professionals and also offers customized computer classes. She offers us her favorite reference websites: http://www.columbia.edu and http://www.word-detective.com. She also states that she belongs to a local PC user's groups.

Typing Tips For Manuscripts
You also want to be familiar with proper setting up of manuscripts. The *Writer's Digest Guide to Manuscript Formats*, by Dian Dincin Buchman and Seli Groves, published by *Writer's Digest Magazine* is what most word processors use. To obtain this book, look through the latest issue of the *Writer's Digest* or call (800) 289-0963.

Many authors will seek your help in the proper formatting of their manuscript. Mark Garvey, in the *Writer's Market*, states, "There are no 'rules' about what a manuscript must look like." Check the *Writer's Market* website (http://www.writersmarket.com) for a complete description of how to properly prepare and submit a manuscript.

You will need special skills for targeting writers, but you can obtain these skills through books, research, or perhaps a college course. First, you should possess a good understanding of the English language and good grammar and editing skills if you are helping them with edits. The *Writer's Digest* has several books written on grammar, word usage, etc., that you may find beneficial. These books are listed in their magazine. However, don't feel that you need to know everything. You don't!!! You absolutely do not need to be an English major. Just have a good understanding of the English and/or how to find out what you are unfamiliar with. If you are helping authors with publicity and marketing, you'll need good marketing skills, research skills, an understanding of submitting press releases online, and so forth.

Patsy states, "I basically use the generic 1.25 inch left and right margins and 1 inch top and bottom with New Times Roman 12 pt. unless the writer has guidelines that they need to use for a specific purpose, i.e., publisher's guidelines, self-publishing, etc. It's hard to know what to do sometimes because there isn't a set format, no matter what others say. Each publisher or agent decides what they want and if the writer is sending to a specific one, they need to get the guidelines they want the manuscript to follow, or have you request them or look them up on the Internet."

Patty offers the following advice: "The most commonly accepted format these days is 12 point Times Roman (or Times New Roman) with 1-inch margins all around. Put a header at the top left in 10 point Times Roman italic with the author's last name, the story or book title, and the page number. There should be a half-inch between the header and the beginning of the text. Make sure widow/orphan protection is on—there should not be single lines of text at the top or bottom of a page. Use ONE SPACE at the ends of sentences—using two spaces after a period went out when everyone stopped using Courier font."

Vivian states that the most often requested format she uses is double-spaced, 1 1/4" margins, in Courier or Times New Roman font. "I handle a great number of scripts and plays, which require specialized formatting. I receive less than 2% of work by e-mail. About half the work is handwritten and half already typed."

Ginger Brown states that unless otherwise requested, she always uses the standard 1-¼ margin all around. She further states, "I try to dissuade clients from using 10 pt fonts, always recommending 12 pt. And common fonts like Bookman Old Style or Times New Roman."

When asked her favorite manuscript, Patty states, "I like them all." When asked her least favorite, she replied, "A science fiction piece that was so disjointed and poorly presented that I could barely make sense out of it. I tried to gently tell the author he really needed an editor to work with him (what he actually needed was a ghost writer!) but he insisted that I just type it up. I hate giving back work that is not up to my standards, but in this case there wasn't much I could do."

NOTE: I highly recommend that you do an online search and just familiarize yourself with the different formats. Yes, you will get different ideas. But the majority will be the same. It's just good to have a good understanding before you start typing. When I do a search, I normally lose a couple of hours, but come out with lots of great information. I hope you do the same!

On every manuscript I have typed, the author has asked for tips on editing and any other suggestions I could offer. Most authors appreciate your assistance. Therefore, the following are items I frequently encounter or that were pointed out to me with the editing of this manuscript:

- It is *strongly recommended* to have a signed contract and to get a deposit *before* you begin any work. Also, before you send the final manuscript, collect the total payment. Most authors are honest and you will have no problems, but as you are dealing with people outside your immediate jurisdiction, there is a greater risk of nonpayment. Unfortunately, several word processors indicated they never received payment from authors who promised to pay when they received the final manuscript. Some VAs ask for payment in a money order or certified check. You can also accept Visa or MasterCard, or PayPal.
- Set aside time each day to type the manuscript. Don't wait until a week before it's due to start typing. This can easily happen when you get busy with your other assignments and keep putting it off because the deadline is weeks away.
- Allow yourself flexibility when determining the completion date. Sick kids, a sudden rush in business or a personal illness can set you back. I try to allow at least an additional week as I don't exclusively target authors and have full-time commitments with my regular clients.
- Proofing is an essential part of this type of work. Unfortunately, typing a long document, such as a manuscript, can become a tedious process and you're more prone to overlook mistakes. I would recommend reading the final manuscript at least twice. If time permits, read it several days later when it's fresh. Sometimes you're too close to the material and you overlook typos that become blatant the second time around. I always try to do the final proof away from the office. With no interruptions and a nice change of scenery, I seem to do a better job.
- Numbers that start a sentence need to be written out.
- In sentences that require numbering of items, use double parenthesis instead of singular. (1) instead of 1)
- In quotations, the punctuation comes before the end quote (." instead of ".).
- In quotations, when you are omitting text and then within the same quotation citing more information, you use three periods with a space in between.
    For example: last word . . . next word

  You would use four periods if a new sentence follows.
    For example: last word . . . . New sentence
- Long quotations of four or more sentences are indented and no quotation marks are used.
- There is no space between dashes--this is correct.
- Avoid overuse of the pronoun *it*. Instead, describe what it stands for. Also, make sure when you use any pronoun that the noun it modifies is clear to the reader.
- If the noun is singular, then the pronoun must also be singular. If the noun is plural, then the pronoun must also be plural.
- Titles of books and magazines should be placed in italics.
- There is no comma between a month and a year in text.
    For example: April 20012 issue (correct)
                April, 2012 issue (incorrect)
- Use a margin of 1-1/4 to 1-1/2 depending upon the publisher guidelines.
- Always double check the Table of Contents and Index are correct.

Typing Query Letters

Many authors will ask you to type a query letter. A query letter is the letter authors send to a publishing company trying to get their work published. Most publishing companies request a query letter before a complete manuscript is forwarded. These letters are sent to the publishers handling that particular type of book. For example, some publishers specifically state that they handle only nonfiction military books. Therefore, if you were to send a book on how to start a business to these publishers, a rejection is sure to follow.

Publishers are listed in the *Writer's Market*. Often a client will compose a base letter and want you to send personalized letters to all publishers who would be interested in their book. Always personally address the letters to the person listed. Use their title and check that you have spelled their name correctly, both in the inside address and the salutation. In the salutation, you should address the letter to Mr. Jones and not their first name. Finally, make sure that the letter is 100% correct.

Enhanced services to offer authors:

- PR & marketing campaigns
- Book for reviews
- Schedule virtual book tours
- Social networking
- Coordinate teleseminars
- Schedule book signings
- Website/blog services
- Manage ISBN numbers
- Coordinate book printings
- Cover designs
- Web graphic design
- Affiliate management
- Product fulfillment
- Shopping cart maintenance
- Copywriting

Publicity and Pitching the Media

You'll likely discover that the majority of your clients are always looking to get into the media and gain free publicity, particularly authors and speakers. They want to get more exposure for their books or products and just may need your help to get them the desired exposure.

Pitching the media is not for faint at heart. It's imperative to do it right and build the necessary relationships with the media to achieve positive results. You surely don't want to get the media on your bad side. So here are some tips you'll find useful to help you become a master at getting publicity and provide a valuable specialty service to your clients.

Be sure to apply them when seeking media coverage for your own product, service, or cause!

- Do it right. You want to build relationships and not do more damage than good by annoying those you pitch.
- Personalize your pitches whenever possible. Think how good you feel when you get an e-mail that's directed to you. It also shows them you have done your homework in seeking out the right person for the pitch.
- Plan results. Know whom you want to target and why it's a good match.
- Keep an updated contact database so it's easy to locate the right media to fit your products, service, or cause. You don't want to constantly be looking for e-mail addresses and phone numbers. Your database is true gold so take good care of it.
- Think angles and hooks and be ready to tell why your story is relevant and newsworthy.
- Watch the news constantly. What relates? It's amazing in PR how every week something else tops the news. It just shows the potential for getting your product or services out there connected to a news event.
- Make sure to give reporters something they don't already have. You can report on a story that's in the news now, but don't just reiterate what's been said before, over and over again. What do you have that's new and can add more to the story? Again, goes back to the angle--what angle do you have that's new and informative?
- If you see an upcoming event unfold before the media gets it, GO! They might not see the angle yet, and you can get a lot of press by being the first.
- When pitching, lead with that pitch. It's your most important point and the reason they need to hear what you have to say. Don't wait to get to the point.
- Visualize your pitch and be able to visualize your story as well. When you get the opportunity to talk to a journalist, you can even say, "I can see an interview with (person) and we would discuss (topic)."
- Provide complete stories. Often times, you can have other experts that can help your story, making their job so much easier. For example, Diana was on a segment for CBS4 News and they were interviewing her on being a virtual assistant and how that can be a great idea for those unemployed. They wanted to also interview a company that was utilizing a virtual assistant—BAM!—she quickly contacted her local clients and bingo, they had an awesome story.
- Think trends in business. This is ever changing, but exciting.

- Be aware of the PR Calendar and when to submit news. Magazine times are different than newspaper times. You need to plan ahead when to submit. By knowing the calendar, you can think ahead to how your company fits in with an upcoming holiday or event.
- Pitch human-interest stories. What inspires those in your community? What have you done that helps those in your community?
- If you are pitching on a problem that's current, don't just mention the problem; pitch the solution, too. For example, unemployment is at an all time high, start a business to succeed.
- Be aware when a topic has reached its due date. You know when it's just been in the news so much that no one can bear to hear it again. It's time to change it up.
- Be honest and truthful. Often times when a reporter asks additional background questions, it can be easy to just say, "yes" to questions that are maybe not 100% truthful. It's okay to let them know the truth. Try, "Well I've never actually done that before, but I have done … " and emphasize a related strength.

The Art of Pitching

- Know the media outlets you want to pitch, dependent on what and who you are pitching. Is your target audience moms, CEO's, or baby boomers? That makes a big difference.
- Decide what methods will give you the best results. Some pitches are made for radio, others for newspaper and TV.
- Make sure that the magazine, radio, TV companies you are pitching would be interested in your topic. Why waste both of your time by submitting a sports topic to a business website?
- When pitching, don't just say go to my blog or website and see for yourself. Take the time to write why you are a good fit.
- Think outside the box. Whatever makes you unique in your business can help to make you unique in your pitch as well
- Know how to pitch that particular person. Do they want e-mails sent to them, a form filled out on their site, comments to their blog?
- When pitching via e-mail, write a brief introduction. Just a sentence or two that tells why the story you are submitting is news to them and worth reading further. Tell why you are the person who should be reporting on this topic.
- Subject lines count BIG Time! Don't just rehash the title. Grab their interest.
- Never send an attachment unless requested.
- NEVER EVER do multiple e-mails to numerous reporters so they can see it! (CC everyone. YIKES!!! It's scary just thinking about it.)
- When you do get mentioned in a publication, make sure you follow-up and thank them.

Who to Pitch

- Send your press to reporters who regularly write on your industry. Be sure to build your credibility, show your qualifications and provide great insight into that topic.
- You can find reporters by Google Alerts, reading newspapers, magazines, blogs.
- Set up Twitter searches and utilize Twitter. Media is all about utilizing social networking today. Follow them on Twitter. Join their Facebook Page. Go to PR

Twitter Chats, which you can find by searching PR related hashtags. See who you can find on http://www.mediaontwitter.com

- Find out if the reporter you are interested in targeting has a blog. Familiarize yourself with that blog. Add comments and build a relationship – "I agree with you. I love your "specific comment. Would like to see more ... "
- You can purchase media lists. But, however you get your lists, keep them current and updated, and treat them like GOLD.
- Sign up for services like these where you can find journalists looking for experts to interview:
  - HARO – http://HelpaReporter.com
  - http://www.reporterconnection.com/
  - http://www.pitchengine.com
  - http://www.pitchrate.com
  - http://wwwRadioGuestList.com
  - Other sites I use to find where to submit PR – http://www.mediabistro.com, http://www.newslink.org, http://www.pitchengine.com

Resume Writing

Many VAs add resume composing and typing to their services, and specialize in it. Fortunately, resumes can be typed from any location, so it's perfect for a VA business. And, with the success of monster.com and other online sites such as these, you can tell that the future looks even brighter. Posting your resume on the Internet or e-mailing your resume to potential employers is becoming the acceptable business practice in today's busy lifestyle. In fact, many will only accept resumes through their company website.

When doing almost any type of virtual assisting at one time or another, I believe you will get a call to do a resume. At least that's what I've found. That's why I feel it's beneficial to familiarize yourself with the basics. And if you choose to specialize in resume preparation, then absolutely be as knowledgeable as you can be.

It has been determined that one in four executives spend no more than two minutes reading a resume. Many spend only 30 seconds to review a resume. You can help your client make that time count by helping them create a resume that sells the person well. The top half of the resume is what has to catch the eye of the reader in order to entice the reader to completely read the resume.

I have always loved the Martin Yate's series, *Resumes That Knock 'em Dead.* I highly recommend going to the bookstore and getting some of his books. They are well worth having available. Not only do they tell you what to include in a resume, but they also provide samples, cover letters, tips, you name it. It's well worth the money.

I'm just going to briefly go over the basics here. Here is what must always go in a resume. For the heading:

- Name—The first and last name only. No middle initial. No need to add Mr. or Mrs.
- Address—Give the complete address. Use the two letter abbreviation for the state.
- Telephone Number—Don't forget the area code.
- E-mail Address.
- Web Address (Optional)—However, you will find that many do include it today.

Job Objective—This is usually a sentence or two summarizing the job they are seeking. It is also called Position Desired, Employment Objective, etc.

Employment Dates—Very important to include. Employers are leery if not included. Include both the month and year.

Company Name—The names of the employers should be included. There is no need to include street address or telephone numbers, but do include city and state.

Responsibilities—Here you will list the special achievements and other contributions made.

Accreditation and Licenses—Licenses, etc.

Education—Start with your highest level. Abbreviations will be used for Ph.D., M.A., etc. Mention scholarships, awards, etc.

Some of the things that are usually not mentioned on a resume are your salary requirements, reason for leaving a prior position, list of references and phone numbers, personal information, mention of age, race, religion, health, hobbies, etc.

When preparing a resume for someone, what I have found beneficial is to prepare a book of samples, list them on your website for easy viewing, or keep a portfolio of them on your website for easy access and have them pick out a style. You would be amazed how many people come to you who have never done a resume. They are thrilled that you can simplify the process for them by providing this. They can then fill in the blanks with their information.

Try to keep the resume short and to the point. Some of your clients will go on and on about everything they did at a particular job. No potential boss cares! Encourage them to think about what job they would be most interested in and to focus on the skills they know.

Okay, this is where you come in. The resume that leaves your office has to be accurate. I usually try to have the client come back and pick up their resume when possible. They often will continue talking and have you ever had someone watching over your shoulder while you are working? It is disconcerting, to say the least. If the client is hesitant to leave, explain the importance of being able to make sure this is accurate. If there is a typo in that resume, it can hurt their chances of getting a job. But if they insist, I will NOT push the issue. I can type it while they are there.

Here are some tips from a fellow VA in Ohio who has specialized in resume typing. Mary operates a VA business in Ohio. I think you'll find them very beneficial.

> Resume paper should be about 60 to 65 lb weight. I purchase mine at a printer near my home. I do offer a variety of shades and textures, and I buy Beckett linen and Beckett Royal Fiber. Various shades, white, off-white, ivory, cream, light gray, and I also have light blue. I also provide matching envelopes for clients. My favorite is Colonial White, which is an off-white. My clients get five originals and matching envelopes. Of course, don't forget the white bond copy for faxing.

> Since you are writing for VAs, and many will be writing resumes for long distance clients, they should still mail copies to the client, e-mail it, or submit it to the companies the client is applying to. Many also now want their resume on a CD. Although my feeling is if you upload or e-mail the file to a client and the programs are compatible, then, that can take the place of a CD, or they can burn their own. For online submissions, I will also include a clean plain text file that they can easily cut and paste. I package everything in a nice resume folder with a label I have printed and put on the front of the folder, with my business name, address and phone number. Have to use those larger labels for that. Of course, the business card on the inside, and then I have a form printed that is pretty neat; my friend created it for me, for

clients to use and track where they have sent their resume. I also include a packet of interviewing tips.

The cover letter introduces the resume and the resume introduces the person. Cover letters are, of course, very important, but I have found that since many people e-mail their resumes, they don't want to use a cover letter. But some of the sites online still request a cover letter. When faxing, I encourage clients to send a cover letter. Of course, some ads have reference codes nowadays that have made the need for a cover letter less important.

I use an Areas of Expertise, or sometimes I call it Technical Expertise, or Equipment Operated, and many times I still include Areas of Expertise along with another heading. Then I have columns, three usually, with one, two or three words describing, such as Team Building, Training & Development, Budget Formulation, Inventory Control, words that will give the person reviewing the resume, a quick and brief description of the person's skills, before they read the bulleted sentences describing the person's position. I like to include a heading on the left margin when there are accomplishments, in bold; I type accomplishments to catch the eye of the reader.

I feel that people need to totally rethink what a resume is and what it needs to do for them. We are stuck in the traditional chronological format with a job description under each job.

If I can't get a resume to one page, then I try really hard to get the most important information on the first page, so that an HR person will find the resume interesting enough to read the second page.

I have four pages of skills I typed up to include in my book, and put little boxes next to them so that someone reading them can check their skills or bring to their attention what they need to put in their resume. I go back periodically and add more skills as I do another resume and find some new skills I hadn't thought about.

The focus of the resume is what dictates the verbiage and format. Those are the three basic elements of a really marketable resume. That's why when a client is either changing fields or has two focuses, I advise two resumes, and they don't have to be that different, but, sometimes they are.

You can tell, Mary has been doing this a while. Many VAs starting a VA business will find resumes to be their niche. The very best advice I can give you is to learn everything you can and keep updated. I suggest buying the latest resume books instead of going to the library, as those are often outdated. Also, go on the Internet and get tips there. Write everything down. Know that every client is a bit different so be flexible in preparing his or her resume.

Here are some additional tips:

- You will want to make the resume pleasing to the eye.
- You will want to make the resume short and to the point.
- Important areas of interest should be standing out so a cursory examination of the resume will point these areas out.

Another VA who has some tips to provide is Kathy Keshemberg. She has compiled a package of sample tips that I highly endorse. Her website is packed full of great tips on writing an effective resume, including samples you can view. She also offers teleseminars that you will find beneficial. (http://www.acareeradvantage.com)

The Insurance Industry

Insurance agents and insurance adjusters are excellent target markets. No matter what type of insurance they offer—property, auto, life, medical—they often need help with just about everything; and that's good news to us. We can help them with their daily correspondence, regular mailers, late notices, large insurance claims, accident claim reports, scheduling appointments, making sure applications are filled out completely, and so on. Many insurance agents don't have a private secretary so they can utilize us on an "as-needed" basis. I know you hear that phrase a lot in our book, and keep that phrase in mind, it can be a key phrase to use to sell a client on your services. Keep reminding your potential client that they pay us only when they need us.

Insurance adjusters often have long client statements to be transcribed. They will have taken a client's statement for their client, and need to have it transcribed so they can forward it on. They can sometimes be long and tedious, but very profitable. Pay close attention to detail. This statement alone can sometimes make a difference in the outcome of a claim. Sometimes it can be quite exciting to see it unfold. In my 25 years, I've discovered that there definitely are some people out there who are trying to scam the insurance companies. It's pretty neat when an adjuster can catch them. Often as you're typing along, you can see it coming. And we thought being a virtual assistant was boring!

What's even better is that insurance agents are great to target in the online world. The majority now have websites and are active online. In most cases, they are no longer confined to one particular area. For the small agents who aren't with big companies, they are thrilled to have our expertise not only in web design but also in setting up and customizing their work, building their brand, promotional and marketing help, digital transcription, and with the day-to-day e-mail and follow-up correspondence. You'd think in today's world that everyone would already know this, but they don't! Agents were taught to sell insurance. I've developed a great network of agents now and I can tell you that they appreciate the support that the VA community is providing them.

Many agents are actively engaged in other organizations in their spare time and can use assistance there as well. For example, Jack Goldstein Jr., an insurance agent with one of the leading insurance firms in Columbus, Ohio, uses VAs on a regular basis. He is also very active in the local JayCee's and requires help with their correspondence typing, as well all of their promotional materials, flyers, newsletters, event scheduling, etc. He states that he doesn't have the time required to do the typing and composing of these, but he gladly pays a VA to help him out. He states that his office runs more efficiently with the use of his VA (ME!).

Mr. Goldstein goes on to state, "They can be instrumental when you are planning a big event, like the 4th of July celebration. I needed help with almost all aspects of it. My VA was able to schedule the event, keep track of all the income and expenses, contact contributors and follow-up with written authorizations and letters, etc. I couldn't have done it without her." I was able to continue doing my insurance work and she was able to keep the event rolling. By the way, the event went off as a huge success."

When typing for insurance adjusters, make sure that you are clear on the claimant's correct name and address. Normally, the adjuster will spell it for you. Details are important such as the claim number, address, date of loss or accident, etc. If by any chance you are having any difficulty with the dictation, don't hesitate to ask the adjuster to speak more clearly or to spell out any pertinent information in the future. They will appreciate it as much as you will.

Be careful when determining your turnaround time. Some tapes can be short, a simple letter to the insurance company—a page or two. The next tape may be a detailed insurance report that is fifteen pages in length. You'll get accustomed to this. Just be aware that you don't want to offer 24-hour turnaround on this type of dictation. Also, often times the adjuster will drop off the tapes after hours. Make sure he is aware that that does not count as a day.

To obtain insurance clients, there are several means that you can utilize. NOTE: These marketing methods are universal and can be used for all specialty services.

- Direct mail--sending your business cards and/or brochures.
- Composing a website.
- Dropping your cards off at local office supply companies and printers.
- Networking at local organizations, Chamber of Commerce Business Fairs, etc.
- Advertising in community newsletters.
- Yellow Page advertising.
- Word of mouth.
- Volunteer work.
- Social networking sites like Facebook, Twitter, and LinkedIn
- Send out press releases and articles detailing how a virtual assistant can be of value to an agent, broker, or adjuster.
- Use keywords wisely in your web content to make sure your site comes up for "virtual assistant insurance agents."
- Get listed on VA directories.
- Respond to RFPs.
- Ask for referrals.
- Work-at-home sites often have listings of companies looking for help. Just make sure it's a good, legitimate site and that you get paid what you're worth!

The Real Estate Industry

The real estate industry for VAs is always a viable specialty. In fact, a number of former real estate agents have opted to become REVAs (Real Estate Virtual Assistant). National speakers such as Michael Russer are continually proclaiming the benefits we can provide this industry. The late Janet Jordan, who was a true pioneer in our industry, once stated that Allen Hainge is another seminar leader promoting the VA industry who coaches top producers across the country, telling them they need a VA. He is known to work with several VAs.

Fueled by today's technology, and driven by such dynamic people as these, we are but one step closer to seeing our industry step into the future. It's a future we VAs are creating. Isn't it powerful to see an entire industry, such as the real estate industry, work closely together with ours and start a whole new way of doing business? The days of driving around with your realtor and looking for homes are slowly being replaced by clicks on a computer. So fellow VAs—buckle your seatbelts and let's go!! Let's learn about this exciting new field.

Now before we get started, we need to realize the type of personality that works best. We will be dealing with people who, although they are sometimes having their dreams come true by buying their dream home, are stressed. Moving is a stressful time for everyone. You need to be the type of person who can stay calm under pressure. You're going to be dealing with attorneys, buyers, sellers, other realtors, inspectors, appraisers, etc. You need to be good with people and empathetic to their needs. Gretchen Berg, a VA who teaches one of the training classes, states that it is also important to be detailed-oriented. Even the small details count. Does this sound like you? If so, let's read on and learn about some of the exciting things you can do.

Online Transaction Coordinator

The Internet has now made it possible for virtual assistants to act as transaction coordinators to a real estate transaction regardless of their location, as long as they have Internet access, a phone and a fax. By utilizing web-based software such as GuruNetworks (http://www.gurunet.net), a VA, serving as transaction coordinator, becomes the hub of the real estate transaction by managing the many facets associated with buying or selling a home. Working with either the buying or selling agent, the VA maintains all the listing information, coordinates inspections and appraisals, gathers all the necessary documents to the transaction, provides necessary follow-up, and makes all responsible parties accountable for their tasks.

From the convenience of their own office, the VA manages all these transactions online where each party to the transaction can log in and, based upon their security access, view the status of the transaction. With GuruNetworks, there is a contact database of vendors and suppliers used in the transaction, an intranet for e-mail correspondence between parties, a calendar, and report writing capabilities. This only touches the surface of the power and flexibility offered by GuruNetworks program. What does this mean for your real estate client? No more paperwork, no more follow-up calls, no more babysitting files. Instead, they can be out in front of the clients selling more real estate.

Most transaction coordinators charge a flat fee for setting up the agent's template of checklists. Then there is a non-refundable fee charged for setting up a new transaction, which represents a retainer in the event the deal does not close. Upon closing and disbursement of funds, you collect the remaining balance. Fees for setup range from $200--$275. Fees per transaction range from $200--$300, with an estimated $50-$75 retainer fee due up front.

To learn more about supporting the real estate industry, we recommend getting the proper training and speaking with those currently offering these services. Here are some resources to check:

http://www.revanetwork.com
http://www.guruNET.net
http://www.imprev.com
http://revainstitute.com
http://www.recyber.com
http://www.settlementroom.com
http://www.afhseminars.com

Realtor Marketing
There are other ways to target realtors. I was able to get many real estate clients through my direct mailings, Yellow Page ads, my web page, networking, and presenting at industry-specific events. For local clients, I even drove around local areas and contacted them. Looking for signs in my neighborhood, I wrote to them and introduced myself asking if I could help with their marketing. I did land a regular client that way who turned into a very profitable income to my business. He was looking for something different to catch the neighbor's attention. I had lived in the area for years. I knew what had been done before and I came up with a new idea. It worked. It was a little costly, but he made a great deal of money on it and better yet for him, he became known in the community and the realtor of choice.

It was around Halloween time and he invested in pumpkins, put his cards on them, and gave each home one. We live in a nice area, so fortunately, it was well received. I was initially afraid that the kids would toss them in the streets, but they didn't. One of the things I like about owning my own business is that I get to be original. Some ideas work, some don't. The ones that didn't, you won't hear about in this book! Hopefully, you won't run into my kids, as they love to tell those stories.

Many realtors will want you to do their entire marketing for them. I work with another agent who states he felt that his time would be better spent out there selling houses, so he just said basically, "Go for it." Even in our initial interview he was in between appointments and in a hurry, but I made sure that I had all the information I needed to be effective. Also, knowing that he was extremely busy, I asked what was the best way to contact him when I did have a question. This is very beneficial. All businesses run differently. (For example, I have one attorney who will absolutely not get a computer or have anything to do with it. To e-mail him would be useless. He tells me the time of day to contact him.) For this agent, he advised that the best time to reach him was first thing in the morning. He wanted me to fax my marketing pieces to him for review and he would call and leave a message giving his approval. He has referred me to many realtors throughout the country. We are able to work via e-mail, fax, etc. One thing you will discover, just like with all your clients, word-of-mouth will spread rapidly, with realtors especially. When you start selling and making them money, they are very happy!! And they want to keep you happy!

In addition to marketing, realtors use virtual assistants to answer their e-mail, schedule their appointments, coordinate their closings, update their web listings, research FSBOs, upload virtual tours, and much more. I know of a local realtor who has 11 agents working for him. One agent works here in south Florida, but uses a VA in Orlando. She has a cell phone listing in Orlando. He says it's as if she's right here. He has utilized her services for years for every aspect of his business. According to him, and I quote, "There's no way I could run my business without her today. She keeps on top of everything. She schedules my day. Tells me where I need to be. Does all of the paperwork. That allows me to go out and sell. I rely on her for everything." You know she will get a nice Christmas bonus this year.

When targeting the Real Estate Industry, also consider who else might be interested in your services besides the agents. For example:

- Property appraisers
- Inspectors
- Construction companies
- Closing companies
- Foreclosure specialists

Legal Transcription

Legal transcription can be a major part of many VA businesses. There are so many things they can do for their attorney clients to aid them in their business, in addition to typing their pleadings. For example, many VAs do the researching for the pleadings, scheduling of all their appointments, depositions, arbitrations, travel arrangements, client luncheons, presentations, e-mail answering, gift giving, etc.

Often large firms will have several offices in different cities or their main office in another state. You may be responsible for coordinating multiple flight schedules and accommodations, not to mention making sure that all of the paperwork is complete so that the attorneys can take it to court. It's amazing that this can all be done right from your home office.

If you are responsible for handling flights and hotel accommodations, I recommend using the same travel agency. Find one that's good and stick with it. You will find that they will help you out in a pinch. Plus, they have on record what they have used in the past, leaving less margin for error. Of course, there are a number of online options for making travel arrangements.

It's important to find out from the office's administrative assistant of the visiting attorney, what the attorney's likes and dislikes are. You'd be amazed at the good PR you can create by having their favorite bagels on hand, or a special coffee or tea. You can order these ahead and have them in the room. You are usually given an allowance to spend.

Dawn Mayo of Absolute Document Services offers legal and medical transcription. She was able to get her training through experience. She worked for the federal government for nine years and states, "Transcription and word processing were extremely formal in the government. This formality was a great tool, though, because it helped me to get comfortable with the most difficult transcription. What that means is when a client comes to me with what they think is difficult, I can transcribe with ease because of the extensive OTJ training that I've had."

She states that most of her marketing is done through postcards, Yellow Pages and direct contact. She further states, "I feel it is important to stay in the face of your clients, current and potential. I place an ad in the two major phone books in my area. I am a firm believer that image is everything, so I don't skimp. My website is also a means of marketing for me, but I'm looking to get more into the PR aspect of marketing. (Her website is www.yourremoteoffice.com)

If you specialize in legal transcription, you will have to be very good at scheduling your work and taking care not to take on too much. Attorneys often will need their work back in 24, 48 to 72 hours. As they will probably be your main bread and butter, it's better to skip a resume job or typing of a school paper, than to overextend yourself trying to do it all. I have someone in the area that I will refer work to when I'm working on several tapes. She does the same for me, so it works out great.

To target your market specifically for attorneys, in addition to directly targeting them with letters, advertise in legal publications. Most cities have a newspaper subscribed to by attorneys that relates directly to legal issues. A section of this paper is usually devoted to freelance secretaries. All states in the U.S. have State Bar Associations, which produce monthly or quarterly periodicals containing articles of interest to the legal community and advertisements for lawyers, paralegals, secretaries, typists, and other legal support services. Also, advertise in the college newspapers that have a law school or law-related classes, as well as place your flyer on their bulletin boards. Also, utilize your website and classify it with all search engines highlighting your legal experience. There are some well-known attorneys who advocate for virtual assistants. Research them online and connect via social media or attend one of their events.

In addition, visit local attorneys' offices in your area. You can drop off a portfolio or your business card. You can also send personalized letters to these offices emphasizing how beneficial your services could be to help with the overflow of work often encountered in a busy attorney's office. You might also want to contact other legal transcription services in the Yellow Pages and offer to help with their overload work.

In addition to attorneys' offices, also connect with court reporting agencies, government agencies, paralegal firms, judges' offices, etc. I'd also contact any freelancing paralegals. Often they can get backed up with work and can use your VA assistance. Also, word of mouth, networking through the Chamber of Commerce, Toastmasters groups, or other activities is very successful in obtaining these professional clients.

Most attorneys prefer to be billed hourly and usually pay weekly or bi-weekly. For one attorney's office, I will send an invoice with all returned work and they pay all invoices weekly; and for another office, I just bill them bi-weekly. You will need to decide what best suits you and your clients. Working with attorneys on a retainer basis with payment in advance is also an option to consider.

With attorneys, occasionally you will be asked to do rush jobs so they can get a pleading to the courthouse on time. They will normally fax or e-mail the document. I've also had them e-mail me the document and then fax me the handwritten changes that need to be made. Keep in mind that the attorney is not going to be proofing your work well. You need to be the one proofing it, as they are paying you for it and it's your responsibility. Even in rush situations, proof well.

You probably will be dealing a lot with the office manager. Make sure to keep on her good side, and whenever possible, make her job easier by helping the office out in some way.

In legal dictation, it's advisable to create macros for the items that are repeatedly used. For example, create a macro for the caption, the prayer (wherefore section), the signature line, the notary block, etc. This prevents you from having to retype and reproof the information in those areas.

Be very careful when typing citations. Make sure you type them correctly as the attorney and judge will often be looking for them, and it can be an embarrassment to the office if you have incorrectly cited the material.

You can also help your attorney find the appropriate citations. I use http://www.lawsource.com; it's so easy to use. I recommend if you plan on offering legal transcription, that you go there and just familiarize yourself with the site. It includes everything you need. The Electric Law Library is another great resource-- http://www.lectlaw.com/usforms/realestatecontracts.htm.

It is advisable to get a sample copy of a pleading and keep it in your file for each attorney's office. This will provide an example of how they set up their pleadings, correct spelling of the attorneys' names, and other pertinent information for that particular firm.

In typing for attorneys, it's absolutely imperative you keep everything you type confidential. There is a tendency to bring up the latest hearing at the dinner table as it's interesting and in the news, but avoid this. Your reputation is at risk and your client is depending on you.

Professional attire is normally required for your attorney clients, and if at all possible keep the kids at home if you are delivering or picking up work, at least until you get a feel for the office. I know some of my clients downtown are often having depositions or arbitrations, and children's chatter can greatly disturb the setting.

Attorneys may have you transcribe court hearings or depositions. These can be five or six tapes or more, depending on the case. It's important to find out if they are going to be using them just for use in the office or in court. Here's why: The attorneys I work for often have me transcribe their tapes and it's only for their viewing. They would much rather I just zip it out quickly since they are paying an hourly rate instead of taking my time to do a more thorough job. For the transcription they are going to be using in courts, they need that exact, well-proofed and in good form.

It's also a good idea to save questions for one phone call or e-mail your questions. Most of the time, you can simply e-mail your questions, but be sure to consolidate them into one e-mail. When I complete the pleadings, I'll e-mail them to the attorney, and they can download and make any changes or additions. Don't be offended if they do!! Attorneys are notorious for adding and changing their minds once they see a pleading in writing. They dictate the pleading and once down in print, they can add more thoughts or cases to it as needed to strengthen their case.

Medical Transcription

A medical transcription service can target a number of medical professionals and institutions locally and virtually. These include doctors, specialists, hospitals, chiropractors, physical therapists, home health care agencies, psychologists, laboratories, dentists, and veterinarians to name a few.

You must first decide what medical specialty you wish to target. If you don't have considerable medical experience you might want to target chiropractors, psychologists or therapists at first. Their dictation generally is not as technical as a cardiologist's. You might even want to contact massage therapists' offices or places that offer physical therapy.

I find it truly amazing how much work there is out there. Last year when I went for physical therapy, I got into a conversation with one of the technicians and told him about my medical transcription business. Once I finished saying medical transcription, he immediately stopped right in the middle of the massage, got his boss, and I was negotiating my rates right then and there. (I usually have better dress attire than a gown, but if it works, why not.) They were so far behind and needed help immediately. I was able to not only catch them up, but make a good profit at the same time. My back's all better too!! Another win-win situation.

To be successful in this field, you must have prior knowledge or have taken a medical terminology class. If not, you will constantly be looking up terms for the proper spelling. There are courses you can take at local colleges and courses that you can take online, as well as at home. One popular at-home school is At-Home Professions. It has an excellent reputation in the following specialties: Legal Transcription, Medical Transcription, Secretarial/Word Processing, Bookkeeping Paralegal Training, and Computer Basics. Contact them at: At-Home Professions, http://www.at-homeprofessions.com.

There are also many online places that you might want to check out. MTDaily has been around for years and comes with an excellent recommendation:

- The American Association for Medical Transcription, http://www.ahdionline.org
- MTDaily, http://www.mtdaily.com
- Medword, http://www.medword.com
- MTMonthly, http://www.mtmonthly.com

To obtain clients, you can personally stop by medical practices and hospitals in your area and drop off business cards and/or your portfolio. Ask to speak with the office manager, but don't force the issue. Be brief in your presentation. Most offices are busy and you can jeopardize your chances if you take up too much time. Also, consider the time of day that you are stopping by. Don't go too close to the close of business, as they may be running behind and don't have the time to meet with you. Also, around lunchtime is a bad time because they want to get a break from the office.

You can also call medical practices, informing them that you offer freelance medical transcription services on an "as-needed basis." Advise them that if they are interested, you can forward a brochure or set up an appointment to explain your services in more detail. Another way to find potential clients is to search the want ads of the paper and send a letter or call the offices looking for help. Let them know you work on a freelance basis and you could assist their office until they hire a full-time employee. If you offer this service, make sure you're available for immediate work. Also, look for medical practices that are just opening and send a small gift basket and a letter congratulating them and explaining your services.

Take advantage of all the online opportunities, too. Seek doctor's websites in your area and ask about contacting them that way. Are they on LinkedIn or Facebook? You can also place an ad in a medical newsletter. Chiropractors and other medical professionals receive newsletters that allow advertising for freelance secretaries. Contact local doctors in your area and ask for additional information on these newsletters.

While most work can be delivered through electronic means, if you need to pick up and deliver work, arrange it to your schedule. Most chiropractors and psychologists offer evening hours several times a week. You could then pick up the work after hours and not miss time away from typing.

Some word processors might benefit from a medical spellchecking program or an electronic medical dictionary such as *Steadman's Medical Dictionary*. A computer dictionary will allow you to look up medical terms right on your computer, complete with definition. One company that provides the *Steadman's Medical Dictionary* is Lipincott, Williams & Wilkins (www.lww.com). As Tina Armillotto, a medical transcriptionist in Ft. Lauderdale, Florida, states, "It has been a lifesaver to me. I don't have to spend so much time stopping and looking up medical terms and medicines. You just sound the word to your best judgment and it will insert the word it feels is most likely it. I'm able to keep my typing flowing by not having to stop and get the dictionary."

Tina also utilizes auto correct and macros. She has all her doctor's names and addresses, as well as paragraphs of repetitive type, all programmed in her word processing program. She is able to type just a few letters instead of the whole paragraph or line. For example, say a doctor says one particular phase over and over again; you can program it where you just type a few letters and the whole phase types out. She also uses them for full letters, like thank-you letters. One click of the key and she's done!

I have found that charts of the human body are extremely beneficial for finding the right term. *Dorland's Pocket Medical Dictionary* contains a complete section of detailed charts. I feel this dictionary is a must for all medical transcribers and can be found at most bookstores.

It's very important to be aware of the laws that affect your business. One such law is HIPAA. You should do research on HIPAA.org and other HIPAA sites to learn about this law and how it effects your business. HIPAA is the Health Insurance Portability & Accountability Act passed in 1996. One aspect of HIPAA is that it is the founding authority for the releasing of medical records for inspection of medical records pertaining to an individual. Since you will be dealing with confidential patient files, you need to learn the essentials of this law.

Bookkeeping Services

Bookkeeping services can be a wonderful addition to any VA business. I was surprised once I started offering this service how many clients were interested. I hadn't planned on adding bookkeeping to my VA business. It just didn't interest me. However, one day one of my best clients asked that in addition to doing their correspondence, would I be interested in keeping their books as well. I was familiar with Quickbooks, having kept my own business records on it, so I said I'd give it a go.

If you don't have a bookkeeping background, we do recommend taking some online classes, taking an adult education class, reading some books, or educating yourself. You will want to be familiar with the latest laws, as you are dealing with the financial status of the client's business when you offer these services. Make sure you know what you're doing. Although you may know how to use the accounting software package, each business is unique in its own right, and that means there can be variation in the way they conduct their business and keep their books. If you don't feel comfortable, don't accept the job or offer the services in the first place.

Many new businesses are looking to have someone help them out with their monthly invoicing, bank reconciliations, payroll, online bill payments, shopping cart transactions, and reporting. If you do invoicing, payroll, billing, etc., make sure you keep a backup of your work. Quickbooks will also ask that you do. Always check the number of the check when printing it, if it says it's a duplicate, find out why, and don't just assume its okay. DON'T delete checks; void them. Reconcile your checking account monthly. There are additional risks involved in offering payroll services. Be sure you are educated on the current employment laws and appropriate filing dates.

Here are some tips that we've found helpful:

- Take your time and look over your work at least twice to make sure you have it correct.
- Prepare a schedule and follow through with it. For example, I have to call in one client's weekly taxes. Even though I have several days to do it, I always call it in the first thing Wednesday morning, which is payday. I've created the routine and follow it religiously so I never have to worry about forgetting.
- Establish a good rapport with the accountant that they use. It can come in handy when you have questions.
- Don't let things get behind. Process and close all transactions monthly.
- Have clients keep an envelope in their car or computer bag where they can toss receipts. You can send them preprinted envelopes or labels for easy drop off at the post office.
- Know that there will be times of the year when you will be busier. Naturally, January for 1099s and through April tax season will be your busiest times. Plan accordingly.

Academic Typing

This is typing papers for students, teachers, etc. Academic typing is also the most readily available market for virtual assisting and word processing, and is relatively inexpensive to target. You can put ads up at school bulletin boards for free, and the campus newspapers and local weekly publications are a fraction of the cost of advertising in daily publications. Most ads you place in any newspaper will generate school papers, even if you're targeting other areas. The best advertising will be from word-of-mouth. Students inevitably go back to class and tell others of your services.

If you decide this is the area you would like to target, spend a day visiting the various colleges in your area. Place your flyer or business card on their bulletin boards. To place your flyer or business card on the main bulletin boards, you will need to obtain approval first at the Information Booth or Student Services. However, there are other bulletin boards throughout the campus where you can post your ads that are not monitored and don't require prior approval. When I dropped my son off at college, I was amazed at the opportunities for advertising at this campus town, the University of Florida. The hotel that we stayed at had business card holders in the front desk and had advertisements for massage therapists, room cleaners, etc. No virtual assistants…the perfect opportunity. The Wal-Mart that we shopped at for the last minute items that he needed was absolutely bombarded with students, and they said it was always busy. They had a bulletin board that allowed advertisements. Again, the perfect place for an attractive business card. The restaurant we ate at actually had a turnaround business card holder. It did have a word processor in it. The opportunities were there. Not only did it get my mind off of leaving him, but it really made me realize the potential besides the obvious.

Provide tear-off sections on your flyer with your name, phone number, e-mail address and URL. Make your flyer stand out by using an impressive or unique design or colorful paper. There are usually several typists listed, so your flyer needs to be the one they look at. You can find bordered paper or specialty designed paper that is perfect for these eye-catching flyers at most office supply stores and online sources such as Paper Direct or Idea Art.

For those schools you don't personally visit, send letters asking them to place your flyer on their bulletin board. Advise them in the letter how reasonable your rates are and how your expertise in this field would be beneficial to their students. Advertise in the college campus telephone directories or other directories targeted to students. College newspapers are also good advertising tools. As previously mentioned in this book, it's good practice to be a consistent advertiser. Consider sending articles to them on a regular basis. Most college newspapers are listed at http://www.newslink.org and do accept articles.

Other areas to target would be the public and private elementary and secondary schools in your area. I suggest that you offer their professional staff a courtesy discount of 15% to 20% (if you choose). See if they offer advertising in their yearbook or other publications. For example, my son's school has a cookbook that they sell each year and the school accepts advertisements for it. It's only $10.00 and I always get responses from that ad. One method to get your services recognized is to become active at the schools. Volunteer for the yearbook staff or helping with the school newsletter. Join the PTA. This free advertising is well worth the time spent. Your kids will appreciate it, too.

I have found that the majority of my typing is generally double-spaced text. The majority of the time, the student even brings along instructions. However, you might want to familiarize yourself with the following books as well:

- *APA Publication Manual* - APA
- *MLA Handbook for Writers of Research Papers, Theses, and Dissertations* - MLA
- *A Manual for Writers of Term Papers, Theses and Dissertations* - Turabian

Academic typing is normally charged on a per page basis instead of an hourly rate. Students like to know exactly what they will be paying. Single-spaced text is generally charged differently than double-spaced text.

Here are some additional pointers:

- Charge an additional fee if the work is illegible.
- Be firm on your turnaround time and charge extra for rush jobs.
- Minor editing is allowed, but if it requires extensive editing, charge more.
- Always give the student back both their original and typewritten copy.

The secret of joy in work is contained in one word – excellence.
To know how to do something well is to enjoy it.
–Pearl S. Buck

Operating Your Business

A Typical Day in the Life of a VA

One of the joys of writing a book is getting to interview others. It was absolutely amazing to see just how many people were so happy with the business they have chosen. They love what they're doing. The energy and the enthusiasm for the virtual assisting industry are astonishing. Our hope is that you, too, will find the happiness that we have.

This is an interesting chapter for me. When I think about it long and hard, I could probably identify some things in my day that are "typical," but for the most part, nothing is typical—and that's exactly why I love doing what I do. The wide variety of tasks and the different types of clients I serve throughout the day, or the week, is the best part of my business. The flexibility I have in scheduling my own day around other obligations is something I strive for—I'm accomplishing this because no day is typical.

For those tasks that are routine for the day, consider these helpful hints for keeping it all together.

- Work your plan. Make note at the end of each day of what needs to be accomplished tomorrow.
- Be consistent and stay organized. Make every minute count.
- Utilize a Daytimer, online calendar, or project management system to stay focused on the time constraints that you have set in advance.
- Keep any client visits to a minimum. It's great to be personable, but don't let it go overboard. Client visits can consist of online meetings, in-person meetings, and phone calls.
- Make it a policy that all clients call before stopping over.
- Avoid interruptions as much as possible.
- Stay focused on the job at hand. Don't get sidetracked with other tasks, surfing the Net, checking your e-mails, Tweeting, or following a listserv discussion.
- If you feel overwhelmed, stop, take a walk, and get away from the work for 10-15 minutes. You'll find a whole new person when you come back.
- Avoid isolation by participating in online networking groups. Beware! Do not allow yourself to be consumed by the e-mails generated by the networking groups.
- Manage your time wisely. Schedule certain times of the day to read and respond to e-mail just like you would schedule any other task.
- Use a timer to help keep you on track.
- Focus, focus, focus!

In Their Own Words:

Tess Strand Alipour: I think like most WAHMs I have a pretty atypical day in that I juggle a business, family, and personal time. The hours I work have changed drastically since I started my practice. Initially I was working up to ten hours a day some days. It was all new, the ability to work from home, doing things that were challenging and fun at the same time and I loved it, and worked almost constantly the first few months. At the time I was living in India, and my clients in New York loved knowing that I was working on their business growth literally while they were sleeping. After a few months though, I realized that I needed to seek more balance in my schedule and tried to keep work time to more traditional business hours - still abroad, so still working during my clients' evening and night-time hours, but being more reasonable about when I was available, etc. I made changes again, in 2009, after my daughter was born and cut back my work hours drastically - choosing to work only with select clients and on a somewhat limited availability. Now, I usually work 3 hours a day, 5 days a week, focusing on business growth for myself and my clients when it is convenient for my family [i.e., when my daughter is sleeping or playing with her daddy or grandma.] We believe strongly in attachment parenting and are so blessed to have the luxury of that parenting lifestyle. It is also immensely helpful that my husband and business partner is home as well. Since day one however, weekends have always been sacred and are strictly a time for family and personal life. We do also enjoy exercising our 'entrepreneurial prerogative' and taking a three or four-day weekend now and then, as well!

Shane Bowlin: Is there such a thing?? Start working around 9 a.m. Check and respond to new e-mail (quick answers only). Prioritize the rest of my messages. Get out the "to do" list I made the day before and start at the top. I try to NOT answer the telephone if I am in the middle of a project. I end my day by compiling a "to do" list for the next day. I schedule a lot less than I can accomplish so there is time allowed for "priority" projects.

Jeannine Clontz: Most days are 8-10 hours long – but I still control how many of those days are 10-hours long. Most days start out with checking and clearing my e-mail. Then I check the previous days' task list to see what projects are still to be completed and the time frame I have to complete them. Then I dive into whatever task(s) are next to be completed. Around 10:00 a.m., I usually head to the post office to check my mail, and pick-up the mail for my association management clients. Upon my return, I sort through the mail and handle any tasks that need to be accomplished from that days' mail. Then, it's back to more client projects, and handling incoming association and business calls. Towards the end of the day, I update my "To Do" list so that it reflects any completed jobs, and add any new jobs to the next day's "To Do" list. I finish the day by checking my vendor and client invoices to see if I need to send any payments or contact a client that has yet to pay their most recent invoice. Some days also include out-of-the-office client and networking meetings. No two days are exactly the same, and I really like that part of being in my own business. I also like volunteering my time to great causes, and in areas that help support women and children. It's very fulfilling.

Alyssa Gregory: I don't have set business hours, but instead work when time allows. I do tend to limit my client interaction to standard business hours, however. I would estimate that I probably log 40+ hours per week total, billable and non-billable time.

Kathy Ritchie: Typically, I'm at work as soon as my husband leaves for his work, about 6:30 AM till 5:00 PM and other hours during the weekend, if needed.

Nora Rubinoff: I check in very early – usually around 6:30 am, after my son is out the door to high school. I begin by reading e-mail, catching up on news and social media, then craft a "short list" of must do tasks for the day for myself and my team members.

I try to spend at least 30 minutes on the treadmill, make a healthy breakfast for myself and my husband.

I try not to schedule more than 3 conference calls per day. The rest of the day is spent fairly heads down on projects and tasks. About 3:30, I review where I am and my team is regarding projects and tasks for the day, adjust any expectations or deadlines, and try to wrap by about 4-4:30 in the afternoon. I close my office at noon on Fridays to give myself a little administrative time in the afternoon – one of the best business changes I made in the last few years!

Nancy Seeger: Ten hours on average. One to two meetings, correspondence, project management of sites, coding and designing elements for websites or e-mail templates, graphic layout or e-books, and occasionally artwork for multiple social media usage (Twitter backgrounds, etc).

Donna Toothaker: My typical day starts with going through e-mail. Then catching up on my forums and groups, and doing a little social media work. I may have client calls scheduled throughout the day. I handle client work early in the day, which usually is some 1SC or e-zine work for them. My day starts early, 5am, and I finish by 3:30 when the kids get off the bus. I typically work ON the business the majority of the day, and work IN the business a few hours - depending on client calls scheduled or potential client calls. My team handles the majority of our client work.

Daily Operational Procedures

It's so important when you're in business to learn what works for you and what doesn't. Each individual VA will have different techniques. It is important to find just the right combination for you.

One of the things that I discovered was to find out when my peak time of work was and to focus my main work efforts around that time. Fortunately, when you're the boss, you can do just that. For example, I'm a morning person. I love getting up early, getting that cup of coffee while it's quiet, and getting started. I've had more fun writing this book during those early morning hours. Without all those daily interruptions, you can get so much more accomplished.

Determine your peak time of the day when you're most productive. This is when you want to schedule your proofing or more challenging jobs. Log your time. Find out where your energy lies and then work around that.

Letter Perfect Work

We can't emphasize this enough: your clients are going to be relying on you to get their work done properly. You want to make sure that they can depend on you and that you won't let them down. You will have a deadline for the work to be completed. If you are constantly missing that deadline, your clients are probably going to look elsewhere. That's why I usually have all the work done for my clients well in advance of their pick-up time.

Also, if they receive their work and find errors, they will find someone else who can do it correctly. What works well for me when proofreading handwritten documents is to use the ruler technique. I have two rulers and go down the page sentence by sentence. When I find an error, I circle it, write the correction, and then make a check in the left margin and the top of the page. That way, when I go back over the document, I can tell quickly the mistakes that need correction. Even if you're not using a ruler, you can utilize the check to help with proofing

I will also, whenever possible, proof my work at a later time. For example, if I have the time I'll put it aside, go onto something else, and then I go back to it. I also try to do any proofing when I'm at my peak of energy.

Turnaround Time

Many VAs eager to start a business make the mistake of offering their clients turnaround time that is unrealistic. For example, when I started I offered all my clients 24-hour service. In other words, they would get it to me one day and the next day I'd have it done. Often my table was full of different client's work. It didn't take long before I burned out.

Plan carefully and set a standard time to have work done. Many of you will be doing some tasks on a daily basis, such as answering e-mail and scheduling. Figure out how much time you feel that would take, and make sure you allow for all your daily operations.

Keep in mind that each individual VA practice is set up differently. In researching for the book, I discovered some VAs who offer 24-hour service to their clients as part of their regular service. They often have other VAs to assist them in meeting deadlines. In setting up your VA practice, you have to do what is right for you and your business. If you feel you can offer your services 24-hours a day, then go for it. But, this is a decision that needs to be made prior to starting your business. After starting, you can change it, but it's more difficult to do, as clients will expect the turnaround that you have offered in the past.

Take transcription, for example. In reference to turnaround time, you will need to know approximately how long projects will take. It gets easier with practice. As a general rule, the ratio of 3:1 to 6:1 applies, depending on the quality of the tape with 3:1 to 4:1 being the norm. However, many factors come into play including how many people are being recorded, where the tape is being recorded, if background noises are a problem, etc. The Office Business Centers Association International (http:www.obcai.com) publishes an Industry Production Standard Manual (IPS) that has an entire chapter devoted to this.

Another trick that I have done is to transcribe what they have given me for 15 minutes and time it. This can give me a rough estimate of how long the project will take me if they are looking for a time frame. I always tell them this is an estimate and the final cost will be based upon the total amount of time worked. I do the same with sending out press releases and articles. Send out to a few places to see how long it takes then estimate the total time for completion.

Pick-Up and Delivery
For VAs who are also going to target your local community, you will need to decide on whether or not you wish to offer pick-up and delivery or have the client drop off the work. There are definitely pros and cons for both.

Some VAs live in condos, apartments, or communities which don't allow home-based businesses. Thus, they don't want to have traffic coming in and out of their homes. For those VAs, they can arrange their businesses so they stop by to pick up the work themselves. This is also an option for those who don't have an official office set up.

The main disadvantage is that it takes time away from your business. But there are ways that you can minimize this. First, set up your travel time for early morning or late in the afternoon. If possible, arrange to drop it off in the evening. Second, make sure that you don't have to meet with anyone each time you drop off work. It should be a quick in and out and back on the road.

Time Management
Here are some tips for scheduling your time:

- Be sure to schedule work for retainer or regular clients first, then you can add other projects that come up during the idle times.
- Set your hours of operation and make sure that all clients know this in advance. This includes notifying clients of days off.
- Ideally, you should always be looking out over a three-week horizon when preparing your schedule. Be sure to pencil in personal matters first, then take care

of your retainer clients, and then you know what time remains for scheduling other jobs that come up.

What works for me is to look at each upcoming week toward the end of the current week. I then make sure I have noted my children's school schedule for early dismissals and days off. I have to account for Chamber meetings, other networking events, scheduled phone calls, etc. I then take a look at my regular clients and give them a call to see what they will require to be done the next week and pencil in these times. You will notice that I keep saying "pencil in," and I literally mean use a pencil. Your planner could become a real mess if you use ink and your schedule changes constantly. The time remaining is used for marketing your business, spending time with your kids, calling potential clients, or other miscellaneous tasks.

For me, this schedule then becomes a source for invoicing. As the week goes on and I begin to complete projects, I note the start and end time, in addition to the work being done, in my client's notebook. I have a notebook for each client where I keep track of hours worked, in addition to notations of projects, telephone conversation notes, additional charges for the month, things to do, etc. In this notebook I will draw a line at the end of the billing period and note the number of hours invoiced. At the end of the billing period when I generate invoices, I can easily go through my client's notebook and see what needs to be invoiced by client.

As I said, this is what works for me. There are other alternatives such as setting up an Access database, your accounting package may offer job tracking, and there are online services for time tracking such as Open Air (http://www.openair.com) or Time Stamp from Syntap Software http://www.syntap.com).

Due to the fact that I may work from my outside office or at my home office, I like the flexibility of having all my client data in a notebook that I can take with me. It allows me to capture the entire history of my relationship with this client. It also acts as a quick reference tool when checking to see if something was completed or notations of a phone conversation. I also like not having an online time tracker because I don't need an Internet connection all the time nor do I have to log it on paper and then transfer it over to a different system—that's double work! Do what works for you.

Client Scheduling
Here are some tips that I found helpful:

- Always have your clients call in advance. Make this a rule that should rarely be broken.
- Be dressed and ready at least ½ hour before their arrival time just in case they come early.
- Never plan on having two clients at the same time.

Also, many of you will be scheduling your client's appointments and keeping their calendar. Once in a while you might make a mistake and miss one. However, if this becomes a habit, your client is going to look bad and he is not going to like it. Take the time you need to set up a system that works. Organization is so essential here.

Here are some tips that I found helpful for me:

- Have a separate calendar for each client.
- Keep all client-related material in the client's file.
- Write down specifics such as who you confirmed the appointment with, any directions the client might need to get there, etc.
- If the client wants a reminder the day before, work out a system that works best for you. What I do is print out each client's schedule and then e-mail it to them the day before. This works for me because all my clients look at their e-mail in the evening. However, if they don't, you might need to call. Some clients might have you call and leave a message on their voice mail. Some online calendaring systems, like http://www.Airset.com, will actually e-mail a schedule daily at your designated time of day.

Handling Interruptions

This is a tough one. When doing this type of business at home, often you will really get into what you are writing or proofing. I joke with my family that I'm in the "ZONE." But it's true; I'm absorbed in my work and an interruption can really put me back. Sometimes, I never fully get back into the work as I have lost my train of thought. Therefore, I'm very firm with my family, friends, and even some clients.

Here are some tips that I've found useful:

- Have an approximate time when they can call back when they call and you aren't available.
- Make your rules clear and try to stand by them.
- Don't feel guilty.
- Stop at a good breaking point to return calls.

Liz Folger in her book, *The Stay-At-Home Mom's Guide to Making Money From Home,* has suggestions for keeping your children quiet while you're on the phone. I think you'll find these beneficial.

- Teach your children that when you pick up the phone, they are to immediately pick up some paper and a pen and draw quietly while you're talking.
- Tell the kids every time the phone rings to pick up a book and read it quietly.
- Use a portable phone and hide from your kids in the nearest closet.
- Buy a phone with a mute button so when the other person is talking they can't hear little Betsy screaming in the background.
- Have a special toy close by that can be played with only when you're on the phone.
- Have a second phone line put in so that your whole family knows whether it's a personal or business call.
- If your house is exploding and you do get a phone call, let the call go to voice mail.
- Fill a jar with chores written on pieces of paper. If your kids bother or interrupt you, get the jar and give them a chore to do immediately.
- Forward your calls after business hours to an answering service.
- Make your phone calls during your child's nap time.

Supplies

This is a topic that is near and dear to me at this time. We are revising the book during the summer. The kids are home, which is always a bit more challenging, but wonderful. Now, I've ran totally out of envelopes, I'm on my last box of paper clips, have one ream of paper left, and if I could find a pen right now I'd be the happiest person in the world. This is so not me! The moral of this story is to buy your supplies and keep an abundance of supplies on hand. Thank goodness I do. That's why I've been able to make it months without going to the office supply store.

Here's what I do, and it works like a charm. I have a list typed up of all my supplies that I use, complete with ordering number. When I start running low, I check the list. When I see that I have several things on the list, I order the supplies. It's a one-time investment to make the list, but it is so worth it. When I get new equipment, I simply add it to the list. This also enables me to keep an eye on sale items in the paper. It seems easier just to pull out a piece of paper, then to look for the cartridge, etc.

I buy in bulk and I buy at the very lowest prices. Just like with my groceries, I save as much as possible on everything I buy. I also utilize online services, as well as places like Office Depot.

I like Office Depot. One of the things I like about them is that when you order from them via phone you get a real live person every time. What a pleasure that is in today's world. Plus, their prices are reasonable; they keep good track of your prior purchases so if you forget a catalog number you're okay; and they ship the same day or next day. In my book, that's a company that's got my business!

While most office supply stores offer the convenience of ordering online and delivering right to your door, don't discount the opportunities that exist to make potential client contacts shopping at the store. I know of several VAs who have been able to secure clients just by being helpful to customers in the aisles – never miss an opportunity to share your knowledge and talk about your business.

Here are some other suggested office supply stores.

- Office Max – http://www.officemax.com
- Office Depot – http://www.officedepot.com
- Staples – http://www.staples.com

Know When to Get Help

Just like we tell our clients, there are certain tasks we need to do personally and certain tasks we need to delegate to others. It just makes sense from a time management and financial standpoint. Take your own advice!

Planning your business with the big picture growth in mind from the start will help you to stay out of overwhelm when the client load picks up and you begin to feel like you just can't take on anything else. Or, perhaps your business model is designed to where you will be the marketing machine and subcontract all the client work you secure. Whatever the case – plan accordingly and select your partners wisely.

Let's face it; there are only so many billable hours in a day that you're capable of handling personally. Partnering with others in some fashion is the only way to grow your business and stay sane. Maybe you need to hire an in-house assistant to help you with certain tasks that absolutely must be handled in the office or that you need to have complete control over. Maybe you partner with other independent contractors or VAs to subcontract work to them. Or maybe you partner with a web design company, graphic designer, a bookkeeper or some other industry specialist to handle those aspects of your business that free your time for business development. You can also partner with others to help complement your service offering for those services you don't wish to handle in your business. Maybe it's a combination of all. However you want to design your business model is completely up to you. Just be educated about your options and plan accordingly.

CAUTION! There is a fine line between a contractor and an employee. Consult the IRS guidelines on the different classifications. Here is the latest we found: http://www.irs.gov/businesses/small/article/0,,id=99921,00.html

There are a fast-growing number of VA companies who are working with entire teams of other VA companies behind them. You may hear the term "Multi-VA company" being used as well as other VAs referring to their "team." Then, there are those who completely refer a client, fee paid or no fee, to another vendor company that releases them from the client relationship all together.

The key to these successful alliances is finding the right people to partner with. Not all VAs and not all vendors are created equal. You want to align with those who have the same standards and values as you do, particularly if you are subcontracting, because ultimately it's your name that's associated with the work. Keep your reputation intact.

Where do you find good people? That's the golden question! Talk to others and see who they are working with. Keep an eye out for people on the social networks and message boards who are being recommended, answering questions, and that stick out to you as being very knowledgeable and professional. This is a practice you should exercise at all times, whether you're currently in the market for help or not; make note for future use. Attending industry networking events such as the IVAA Summit allows you to meet personally with other VAs.

When you find someone of interest, you need to be sure to: check references, review portfolios and work samples, and interview them. Get a contract in place that outlines all expectations and deliverables to leave no room for question for either party. Payment terms are an essential part of the contract. Whether your client pays you or not, you are still responsible for paying your subs. Make the payment terms reasonable while still taking into consideration your cash flow.

And while it's nice to get assistance from friends and family at little or no charge, keep in mind that working together can bring about other issues in a relationship that are less than desirable and put a strain on the business. We know they can be cheap, but cheap is not always the best way to go. Involving your kids in the business is great, too, but don't make them feel obligated or they will soon resent you and the business. Or, they might love what you do and follow in your footsteps, which would be fantastic!

Client Relations

It takes less time and money to keep a client than it does to find a new one. Building solid client relationships is key to building longevity in your business. It all starts from the first contact so make a good impression from the start, and continue to make them feel like they're the only client you have throughout your partnership.

Shane Bowlin states, "Start with a good business foundation, set boundaries, be nice but firm with your clients. It's best to give an honest opinion when asked for it. Treat your clients like you want to be treated. Remember special occasions and check in periodically to see how they are doing if you haven't heard from them."

It's important to learn the essentials of meeting clients and being able to effectively promote your business. You need to convince these clients that your company will be an asset to them. The uppermost important thing that you must relay to them is that you truly believe in your business. You absolutely, positively, without a doubt, know that you can help make their business better, and given the opportunity you will!! It all comes down to CONFIDENCE!!

We know when you're just starting out, having that confidence can be difficult. Don't let it be more difficult than it really is!! Think about how long you've been in the business world supporting someone else's business. Think of how many times you have saved the office by remembering an important appointment or preventing a near crisis. Think about a time when you finished a job and you knew you did a great job. That's the confidence we're talking about. You always want to leave your client with a favorable and positive impression of you.

Confidence is a frame of mind. Remember that you no longer have to justify your actions to a boss in the corner office or to an overzealous co-worker. You are the boss. The only ones you have to prove anything to are you and your clients. Remember all the times you made suggestions to your boss about how to make the office run smoother? You just know that had they listened to you at least once it would have worked. Well, now you have the chance to shine. Clients will listen to you because you know more about your business than anyone else. Developing a partnership with your client will allow you to know their business as well—maybe even better than they do, in time. You are the one with the solutions to their problems. Doesn't it feel great!!

Now, on the flip side, don't be over-confident—that can be a turn off to some. And remember, you can't be all things to all people. This might be a good time to revisit your mission statement and your business plan to make sure you have developed a niche that you can easily profess and sell as your specialty.

To aid in creating a positive impression, practice the following:

- Maintain a professional demeanor and company image at all times.
- Believe in yourself and the benefits you can bring to a client's business.
- Be willing to go to great lengths to build client relationships.

- Listen to your clients' needs and find ways to meet those needs. Follow the 80/20 rule for communication: listen 80% of the time, talk 20% of the time. You'll be amazed at what you can learn about your clients.
- Ensure clients that you have extensive knowledge of their particular field and that you have the experience to back it up.
- Don't make excuses or try to cover up for lack of knowledge.

As a VA, you will be doing the bulk of your work over the Internet. Even here you can display a professional appearance. Make sure that all e-mail correspondence is typed accurately and is short and to the point. For example, I once had a VA who was working with me on a large project. Timing was critical and I was far behind schedule. She did excellent work, however every e-mail back to me was like a small novel. I was frustrated to have to read through the entire e-mail to get to the points I needed. I would have preferred to have the points highlighted and concise, so I could spend my time on the project and not her e-mail. Write e-mails to clients like you would write a letter. And forego the use of Internet emoticons such as LOL and :). As cute as you might think they are, the recipient is a business relation, not a family relation.

Using Portfolios For A Better Image

Here's another way to convince clients to use your services. Create a portfolio that shouts of all you can do for them. A portfolio is a folder that contains pertinent information about your services. This is a valuable marketing tool and I recommend you spend some time to make a good one.

I recommend a black or navy blue folder with two inside pockets. Staple your business card to the inside right-hand cover. You can also purchase folders with a pre-cut slot for business cards already provided. In the right-hand side, include an introductory letter about your business, your brochure, copies of articles about you and the virtual assistant industry, a press release, any press you've been mentioned in, and your bio. You can really hit home if you can find an industry article showing how a VA has proven beneficial. On the left-hand side include sample business correspondence, a sample targeted directly to the client's specialty, and testimonials. Some of the items you include will depend upon the type of client and how far you are in the sales process. You might also want to include a bulleted proposal of some of the work you can do.

Maintaining an online portfolio or business presentation can prove beneficial in sharing this information with your potential clients. You can have this presentation available for online meetings with potential clients and really show them how you are a step above the rest. You can also personalize the presentation to the prospective client needs.

I maintain an extensive portfolio of PR I've received, copies of certificates of achievement, and samples of my work. All of these items are in protective sheet covers and stored in a binder. In corresponding or meeting with potential clients, I'm able to adjust the portfolio based upon the type of work the client requires. If I have to mail out company literature, I put together the type of portfolio mentioned above, in addition to a brief history of my company, a synopsis of successful client partnerships, and a client self-assessment form.

Others may disagree, including Diana, but I do not recommend, unless the prospect specifically requests it, to include a copy of my contract or my current rate schedule. Why?

Because you should do such a great job selling the benefits of your services that price will be the last thing you discuss, if it's discussed at all. If it's an issue, it will be brought up when you send them the contract outlining all terms and conditions. If, by chance, I do include a contract, it is indicated as a "sample contract" so that I'm not tied to anything that might currently be included in the contract, which might not apply to this particular client situation.

Contracts

You will want to get a signed contract from most, if not all, of your clients. This ensures you are both in agreement about the terms of your working arrangement. Tena Cummings, owner of A Page in Time Designs, has the following recommendation for composing a contract: "My contracts include the basic information: What services are to be done, cost of the services, how payment is to be made, when services are supposed to be done, and a confidentiality clause." I also recommend that you include all the specifics for that particular job. See a sample contract and Contract Checklist in the Appendix.

For one page letters or small assignments, I'll often forego the contract. However, for all regular clients and larger assignments, and all virtual clients that I don't see in person, I'll make sure they complete and sign the contract. I've never had any problem with clients refusing to sign or not wanting to go through the process. I feel it shows them in another way that I'm a professional business.

Your contract is a legally-binding document meant to protect you. Make an investment in your business by having a professional review your contracts. While we don't like to have to reinvent the wheel if someone already has a contract, you cannot be assured that a sample contract you receive, from any source, protects your best interests. What works for someone else might not work for you. Seek your own legal counsel and make sure you are protected. It's well worth the legal fees do to so.

The Demanding Client

In the beginning, many VAs are so anxious to get work that they will allow clients to "get away" with things. When you only have a couple of clients this isn't a problem. However, once your business grows, it definitely can hurt your business. That's one of the reasons why I tell VAs that I don't feel it is necessary to tell clients they are new to the business.

This is your business and you need to, right from the beginning, set the rules. Let clients know your normal turnaround time and—be specific. I've had clients who constantly would call with rush jobs. Even though I got paid extra, often it would throw off my day and I would miss deadlines for my other clients. I found that after I said "no" a couple of times and didn't do their work on a "rush" basis, they were easily able to get the work to me on time. Amazing, isn't it?

Plan Ahead

After you've been in business a while, many of your clients will consider you to be their own personal assistant. They will depend on you to keep their business afloat. That's one of the reasons we recommend letting your clients know in advance if you plan on taking a vacation or will be out of town for a couple of days. Providing them with advance warning will enable you to put a plan together for any tasks that might need attention during your absence. Or, you might collaborate with another VA to handle urgent client tasks until you return.

Another way you can plan ahead is to have complete instructions to your office written out, if you have local clients coming to your office. I found this to be extremely important in the beginning of my business. As I normally just drive on familiar roads, I needed to be aware of what streets connected to my home from different directions.

Also, you'd be amazed when talking to clients how easily it is to forget your web address, fax number, etc. That's why it's beneficial to have everything handy. Your business card should be in reach so that if you are talking to clients on the phone, you can give them correct information. You don't want to send them to the wrong place and have them have to call you back and have to say OOPS, it's really this....

Setting Boundaries
This is something that applies to some clients more than others. Once you start working for some clients, you'll know right away which ones you will need to apply these ground rules to. It's extremely important to set your boundaries and keep them. For example, I have one client who is on retainer and is actually one of my larger clients. They are quite aware of that fact too, unfortunately. However, that does not mean that they are my only clients and that I can cater exclusively to them. I believe one of their most annoying habits is this: I have call waiting and when on the phone I am beeped when another call comes in. I usually will not leave another client to take that call, however, if I'm on a personal call and not important I will. They would continually call while I'm on the phone. Call, hang up, call, hang up, call, hang up, you get the picture. How did I handle it? Naturally, I told them politely that this was disrupting my business and I needed them to please refrain from doing this. Unfortunately, it continued. After repeated attempts, I finally had to tell them it had to stop, period, or I could not continue to work for them. Now if anyone knows me, you will know that I'm not one for confrontations and this one was extremely hard to do, but it was necessary. They have never done it again. I stood up for myself, my business, and also for my other clients. You will find that it is necessary to set boundaries for your business. Do it and you'll keep in charge of your business; and your clients won't take advantage of you.

This is just one example, and I could list several. I think you get the picture, though. Once you have set a boundary with your client, you need to keep that boundary. That's not always easy, but a necessity. What I do is to remember how good I felt when I initially stood my ground in the beginning. That visualization technique works for me.

Understand though, that while we are in business for ourselves we would be nothing without clients. Setting boundaries is great, but you also have to be flexible. Before enforcing ground rules or boundaries, ask yourself if the situation deems the risk of losing the revenue generated by this demanding client. When all else fails, put yourself in your client's shoes—how would you react if you were told you're overstepping your boundaries? Be firm when necessary, be flexible when you can shine and show that you are going the extra mile for client satisfaction.

The Crisis Client

"Poor planning on your part does not constitute an emergency on my part." – Author Unknown

This type of client will drive you nuts if you let them, and you can't let them. Everything is a crisis for them. They are always in high gear and in an emergency situation. It absolutely has to be done or else. It is easy to fall into this trap. You get so caught into the adrenaline rush. Sometimes there really is a need to have a rush job and there is a need to have something done immediately. Attorneys are notorious for crises. Falling into this trap can put undue stress on you. You need to have an open and honest relationship with your clients. You need to tell them that if it doesn't actually need to be done and you have other work to do, you can't do it. They would want the same if it was their work and you were trying to get their work done for them. You will find when you put it that way; they tend to be more understanding.

Again, I have one particular client who is a crisis junkie. Everything is a major crisis. They will call and although I am calm at the time, by the time I solve their problem, I'm in that crisis mode as well. What I found is that they will never change. I had to change my reactions to them. Dealing with clients can be challenging, but the majority of time you will find a way that works for you and them.

Client Files

You should have a separate subdirectory for each of your clients. Keep all correspondence in that directory. Label their work so you can easily access it. I usually use the person's last name that it's going to and the date. For example, a letter going to John Smith would be called Smith-2-22-12. That way if the client calls and says he needs to add something to the letter he wrote to John Smith on February 22nd, I can easily pull it up in a search on my computer.

You will also want to make sure you do regular backups of your computer. Can you imagine even losing a week's worth of work? We highly recommend getting an online drive through http:www.carbonite.com or http:www.getdropbox.com. You may also consider investing in an external hard drive that you can transport with you. Back up on a regular basis, one or two times a week, even daily if you've done a lot of work that day.

It's also smart to leave a backup set away from your office. Just in case you have a fire or theft, you will have a copy of all your work. For me, it's as easy as giving a copy to my husband to take to work. Using an online system well as an off-site method.

Keep your client's letterhead, envelopes, etc., together in their file, preferably in a file cabinet close to your desk. For those of us with little ones who might get in the office, make sure the stationery is off limits.

All bookkeeping supplies such as checkbooks, payroll books, rubber name stamps, etc., should always be locked in a file cabinet, or better yet a fireproof safe. At least this is what my clients prefer. They trust my family and me and have known us for many years; however, they feel more confident knowing that their valuables are under lock and key.

Bookkeeping/Collecting Payment

 It is vitally important to keep good books. You want to keep accurate records of all income and expenses that you receive. Keep all your receipts and make sure to use your business checking account for business-related expenses and income only. Checks that you receive as payment will be deposited in your business checking account. You will want to write checks for your business expenses. Or you can opt to get a company credit card that needs to be used for only business related expenses and paid off monthly, whenever possible. If you use PayPal or accept credit card transactions, the funds will be deposited in your business checking account.

It isn't necessary to get an accountant, unless you would feel more confident having an accountant who handles this aspect of your business. However, if you stay organized and keep good records of your income and expenses, you should have no problems. One benefit of an accountant is they can find deductions you may have missed.

There are excellent software programs available to help you. Quickbooks is one example, and the one that we use. You are easily able to input income, and categorize expenses by writing checks for expenses and marking the appropriate category (i.e., office expense, equipment, advertising, etc.) You're then able to obtain valuable reports to can see if the business is making a profit or a loss. For example, you can print a report of how much you made in say May, each amount divided by client, and also categorize it by work (word processing, tutoring, bookkeeping virtual assisting, etc.), see how much you spent in advertising, office expenses, etc. Thus, you know how your business is doing and can see if there are areas you need to improve upon.

Every year when I send my tax information to my accountant, she just raves about how well I keep my books and how she wished all her clients were as prepared when they walked through her door. I attribute my system to a previous desire to be an accountant (too many accounting classes in college!) and my corporate days of budgets and sales forecasting. Some people are numbers people and some aren't – I'm kind of stuck in the middle. I really don't do anything magical except I close out everything for a month each and every month so nothing gets behind. From all deposits, to all expenses, all bank accounts and credit cards being reconciled, credit card receipts are attached to the current statement, and all income is tied to a client as well as a type of service. All expenses are tied to a customer or vendor. Throughout the year I also maintain records of charitable contributions along with receipts as well as any major purchases. As I said, it's nothing magical. It's more about the distribution of the process throughout the year instead of that mad dash to get it all done at year-end.

If you prefer manually keeping your books, the main basics you want to have down are all income and all expenses divided by months. When I started my business, my bookkeeping simply consisted of an income book, an expense book, and then a file for all receipts. At the end of the year, I was easily able to figure out my taxes. I totaled all the income each month and all the expenses each month. You should have receipts and bank statements to match up each item. Bernard Kamoroff's book, *Small Time Operator,* has a sample ledger sheets in his book that you can use also.

Keeping Track of Expenses

While tracking expenses is pretty common across the different business entities you can work under, it might be necessary to track some items differently. For example, I operate as an S Corporation. For any items I purchase with a cost in excess of $100, I have to make sure I log the item and the date of purchase. My accountant reviews the list at tax time to determine what is subject to depreciation and what is not. Check with your accountant or tax preparer on the proper way to handle your expenses.

Here is a list of items you should be keeping track of throughout the year:
- Car Expenses - gas, license, parking, tolls, sales tax on purchase of vehicles, depreciation cost. Car expenses can either be handled by the actual expenses incurred or on a per mile basis. Most likely you will come out better on the per mile basis and you will need to maintain a mileage log. You can get a book at office supply stores for car mileage and then keep it in your car.
- Telephone Expenses - this includes long distance calls only on your home phone unless you have a separate line for business use, then you can deduct the whole bill.
- Cell phones and broadband card expenses used for business purposes.
- Advertising - yellow page ads, newspapers, directory listings, press release submissions, and community ad support.
- Office Supplies and Equipment - postage, stationery, pencils, stapler, rubber stamps, notebooks, computers, scanners, envelopes, fax machines, printers, photocopies, etc.
- Sales Aids - brochures, business cards, ad specialty items, etc.
- Legal and Accounting Fees - all professional service fees.
- Education, Conventions, Seminars - brochure, receipts of registration, room fees, transportation, food, cleaning and laundry expenses, tapes, etc.
- Gifts for Clients - birthday gifts, thank-you gifts, etc.
- Entertainment - client lunches, dinners, etc. Be sure to note on the receipt the place, date, amount, client name, and purpose.
- Licenses and permits - annual city fee, resale numbers.
- Filing fees – annual business filing, annual report submission.
- Basically any expense directly related to operating your business should be deductible.

Don't forget about taxes. You will be required to pay quarterly taxes on your NET (income less expenses) income. Contact your accountant for details on this procedure. We recommend setting a certain percentage aside from each check you get for payment of taxes. It's a good idea to deduct 25% from each check just the same as if I were on someone's payroll and put it in a savings account. Doing it this way, you won't be so shocked at the end of the quarter when you have to pay your taxes.

Collecting Payment

There are several methods of collecting your payment. This is going to be discussed with your client, well in advance, with a contract drawn up, terms disclosed, and everything determined prior to the work being started. A client can either pay you when they pick up their work, weekly, bi-weekly, a monthly retainer payment, or whatever works best for you. The best rule of thumb to ensure you get paid is to not release any work to them if they don't pay you. In the case of ongoing work or retainer clients, you simply cease to do any further work until payment is made. If they don't pay on time, they know that you won't be doing their work for them. With VAs not seeing their clients, this still isn't a problem as you have your agreement. The key is to enforce the terms of the agreement. Remember, this is business, and, thus, you need to make sure to collect payments accordingly or you'll soon be out of business. We all know things can happen that impact our cash flow, the same is true of our clients. Be professional but be reasonable on the enforcement based on the overall value of the client and how much you're willing to bend to keep them.

Different methods of payment include:

- Check or money order sent directly from the client. Online banking makes it a snap for clients to setup an automatic payment to be sent every month at the same time to ensure on-time payment to you.
- PayPal link on your site or send a request for money via the PayPal site. In Quickbooks you can tie your PayPal account to it and when you e-mail the invoice to the client it will include a link to pay right there. Freshbooks offers similar invoicing and payment collection.
- Credit card. You can either invoice by your determined frequency and collect payment authorization on each transaction, or you can have a standing credit card authorization on file for charge them automatically each month for services rendered. When accepting credit card payments you just need to be sure you are compliant with the merchant service provider security regulations on maintaining credit card numbers.
- Automatic deposit. This can be set up by filling out the appropriate paperwork from the client to deposit directly into your bank account.
- Barter agreement. Bartering is still a method of payment.
- Good old cash is always an option!

But what if you don't get paid? It's bound to happen, all you can do is put your best foot forward in preventing it at all costs. Hopefully the advice from others experience below will help you in establishing your payment policy and handling of bad debts.

In Their Own Words:

Jeannine Clontz: "Well I'm sure we all have had them. But I've only had to write off a little less than $100 from two different clients. One passed away...didn't even go after the money, and one was for an attorney that deceived me into giving him a lower rate on an icky project with the promise of additional business that never came...which was okay because neither did his check for the icky project. I ended up filing a small claims suit against him and got immediate payment...guess as an attorney it wasn't good to be listed as the defendant in a lawsuit! Normally I will call when the invoice is 2-3 weeks overdue, and ask when it's due to come up for payment. If they don't respond as promised, I follow it up with a nice, but firm letter requesting payment. Once it gets to 60 days, I hold up any additional completing of projects until the old invoices are paid in full. I've only had to do that once."

Patsy LaFave's method of collecting payment: "If they are a long-time customer, a personal check or cash. If it is a new customer, I ask for at least half of the estimated cost in a money order or cashier's check with the balance due upon completion of the work. I used to not ask for any upfront but some didn't pay so I had to stop trusting people. I don't like to feel that way, and 99% don't stiff you, but you never know when that one is going to come along. Like the one deadbeat spoils it for everyone else."

Kathy Ritchie: I highly recommend a good filing system, also, an electronic filing system, tickler file, and software for maintaining client time logs. (I use TimeStamp.) I use PayPal and Yahoo! PayDirect for accepting credit cards.

Nora Rubinoff: Yes but not often. I make sure I state up front that to "avoid an interruption in service, payment is due by_____." If payment isn't in, and I've not had success in reaching the client to find out why, I do no additional work until the invoice is paid.

Using Authorize.net's services, I maintain secure online profiles of my clients' payment information in their compliant system. That way, with the client's agreement, payment is processed after the invoice is sent.

The following collection tips were provided by Michelle Dunn, of the MAD Collection Agency, with her permission. We think you'll find them extremely beneficial.

By Michelle Dunn
MAD Collection Agency

Let your customer know the terms of sale when you make the sale or at the time of the order. Customers are usually happy to comply if they see your stated credit terms right from the beginning.

Send a friendly reminder notice. Many businesses pay 90-120 days after purchase. Send a reminder notice to speed up payment. E-mail or fax is a fast, good way to touch base with a slow paying customer.

Make a phone call. You should always assume payment has been made and ask, "When did you send your check?" Then don't say anything; let them break the silence, no matter how long it may seem.

Pick up the payment in person. Once you show up in person to pick up a payment you should never have to pick up a payment again, if your customer has every intention of paying. If you repeatedly have to go to their place of business, you may want to put them on a COD basis.

What if I receive a bad check? This question is asked of me by so many people that I decided to write an article about it. Most people get a check for payment of services or merchandise and deposit it into their account and forget it. Then suddenly the check is returned for insufficient funds! Most people don't know what to do when this happens.

When people ask me "what should I do with this check?" here is what I advise:

Call the customer immediately and tell them what happened, tell them to send or come in and pay with cash or a cashier's check or money order right away. Be sure to add any NSF fees that are allowed by law. Be sure to make a note on their account that you have received a bad check; you may want to only accept cash or money orders for future payments. Though, if it's a long-standing customer and this was truly just a mistake, you may not want to do that.

If you do not get an answer and can only leave a message, send out a Demand For Payment notice, and send it by certified mail. On the bottom of the notice make a note that a copy of the notice is being sent by regular mail to ensure delivery. That way if they do not sign for the certified letter, you can be sure they received the notice by regular mail.

In your Demand For Payment notice, state the check number, amount, bank name, and who signed the check. I like to advise them of the penalties by law for writing a bad check. Also let them know of any bank fee that has been added. Give them 14 days to pay you. If they do not pay you within 14 days, let them know you will pursue the collection of the check through the appropriate legal channels.

After the 14 days, depending on where you are located, there are different avenues you can take. In some states, you can call the police in the town where the check was written and they will go visit the debtor. In other states, you have to file with the courthouse. Some businesses do not want to do these things and will turn the check over to an attorney or collection agency.

The worst thing you can do is just hold the check and wait for the debtor to make good on it. Act immediately! Your chances of recovering will be much better.

Let's say it's a sizeable amount and you want to take it further. First, you can file a complaint at the State Attorney's Office in your county. Because the writing of a bad check is a criminal offense, the State Attorney's office has the jurisdiction to do something about it and take action. Most of the time the person is willing to pay what he owes rather than have criminal charges filed against him. If the State Attorney's office cannot assist you, you should consider filing a small claims action against the person who wrote you the bad check.

Advantages & Tips for Collecting by Telephone
- Inexpensive – Compared to personal visits and individually typed letters.
- Immediate – Produces some sort of answer the moment the contact is made.
- Personal – Allows an exchange between two people.
- Informative – Allows you to ask questions, obtain information and take appropriate action.
- Flexible – Approach can be varied as changing situations demand. It should result in agreement as to what is to be done.
- Use voice mail or answering machines, if available. Leave detailed, complete messages and speak slowly.
- Always be courteous.
- When asked why you are calling, never say it is in regards to a debt, regarding an invoice is better.
- Create a sense of urgency by leaving a deadline time to hear from them.
- Get the name of a person in charge of issuing checks or paying bills.
- Ask for the best time to call them in the future.
- Leave complete messages, your name, company name, phone number, and the request for a return call.
- Get the name of the person taking the message.

Preventing Failure/Overcoming Obstacles

One of the most rewarding aspects of managing discussion boards and interacting with VAs regularly is getting to see success stories in the making. You can just imagine how exciting it is when someone writes that they landed their first client. You can practically hear the excitement. Then I get to watch them grow their business and gain confidence all along the way.

One of the most important concepts I try to relay to the new VA is motivation. You really have to want it. You have to be determined that even though there might be a few pebbles in your way, you are going to pursue your dream of a VA business. Yes, we all are going to be disappointed at times, but don't let that stop you.

If you've ever seen me online you've heard me say this is a zillion times – "Start Fresh" – it's my main motto. If one marketing idea doesn't work, try another. If yesterday was a real bummer with nasty clients or a missed deadline, today is new; start fresh and make it great. You have the power to make a difference in your business and you can.

Here are some points that I feel are important to consider in preventing failure and overcoming obstacles:

- Have a good understanding of the business and a thorough knowledge of exactly what you want to do in your business. Then read, read, read. Knowledge is power and the more you learn, the better your business will succeed.
- Have a solid plan of action outlined and stay within its course. Yes, you might need to re-navigate somewhat, but try to stay within the guidelines you have determined you want. Revisit the Business Planning chapter for reinforcement in this area.
- Money is important. Plan every expense and make sure that it's a necessary one. Don't spend money needlessly. For example, when going to the office supply store do the same as you do for grocery shopping. Write down exactly what you need and keep to the list, at least initially. It's easy to get sidetracked and buy things that aren't essential.
- Find the very best price on everything you buy.
- Plan your expenses—don't have all your incoming money going out for unnecessary expenses.
- Respect your clients, but don't allow them to run your business.
- Don't put all your eggs in one basket.
- Treat your clients with respect and always do your best.
- Define your ideal client and seek them out for long-term relationships. This is crucial. One of the main advantages to working with a VA is the partnership that is created between you and your client. True VA-client partnerships will be long lasting and preferably on a retainer agreement that allows you to plan a regular monthly income. Going from project to project will drain you and your marketing efforts. Think back to the business planning stage – are you targeting clients that will result in a long-term partnership? Learn all that you can about your clients' businesses in order to help them grow. If you play your cards right, you'll not only strengthen your relationship with your client, you'll also learn a great deal that you can apply to other clients and further enhance your business knowledge. I've

learned a great deal from many of my clients. Sometimes I've learned what not to do in business, but, I still learned something that may work to my advantage in the future.

In Their Own Words:

Jeannine Clontz: Having enough working capital to see yourself through the first 18 months...this is crucial. I only thought I'd need enough to get me through 6 months. Boy, was I wrong. I made that stretch to almost 18 months and then I went back to work part-time nights and weekends. The business supports itself with a little left over, but there's still not enough to be able to take a salary. I think I'll be there by the middle of my third year. They say it usually takes 3-5 years....THEY didn't tell me that until I'd been in business for about a year!

Alyssa Gregory: My biggest obstacle was internal – believing I was business-owner material, and developing confidence in the value I brought to the table. I have since learned that confidence (but NOT over-confidence) is the one ingredient required for a successful business owner in any industry. If you have it, or you can develop it, you can become unstoppable.

Kathy Ritchie: I didn't find the support I needed from my family and friends when I first started full-time. It wasn't until the last 2-3 years that they can see and now respect what it is that I do.

Barbara Rowen: The first obstacle I faced was residing in an area that had little idea of what a VA was, let alone how their business could use one. I chose to focus on the local community, as I saw a huge need right in my own backyard. From the beginning, I was educating the local business community on the benefits of utilizing VAs, and it appears to be working. The second obstacle was being virtual. I was unable to secure clients until I left the safety of my office and actually met them face-to-face, through networking groups and by word-of-mouth. Once the business owners started meeting me and finding out about virtual assisting, they have been more than happy to give me their work.

Nora Rubinoff: Lack of knowledge on how to start a business is probably the biggest obstacle I faced in starting my business. I did a lot of research, made a lot of phone calls and asked a ton of questions. State government isn't always the most helpful or easy to navigate.

Susan Totman: Mostly family-related. When you work from a home office it is very difficult to impress upon family members that your job is a real job. That you are in business and separating the two when family is around, especially kids, is highly challenging.

Staying Organized and Time Management

Staying organized is critical to your success. All of that time spent looking for things can be spent productively earning money instead, and that's what we want! $$$$! Who doesn't want to see those cute little symbols!

I don't know how it happens. You start your day with your desk clear. You sit down. Your coffee is to the right; everything is perfectly lined up ready to be faxed, proofed, e-mailed, etc. Your day is ready to go. Then it happens. The phone rings and you send off the e-mail and attachment to the client who's waiting. So far, so good. You take a couple of sips of coffee and back to work. You continue working steadily, losing track of time, and low and behold three hours pass and somehow the desk has disappeared, along with the pleading that you need proofed in ten minutes. Fear sets in immediately. How did it happen again?

Here are some tips that I have found helpful. I hope you find them beneficial as well. You need to be able to put things away properly, **the first time.** But to put it away properly, it has to have a proper place. I now have a corner desk, which works wonderfully. I now also have a two-drawer file cabinet on the right hand side. Every three or four months, I go through there and take out the excess papers and put them into the regular file cabinet I have in the office.

The main thing that I'd like to emphasize is that having an organized office can be one of your greatest assets. That clutter on your desk and by your desk is a constant distraction. You will soon discover how much valuable time can be wasted looking for things, as well as how unprofessional you look to your clients.

This is one area that I'm constantly working on. What helps me is to keep all clients' materials together in a file. I use black bins for all incoming work and outgoing work. Every piece of paper that I have needs to go either in one of the trays or in the filing cabinets, not in stacks on the desk. Believe me, I'm not perfect, but when you practice this principle it gets easier to follow. Having the file cabinets right beside me made my filing easier and has enabled me to stay on top of it on a daily basis.

When working on a project you will need to have that client's work material out and only that client's work to avoid any mixing between clients. When finished with that client's work, completely put their work away. Clear your desk. Then get started on your next project. Try to have everything you need for your projects close at hand. If you accept phone calls throughout the day from your clients, and get a call from one while working on another, excuse yourself for just a minute so you can switch gears. Completely close the file you're working on and get the other one out.

I have a folder for papers I'm not sure whether to throw away or not. I'll keep the folder a while, filed away in my cabinet. When I do my switch to put my filing to my main filing cabinet (my two drawer to my main cabinet), I simply go through the miscellaneous folder. It's amazing how a couple months later it's obvious what to keep and what to throw away. If I'm still hesitant, I normally will keep it. Something is telling me it's worthwhile.

Most VAs would agree the key ingredient to keeping your office organized is to stay on top of the filing. Figure out a system that works best for you and stick with it. Bring in help if you need it so that it doesn't get out of control. Really think about whether or not you even need to file a piece of paper or is it something you can scan and keep in an online folder. There are a number of VAs who swear by having a paperless office – we don't know how they do it, but it is possible, they say. Scanning and creating PDF files to reproduce a physical filing cabinet on your computer or an online file sharing site is what you'll want to investigate. Check out a system like NeatReceipts for easy organization of the hundreds of receipts and business cards and little notes that you need to preserve.

As for Kelly… I have a dedicated area on my desk or in my file cabinets for each clients work. Since I keep a spiral notebook on each of my clients, to track time and activities, I keep their notebook on the desktop with a post-it on the outside bearing the current task list. The remaining active files for that client are tucked away immediately under the notebook. All other files pertaining to that client will either be found on the computer or in a file drawer. The task lists are easily transferred over to an online project management system, too.

I also maintain a file for "Prospects and Pending Quotes" which contains all the notes I've gathered in talking with a potential client and a targeted follow-up date. I keep the prospect information in that file until I feel I have completely exhausted the lead or I have converted them to a client. Once converted, I create a client folder and affix a Client Information Sheet on the inside of the folder for quick reference on address details, passwords, etc. Under the client information sheet you will find the original contract followed by phone logs and other documentation gathered during the "courting" stages. In the client's main folder, I maintain general correspondence that might not otherwise be kept in my e-mail folder for that client. All other documents, if there are any, are maintained in a separate folder based upon the project, whether it is an ongoing or one-time project. On the outside of the main folder, which stays with the spiral notebook, I keep the immediate contact details such as e-mail addresses and phone numbers, possibly alternate contact details. I also make note of any special charges we have agreed upon such as how much for copies, black and white prints, etc. Finally, I make note of the billing date for retainer clients. Now, you might be thinking how silly it is of me to not keep the client contact details on the front of the spiral notebook. Well, it's because should anything happen and my relationship with the client is severed, I can pull out all their pages, staple and file them away in the client folder then I can reuse the notebook for another client.

Managing your time effectively throughout the day will be a key factor not only in your productivity, but more importantly a key factor in your bottom line. The more clients you take on and the more non-billable tasks you get involved in will make it all the more challenging. Remember—you only make money when you're working on billable tasks. Every second of your time has a dollar value and you can't get time back when it's passed. Keep the same mindset when working on billable tasks—you're only spending your client's money wisely when you are working effectively.

Dedicate the equivalent of two hours per day to your own business development each week, whether you carve out time each day or one day a week. Save time to work on your business so you can stay in business.

Telephone/E-Mail Procedures

You must handle yourself professionally on the phone at all times. I've seen bad telephone etiquette actually lose clients for VAs. I myself have contacted another VA to help with a large project and just by talking with her on the phone and hearing her totally unprofessional demeanor, I decided against her. I want a professional in charge of my work. Actually, it's not that I <u>want</u> a professional in charge of my work, I <u>need</u> a professional in charge of my work. My clients expect it of me.

It's not only how you answer the phone, but also how you conduct yourself during the conversation. Obviously, you must answer the phone in a professional manner, but during the conversation and in follow-up conversations it's vitally important as well. Here's a perfect example:

> One of my clients was looking for another VA to help as they expect to be extremely busy and will have more work than I can handle. I was helping them with their search, screening several VAs, and then sending them the ones I felt would be qualified. One VA met all the qualifications, was perfect for the job, and actually had the job. The only problem was her phone etiquette when they called to tell her she had the job. During all the prior phone calls she was fine. But in this call, she got too giddy and totally unprofessional. She claimed she knew everything under the sun, and would arrive for the job with "bells on her toes." PLEASE!!!! Remember—we are professionals...at all times. Yes, you can be grateful for the job, but don't let on that you are that eager for work. Clients should never think that you NEED the work that bad.

How can you answer your phone in a professional manner at all times? Use Caller ID or the distinctive ring feature to see who's calling so you can put your "professional face" on. Also, you've heard it before, but it's important, you need to put that smile on. That client doesn't need to know how bad your day went. You shouldn't sound rushed or hurried, either. If you are finishing up a job for a client, let the machine get it. You need to make your client feel important, even on bad days. Remember that clients can hear the smile in your voice. If that is true, then they can also hear the frustration and depression in your voice. If it helps, put a mirror on your computer monitor or your desk and watch yourself as you speak on the phone – keep smiling!

Those with Call Waiting will need to decide what to do when another call comes in while you are talking to your client. With Caller ID, you will know who is calling and that will help make a decision. I personally try to not leave a client when I'm talking to them to answer the incoming call. The only exception would be if we are not talking business and have started talking personally about family or something and another client is calling.

If I can sense that our conversation is just about over and another call comes in, I ask the current caller to hold just a minute, then I click over to the other line and say "Another 8 Hours, could you hold please?" Then I click back to the original call and quickly put an end to the conversation or ask if I can call them back in just a minute. For the second caller, this leaves the impression that I am a professional, and quite possibly they might be impressed that I have taken every step to answer the phone personally. The trick is getting back to the second caller quickly, and not click back to the original call and spend another five minutes on the phone. Use your best judgment and be sure to treat each caller with respect, making him or her feel important.

I recently added a Panasonic Plain Paper Fax & Copier/Answering Machine/ Phone that sits on my desk. I have found it to be perfect. I can easily see who's calling me, can get and receive my faxes quickly and easily and best of all, it prints out a listing of all the calls so I have all the numbers that have been called. I can keep a listing of all calls with their phone numbers, just in case I need to retrieve one.

Most VAs today have a cell phone. I don't include my cell phone on any advertisements or promotional material. I also don't freely give out the number to clients. I want my clients to be able to reach me in an emergency, but I don't want them calling me all hours of the day and night either. I make it a point to let them know that this is used only on rare occasions. Other VAs might not have this policy; I've just found it necessary for me. In order to stay in touch with the office while I'm out, I typically forward my office phone to my cell phone. If the situation is such that I can answer the call in a professional manner, then I will answer it as though I'm sitting at my desk.

Also, I feel it is imperative to have an answering machine or voice mail. Clients want to get in touch with you and they don't want to just hear the phone ringing endlessly. They like to leave a message and be able to go onto their next project. You also want to have a professional outgoing message on your voice mail. This is just another way you can sell your business without actually doing anything. Use voice mail effectively. I have been able to transact a fair amount of business through voice mail without ever having talked with the actual person. Leave detailed messages and include the best time to get in contact with you. Don't call someone and ask for a quick return call then leave your office right after you hang up. Most of the time a client seeks the services of a VA because they are extremely busy. Respect their time and be an effective communicator in all forms.

I feel it is vitally important to make sure that you follow-up on all phone calls quickly. If you are out running errands, check your messages as soon as you arrive back and then return the calls. You know how it feels when you are trying to reach someone and they don't get back to you. I have seen VAs lose business by not calling clients back promptly. Clients feel their time is important, and it usually is. They want someone who respects them. If you wait a day or so to call them back, they don't get that impression.

 You also want to have a plan set up with your clients for when they call you near the end of the workday. Tell them in advance to let you know whether or not this call is important enough to require a return call. For example, my clients will always say, "Nothing important, call me in the morning." I know if they tell me to call them back at the end of the day, it's something that needs my attention that day.

Those of you with kids, I know it's hard, but it's important to keep them quiet during phone calls with clients if the kids are around. My youngest has really tested me on this one. All my old tricks I have used for years and written about in prior books just doesn't seem to work on her, lately. My basket of goodies, my dollar store crafts, my portable phone and locking myself in the room, you name it, she's tested me on it. Thank goodness she's finally grown out of the stage, but my best recommendation is to find what works for you and keep trying.

If the children are present and "family life" is louder than the phone ringing, by all means, let the call go to voice mail. Don't put yourself in a situation that you have to excuse the noise and just have to call them back anyway. If you know you'll have to call them back, why answer the call? It's better than trying to understand them with your children screaming in your ear. (Not that my precious daughter has ever done that!)

E-mail Procedures

As a virtual assistant, you will be handling e-mail on a daily basis. It's important to establish a routine and stick to that routine. I believe most VAs do start their day checking their e-mail. However, you need to be careful that you don't get lost doing it and lose valuable work time. With the many groups and associations that we belong to, it's easy to respond to posts and then find yourself an hour later with no work done. Sometimes this is fine. Just make sure you keep an eye on it. However, answering e-mails can be a vital part of your business. I know for me, I enjoy it and it is required. The main thing is to schedule it into your day. This goes for social networking, too – schedule it and stick to the schedule!

Be careful with instant messages as well. I've discovered that family and friends use IMs the same as they do a phone, only it's worse because they know I'm online. When researching, I need to keep online. I have to be firm and tell them I'm working or in AOL, to put the Away from Computer on so that they can't disturb me.

Get in the habit of being brief with your correspondence back to your clients. They don't want to read long paragraphs. Their time is valuable. Summarize what you need to say. Your clients will greatly appreciate it.

No matter how comfortable you are with a client, it's still imperative to maintain a professional image at all times. This means preparing e-mail correspondence in the same manner as you would a business letter, avoiding the use of emoticons. Use a proper closing that includes your contact details in lieu of business letterhead.

Starting Part-Time

Easing into a virtual assistant practice enables a new VA to keep their regular employment while building their practice "after hours." Both jobs can coexist peacefully; however, it will require some careful planning.

Make sure that your clients understand the limitations of your hours from the start, and be certain that you take into consideration the effect this transitional period will have on others in your life. You are sure to be working longer hours as you establish your business, but it is a sound way to make the transition from employee to entrepreneur.

Your decision to become an entrepreneur is a big one. Your decision to quit your full-time job to pursue your business is an even bigger one. You know you've got a great idea and you know you can be successful. But, the reality is you can't give up your regular job because you need it to survive financially. In addition to the financial security, you also have to consider medical benefits, retirement funds, tuition reimbursement, and other insurance such as accidental death, life, and vision.

There are some who can afford to just quit and start their own business right away, but I'd say they are in the minority. So, just how do you go about starting a business and keep that full-time job?

First and foremost, you must make sure you don't jeopardize your current position. Check your company's policy on other employment. As hard as it may be, you still need to give 100% to your current job.

If you have Internet access you will be tempted to keep up on your mail groups, e-mail, social networking, and doing research on your new business. Most companies have very strict policies on the use of computers and the Internet for personal use. I know my former employer monitored this activity. The same goes for phone calls. My advice is to invest in a cell phone, maybe one with web messaging, to make and return calls during lunch. Do not use company time.

Another important reason to stay on the up and up with your current employer is they just might turn out to be a potential client. If they are, you will want to show that you act ethically and professionally. The image you portray on the job will reflect on how you will run your business. Regardless of your company's policy on outside employment, it is still recommended not to discuss your new venture with anyone during business hours. People know that when you start your own business, it is with the intent to be successful and make it a full-time operation. By letting others know what you are doing, it's like coming in everyday and announcing that you have a job interview—they will know you're quitting! This is certainly frowned upon by management. Remember, every office has a grapevine. Even the best of friends in the workplace can become jealous and maybe even vindictive. By telling your trusted friend, you could also put their job in jeopardy if management were to ask them if they know what you are up to. So my best advice is to keep a very low profile and keep it to yourself.

Now that we have the office politics out of the way, let me tell you how you can have the best of both worlds. I realize everyone's situation is different, but I will share with you how I was able to work full-time, start and grow my business, take care of my husband and two children, and attend college part-time. I even had time to go out and enjoy my friends. It wasn't easy and maybe I got lucky, but I contribute it to hard work, dedication, a strong desire to succeed, and a very supportive family. Hindsight will allow me to tell you a few things not to do, as well.

Whether you have a family, a significant other in your life, or just a pet that keeps you company, you will need a commitment from all of them if you want to be successful. I can't stress it enough the support you will need from others. You might want to prove yourself and do this all on your own, but it will be much easier if others are supportive. If you thought life was busy before you started this adventure, you haven't seen anything yet. You will find minutes in your day that you never knew you had because now, you are going to be a successful virtual assistant.

Once I decided that virtual assisting was for me, I spent hours upon hours researching every site I could to find out more information. I checked out all the virtual assistant groups, which were pretty limited at the time. There are a great deal more now. I joined a couple of the groups, lurked around for a while and then felt comfortable enough to start participating. All of this research and joining in on the mail groups was done after the kids were in bed.

I found myself staying up later at night and then I would get up later in the morning. The result would be that I would be rushed and running late for work, so my kids suffered. Don't put yourself in this position.

I find it hard to share with you a "typical day" because since starting my business, I don't think I've had anything typical. Every day is different and progresses in a different way as you reach the milestones in planning for success. I was lucky enough to get my first client in the business through word-of-mouth. Now, I know this business is virtual, but this was a local client and therefore constituted a meeting to discuss his needs. How in the world was I going to do that? I had to work all day. I didn't know whether to tell him I worked full-time or not. After all, this might make it look like I couldn't dedicate enough time to his project. I had a day of vacation scheduled so I scheduled a lunch appointment on that day with him and the gentleman that referred me. It wasn't until lunch that I finally revealed that I worked full-time and was just starting my business. You know what, he thought that was great and said he would be more than happy to have any future meetings with me after hours. It was actually more convenient for him because of his schedule. I could only hope that they would all be this easy. As lunch progressed, I began thinking to myself, "I'm already staying up until midnight every night on the Internet doing research, reading a million e-mail messages, trying to market my business, doing homework, and maintaining my website—when was I going to find time to do this guy's website?" Then reality set in. Hey, this was a paying client, and those e-mails can wait!

My second client also came from word-of-mouth. When I opened my business account at the local bank, I took the opportunity to tell the bank representative what kind of business I had started. I gave her a couple cards and asked if she ever knew of anyone that needed this type of service to please pass one on. She said she had a friend who had just started a business and just might be in need. A couple weeks later, I had a call and secured my first regular client. Regular meaning not just project work, but I'm learning her business and we have since developed a great partnership. Again, this client was aware of the fact that I worked full-time (and went to school part-time) and she was more than willing to meet after hours when we needed to and we spent a lot of time on the phone. She would call during the day and leave a message knowing that as soon as I had an opportune moment I would return the call.

Just prior to securing this regular client, I had done a mailing to over 400 local businesses introducing myself to the community. I had ordered some free webcards that I included with a letter of introduction. Webcards are 4 x 6 (approximately) glossy cards printed with a screen capture of your home page on the front. The back of the card can be left blank or be printed with your marketing message depending on how much you want to spend.

The letter first introduced the virtual assistant concept and then introduced my business. From this I received the expected 1-3% response that resulted in one client. This client, if I could get her, would be the last one I could handle while working full-time.

I had put in my business plan that I would secure three clients on a retainer basis by the end of the year. I did it! Granted, every one of them was not on retainer and there were only two, but the amount of work they provided compensated for the third. The bonus being when I quit my full-time job, I secured my employer as a regular client on contract.

My business plan also contained my marketing plan. While the plan I put in place was a good one, I found I was not in a position to act on it because there was something standing in the way—my full-time job. It got to the point where I couldn't take on any more clients. I couldn't take on any more clients because I didn't have any more time to give; my full-time job was limiting my growth potential. Then I decided it was time to move on and become a full-time entrepreneur.

I sat down and calculated what I needed to make monthly and compared that to what I was currently pulling in from clients. When you do all this number crunching, you have to be sure to consider everything down to the paperclips you need to run your business. In my case, I was carrying the family medical/dental insurance. I knew this could be transferred over to my husband's employer and it would then come out of his check, but it still needed to be considered in the household budget. Outside of normal tax deductions and medical, I also had to account for my other benefits such as life insurance, a savings plan, and tuition reimbursement. Ultimately, unless your income is not relied upon in the household budget, you will want to net out the same amount you are currently required to bring home plus a little extra. Any additional income from project work or non-regular clients can be an added bonus to cover expenses such as office supplies, advertising, telephone, domain registration, hosting fees, membership fees, etc.

Once you think you have it all figured out, run the numbers again. We all know everything comes out on paper. Be sure to estimate high on your expenses and high on your tax estimates. I calculated my tax deductions based on my current payroll deductions. By all means, consult a tax advisor, your accountant, or bookkeeper because every situation is different.

I would actually recommend doing these calculations when you put your plan in place and when you're nearing your target quit date. Calculating up front will aid you in determining what your rates should be and the number of hours you will need to secure from clients. Focus on obtaining retainer clients (partners) and not just project work–this is the money you can rely on. Quitting your job may also mean an adjustment in your lifestyle. You may have to eat dinner at home and go to the Sunday matinee instead of dinner and a movie out on Friday nights. Or perhaps you need to put that new car on hold. It's all a matter of priorities and only you can decide this for your business. One thing that worked for me was to let my full-time job fund the set-up costs for my new business. I sacrificed a few evenings out and put off buying a new car to pay for office equipment, pay off some debts, pay for some advertising, etc. Money coming in from existing clients is a great source for offsetting those start-up costs, as this is "extra" money. When it came time to quit, my office was all set up and I didn't incur a cash flow problem right off the bat. Save every penny you can. I literally save quarters. When I opened my business checking account my first deposit was $140.00--all quarters!

Refer back to the Determining Your Rates chapter to aid you in establishing your hourly rate. In turn, you can determine the number of hours necessary to cover your business expenses and salary. It should be in the neighborhood of two and a half to three times the gross salary you were earning through your employer. For example, if you were making $15 per hour then you should be charging no less than $37.50 per hour in your business. We all operate under a different financial scenario. Do your research and make sure you have covered all the necessary expenses and a comfortable profit for you.

Following are some do's and don'ts of working through the transitional phase:

DO:
- Check e-mail in the morning before leaving for work and answer any urgent requests.
- Check e-mail at lunch whenever possible.
- Return and make calls before work, during lunch, and on the drive home.
- Get a toll-free voice/fax from FreedomVoice or another similar company and have it forwarded to your cell phone. (http://www.freedomvoice.com)
- Be up front with clients and let them know you do this part-time.
- Make your kids feel like they are part of your business and your successes.
- Make sure you eat right.
- Make sure you get the appropriate amount of sleep.
- Keep a calendar or daily planner.
- Mark family commitments first in your planner.
- Prepare a business plan, reference it often, and follow it.
- Set a time frame for quitting your job and outline your plan of action for reaching this goal.
- Take advantage of idle time.

DON'T:
- Spend every waking moment in front of the computer.
- Take on assignments that you know you can't handle due to time restrictions—seek out the support of another VA.
- Think you are superwoman—everyone has their limits.
- Keep more than one calendar – use the same one for everything.
- Lose focus – it's hard to be on the Internet and avoid drifting off into other things.
- Lose sight of your goals – if your business plan needs to be changed, change it accordingly.
- Quit your job before you're ready.

Great Business For Those Families in the Military

The emerging virtual assisting industry is presenting great opportunities for those in the military. With the moving lifestyle that often accompanies this group, a virtual assistant business fits perfectly. This business can be run from any city, and it doesn't matter how many times you move in a year. Best of all, there is a great sense of accomplishment in owning a business.

As Victoria Parham, President and CTO of VSS CyberOffice states: (vparham@vsscyberoffice.com)

> The virtual assistant industry as a whole has grown by leaps and bounds over the past ten years. In particular for military spouses, the VA industry offers one realm of portable career opportunities for those whose career interests are administrative in nature. Ideally, military spouses possess a wealth of knowledge, skills, abilities, and flexibility or the ability to adapt to various circumstances.

> The awesomeness of being a military spouse and virtual business owner is the ability to have total control over the direction of your career. A virtual business, whether a virtual assistant practice or some other creative virtual business concept, offers military spouses portability, career stability, increased client base and steady income & growth levels. With regard to obstacles and challenges, it comes with the territory; it's a part of being a business owner. However, with careful planning, preparation, and a great support network challenges can be overcome.

So as you can see, military spouses face unique career challenges resulting from a lifestyle that often involves frequent relocations—sometimes to remote, isolated posts, high-cost areas, and areas where the prospects for employment are poor. These moves, necessary though they may be, not only impact employment prospects and family income, but the spouse's career progression as well.

Andrea Pixley is one prime example of a military spouse who has been able to achieve a successful VA business. Take a look at her website and you can see how she's taken full advantage of her circumstances and is now happily the owner of her own business. I think she's done an excellent job on her site. It's nice to look at, full of information, and tells potential clients exactly what benefits they can obtain by utilizing her services. http://www.andreapixley.com

Andrea states, "The great thing about being a virtual assistant is that it is one of the few work-at-home opportunities that can be done from anywhere in the world. Since information is shared and work is primarily done via the Internet, reliance on slower means of correspondence is minimal. Start-up costs are comparatively low and, regardless of where the military sends you, a virtual business can be run without most of the expenses associated with moving a brick and mortar business."

She also has a website, 4MilitaryFamilies.com, which could be a one-stop resource site for military families. This is truly a fabulous site; one that I highly recommend everyone stop by and see, even those not in the military. It's a good way to show support for our troops and I think she has done a fabulous job and should be commended.

4MilitaryFamilies.com
http://www.4militaryfamilies.com
E-mail:andrea@4militaryfamilies.com

Andrea was nice enough to allow us to print her article on relocating. For those of you who do this frequently, I'm sure her tips will prove very beneficial! Enjoy!

One in six Americans will move this year. Are you one of them? I am. Relocating is rarely fun and never hassle-free. Add in your own business and the prospect of a move may be terrifying. It doesn't have to be.

Since becoming a military spouse in 1991, I have moved six times. With six states and two countries behind me, when it came time for my latest move, I considered myself a pro. Activating and canceling utilities, printing change of address cards, finding someplace to live and new schools for the kids, and carefully packing up the china had all become part of the routine, but this time was different. I had a business to move. It was time to put all that experience to the test. Here are 10 strategies I have found to help make moving a business a bit easier:

Don't sink your roots too deep. Because I move every couple of years, I have tried to keep most aspects of my business non-geographically specific. The Internet makes this very easy. My business cards and brochures contain my e-mail and web addresses and my permanent toll-free number, while my website has my current address and phone numbers. That way, my business cards don't become trash the minute I move (including all the cards I have given to potential clients).

Do your research. Every hour you spend researching your new location will save you hours of heartache once you arrive. Is there a DSL or cable modem service or at least local dial-up numbers available? Can you get the level of phone service you need? In many cases, you can have everything ready for your arrival.

Prepare your clients. Let your clients know that you are about to move. Tell them that you are confident the only change for them will be where to send payments. If the transition period won't be "business as usual," tell them what they can expect from you until the move is complete. If something unexpected arises, keep them informed.

Tell the Web where you are going. One of the great things about the Web is the incredible number of places to make your business known. Registering your business in a hundred places can pay great dividends. When moving time comes, though, much of that information will need to be updated. I make it a point to record every site I have given my information to. If you haven't done that, a good place to start is your e-mail. If you receive messages from those sites, they can remind you to visit their site to update your information.

Become mobile. There comes the time when you have to unplug your hardware and head to your new home. For a move across town, this may not be a huge event. Moving across the country (or even out of the country), however, makes this moment critical. With a laptop computer and a cellular phone, conducting business on the road can be a snap. For those of us who are less-equipped, a good practice is storing important data online. This can keep you in business until your office is unpacked. I would also recommend hand-carrying all paperwork and backed-up files. This way, if the moving van ends up at the bottom of the Mississippi River, your business isn't sunk as well.

Pay your taxes. The government wouldn't be the government if it didn't add some pain to this already challenging process. A new state means more paperwork come tax time, so keep up with those records. A move out of the country can add a whole new level to your tax situation. Some professional advice in this situation may be warranted.

Get licensed. Find out what sort of licensing, if any, the local government requires. Laws governing business licenses can vary greatly. Generally, the local government's website can give a general guideline so you know what is expected before you set up shop.

Network at your new location. When you're researching you new home, look for local business groups that fit your interests. Although most of my business is generated from my website, I was amazed at the number of new clients that I signed on after joining a couple of local networking groups. Of course, a move to Germany may make this less plausible, but, even then, there are dozens of online networks of working men and women overseas.

Take advantage of geography. I started my business in a small town in north Texas. The small population meant I couldn't rely on local clients to keep me in business. With a move to a metropolitan area, the potential client base exploded. Even if your business is Internet-based and you've never even met a client in person, a few dollars spent on local advertising may pay off. If your budget doesn't include funds for advertising, take a look at some locally-based websites and you might find opportunities to get your name out there for free. If you're moving to a less populated area, anticipate a decrease in local clients and plan your marketing accordingly.

Expect the unexpected and be flexible. Even if you think you are completely prepared, you may still find yourself pulling your hair out. I ordered my telephone service a full month before arriving in the Phoenix area. I had the phone numbers, an order for DSL and the assurance of the customer support representative that I would be able to walk into my house, plug in my computer and telephone and be in business. Of course, when I arrived, not even a dial tone awaited me. It was almost two months before I had telephone service in my office. If this happens to you, ask your local phone company about their compensation program. I was able to get a free cellular phone and service from mine. On the bright side, the delay gave me more time to research and I realized that a DSL modem was not ideal for me, so I canceled my order and purchased a cable modem instead.

In today's business culture, where it is considered a sin to be more than two telephone rings away from voice contact, being out of touch can be deadly for a small business. The easy answer is to stay put. When that's not an option, take control of the process and keep your business booming. By planning ahead, you can take your business wherever life takes you. Instead of wondering if you still have clients when you plug back in, you can worry about the china.

Andrea M. Pixley, Virtual Assistant, http://www.andreapixley.com,
E-mail: va@andreapixley.com

By the way, for over ten years now Diana has been giving away free copies of her first book *Words From Home: Start, Run and Profit from a Home-Based Word Processing Business* to anyone in the military. All you need to do is e-mail her at Diana@virtualwordpublishing.com with the subject line "Military" and she'll e-mail it to you right away.

Tips for Success

The *American Heritage Dictionary-Fourth Edition* defines success as "The achievement of something desired, planned, or attempted: *attributed their success in business to hard work.*" To us, success is a personal thing. Each of us defines success according to our life and our business plan, as well as through our values and work ethics. Establishing measurable and achievable goals will help you identify whether you have achieved success in your business.

First and foremost, we believe that having confidence in yourself, your abilities and the value your services bring to your clients will allow you to accomplish great success in your business. It is possible to be over confident, too, so find the right balance at the right time. You'll know when it feels right.

Also, keep in mind that your clients are business owners, too. Never ask a client to accept anything in regard to terms or working conditions that you would not deem acceptable if you were engaging the services of a company. Always remain ethical in your business practices. Maintain a high level of professionalism and integrity—you'll never go wrong.

The world of social networking has presented a crossover of business and personal that we've never experienced before in the business world. Remember that if you choose to mix the two it could come back to haunt you. Be aware of what you're saying and the information that you're sharing in public forums.

Susan Totman offers some excellent tips for achieving success in your business and your personal life:

1. People will tell you to keep your family separate from your business. That is NOT possible and struggling to do it will stress you considerably more than if you understand that they will coincide and overlap and that you need to become flexible to handle each day as it comes.
2. Clarify to your family that there are times when you need to focus on your business without interruption. This can be difficult, because generally you are the focal point of the family, but it is necessary to the success of your business.
3. Keep family finances separate from the business.
4. Schedule time to spend with your children and/or significant other. This sounds silly, but after you've been in business for a while, you will realize how important this is. There is a tendency to work all the time whenever you are able, because it's convenient and you are working from home. It's comfortable and easy to fall into.
5. Take time off just for you. Do something at least a couple of times a week that is strictly for you whether it be exercise, classes, time out with your friends, doesn't matter what it is. Schedule it and do it. It's important to get away from your work.
6. When you're working, get up every hour or two and stretch, get a cup of coffee, tea or whatever you like, grab a snack and then go back to work. This helps to break up the workday a bit and also truly makes you able to focus better with less stress on your work.
7. When you start your business, sit down with your family and let them know how important it is to you and outline what you need from them. If you are clear and

open as to what you need, it will go a long way toward making the transition to running your own business from home a great deal easier.

8. If you are unlucky enough to have a family that is not supportive, please don't give up. Find support forums to find others who will encourage you and support you and other VAs or entrepreneurs in your area that you can meet with and network with.

Priscilla Y. Huff, author, of *101 Best Home-Based Businesses for Women, 3rd.rev.ed.*, *The Self-Employed Woman's Guide to Launching a Home-Based Business,* offers us these three tips for success:

1. Set goals and review them on a regular basis. It will help you focus on the steps needed to reach your goals and prevent you from becoming discouraged because you are wasting your energies going into too many directions at once.

2. Network often with other home-based workers for tips and encouragements using the Internet (who doesn't these days?!) with e-mails, chats, message boards, and online groups; joining a trade association related to your business to get together for conference and meetings and hear inspiring speakers.

3. Remind yourself often why you are working from home—to be able to arrange your work around the needs of your loved ones? To do work you enjoy? To earn more money for a better quality of life? To be independent? All these reasons and more? Keeping in mind the reason(s) you decided to work from home will strengthen your resolve to get you through the rough times until you succeed.

> *"Success usually comes to those who are too busy to be looking for it."*
> -Henry David Thoreau

> *"Success will not lower its standard to us. We must raise our standard to success."*
> -Rev. Randall R. McBride, Jr.

We caught up with some VA professionals online and solicited their biggest tip for success. Here's what they had to share:

Ruth Martin of http://www.MaplewoodVA.com states, "Trust your own instincts even if the pack is doing something different. No one knows your business better than you."

Kimberley Thomas-Catanzaro of http://www.on-linesecretary.com offered the following: "Keep Learning, Invest in yourself and your business!"

"A white board is a great tool for keeping track of loose ends or a place to brain-storm," adds Janet Ann Janowiak, http://www.ezonesecretary.com.

Stephanie Fish, of http://www.BuckeyeVA.com says, "In order to be successful in your virtual assistant business, be sure to schedule a free day just for you! Take time off from your business, in order to 'recharge' yourself."

Lee Drozak of http://myofficeassist.org recommends, "Collaborate with your colleagues. They will be your greatest source of support, knowledge and resources."

In Their Own Words:

Tess Strand Alipour: It can be difficult to find the time for yourself in the mix of work and family responsibilities, but it is so incredibly crucial and really should be part of your business plan, however informal. Carving out specific time each and every day to take care of your SELF is so important because YOU ARE YOUR BUSINESS.

Jeannine Clontz: Honest, ethical business practices. I think the hardest part for a potential client is to have confidence in someone they may not have a chance to meet in person. It can certainly be considered a "leap of faith." That's why I think that industry involvement is so key to being successful in this particular industry. As with almost every industry, there are good and bad service providers. We have to find ways to make potential clients feel comfortable with our abilities, confidentiality and loyalty. I feel this can only be achieved through referrals, references, and certifications. Having a good sense of business ethics can go a long way in helping our industry thrive and grow. I encourage everyone to take the time to consider ethical options when making business decisions, whether they are for our own businesses, or those of our clients.

Alyssa Gregory: Give up the need for complete control and stop striving for perfection. Be flexible, go with the flow, and don't forget to schedule in time just for you.

Kathy Ritchie: Network, network, network, never miss a chance to tell people about your business! Join one or more virtual assistant organizations/associations. The support and encouragement there is priceless!

Barbara Rowen: Know your stuff, have good equipment and current software, get the training you need, and practice patience and perseverance. Market yourself to the type of people you want to work for and do the kind of assignments you like to do, and it will no longer feel like work. Learn from the past, but plan for the future by focusing on the present. And above all, always have your business cards with you.

Taking Care of Your Number One Asset – You

This is what I believe to be the most important chapter of the entire book. Why? Because your business depends on a healthy "**YOU**" to run it. There are so many ways that you can do damage to your business by not taking care of yourself. And once you're sick, there's often no turning back. I guess I feel so strongly about it because I know the consequences of not taking care of yourself properly.

First off, you need to take time to nurture yourself. You need to be at your peak to maintain momentum. Take at least 20 minutes every day to exercise, meditate, pray, take a bubble bath, etc. Do whatever refreshes and energizes you.

Let's start with stress. According to the American Psychological Association, 43% of all American adults suffer adverse health effects from stress. As home-based workers, we sometimes take on the role of "Super Mom" or "Super Dad." Often we take on even more than if we went off to work at 8:00 and came back at 5:00. Some of us are trying to start a business while working full-time and having a family. It's hard, we know firsthand! We don't claim to have all the answers, but we've researched stress and have some additional sound advice to offer. These may seem overly obvious, but they just might be a good reminder and even come in handy one day by having them all written down together.

1) Don't take on more than you can handle. Learn your limitations and stop before you get there.

2) Stop and listen to your body! Is it telling you that it's tired and needs a break? Learn to know you and what you need to do to remain in good shape.

3) Exercise. We say it too – I don't have time to exercise. Make time! Stretch. Even while sitting, you can stretch your neck from side to side. Take a walk in the morning or before you start fixing dinner after a day's work. Get an exercise bike or a therapy ball. It will make such a big difference in your life. Schedule exercising the same as you would one of your best clients. In fact, aren't you one of your best clients?

4) Learn to say NO and stand by your decision without feeling guilty.

5) Enjoy – Take time out for lunch with friends. Remember why you decided to start a business in the first place.

6) Read, read, read! There are a number of good books out there on stress and stress-related topics. Read these now, before you need them.

7) Forget the "Super Mom" image. Just be the best you can be and be satisfied with that.

8) Get enough sleep. As you are reading this you're probably saying no problem. Just be aware that if you overextend yourself and make promises to clients that are unrealistic, it can and will be a problem.

9) Have a schedule to follow – plan your day well. This helps to avoid that "overwhelmed" feeling.

10) Reward yourself throughout the day!

11) Listen to calming music. Meditate. Get a massage. Practice good self-talk.

12) Eat well. Plan ahead for nutritious meals and snacks. With the interruptions during the day and deadlines to meet, you won't have time to make that salad you want. If you planned ahead, you will have it ready the night before. Prepackaged salads are great, but *boring,* without the little extras in there. Cut up the extras at night; some carrots, celery, cucumbers, etc. That way, you have a nice salad for lunch. Consider stocking up on prepackaged meats, chicken strips, ham, fresh fruits, and bottled water.

13) You're home all day and if you are new at this there is a real tendency to hit the fridge. You must have the right foods available: yogurts, nuts, fruits and veggies; you decide what's best for you, just have them handy. We're not alone on this one and a few of you are nodding your heads with us. If you're used to working at an office and having a 15-minute break, the freedom of a cabinet of sweets and a fridge is delightful. Be careful.

14) Don't be afraid to ask for help. We live by the MomsTown.com mantra – we can do it all, but we can't do it all by ourselves. Asking for help is not a sign of weakness. It's not worth the stress in your life to be overwhelmed when you think of the consequences to your health and overall wellbeing. Nothing will make your family resent your business more than you constantly being on edge and having no time for them.

15) Connect with your friends online. You'll be amazed how great you feel just by reading other postings and Facebook and tweeting with someone. (Be mindful of your time management, though!)

Your goal is a better, calmer you; a you that can handle the demands of your business, your family, your social engagements, etc.

For all you moms, we highly recommend reading, *It's All About You: Live the Life You Crave* by Mary Goulet and Heather Reider for more tips on taking care of you while juggling all the other elements of life as a mom. As Mary and Heather say, "Moms are the pulse of the family." We couldn't agree more and as you can see from the Tips for Success, other VAs agree.

"Where the Heck is My Briefcase and whose little boy is this??"
Learning how to cut back on work hours...

Rebecca Game © 2000
Reprinted with permission.

As I was digging through a pile of papers looking frantically for my to-do list, I uncovered my small son sitting in the pile with it posty-noted to his forehead. I said, "Who are you?" When he said, "Mommy", I realized at that moment that I needed to s-l-o-w d-o-w-n. This wasn't my idea of getting a good "rush". I might be getting tons of work done but where was my sanity? Had I left it in my briefcase? And where the heck was my briefcase anyway?? Where did this child come from? Had I brought home some other busy woman's briefcase? How come I didn't remember that he was supposed to be a happy part of my life with giggles and squiggles?

What happened to all the time I had in high school when I slept till noon on the weekends and planned a lazy day at the pool or maybe even just read a good book by the lake? Where had the days gone when I used to turn to my mother and say, "I'm bored. I don't have anything to do." Where had all the time gone?? There seems to be about 8 hours in a day total instead of the 16 hour days I had as a child. The naps I take now are at 4 am to 6 am and even they are riddled with trips to the bathroom from all the coffee I have consumed.

My sister came over the other day and had on the most beautiful outfit and her hair looked magnificent. Her fingernails were freshly manicured and her toenails painted to match. She seemed refreshed, peachy and bubbly. I imagined how I looked with my house shoes, my hair uncombed and my comfy sweatpants. I had been TOO BUSY to take care of me, BUT.... I had gotten a lot of work done, by golly! She came by to see if I wanted to go to a movie. A movie?? The last movie I saw was the Pink Panther. What's been out since then? Anything worth seeing? No, I can't spend a few hours at the movie. I have 537 e-mails to answer, 16 new web pages to load, 14 directories to print out and then I have to reorganize the filing cabinet because one of my cats decided it was his new litter box. I don't think I could get my shoes on anyway because I've worn these house shoes so much that my arches disappeared along with my round hiney which is now in the shape of a perfect right angle.

As I watched her drive away I thought of all the fun times we "used" to have together. It was TIME for a change! To heck with this working yourself to death. Maybe I could get as much done in less time if I was more structured and organized and MADE time for myself. I can't be superwoman! I don't even have the chest for it anyway! Why try?!

So...That did it! I decided to try a little structure and organization to get back a part of my life that I was too busy to even notice it was missing! Now that I have a plan, where do I start??

I started with the T-T-T theory. The T-T-T theory is "Toss Ten Things". While the theory is supposed to be for tossing ten things out of your house that you don't need anymore, I decided to use the theory to toss ten "job" things that I didn't need anymore. I don't NEED to be on 217 mail lists. I'm pretty sure I can survive with 2 to 3 mail lists that focus only on what I want to participate in. So step one would be...

> Step One: Toss Ten Things that you no longer need to do in your daily work life. It might be hard but choose 10 work things that you can live without doing!

The next thing I realized is that I did not use a daily planner. I had posty notes, index cards, a chalkboard, and a notebook. None of them correlated with each other. Maybe if I used ONE main organizing book, I could eliminate some "hunting" time there that could be used for "fun" time. So step two would be...

> Step Two: Use a Daily Planner to organize your work schedule and tasks, and appointments etc. Crunch work times together to leave times for fun and play and MOST important...schedule your FUN time in your appointment book first! Then schedule your work around those times.

My mail. Geesh! This is a full-time job in itself. I have every computing magazine, every web related magazine, and once I ordered a plate and so now I have every ad in the world that requires four payments of only $29.95 and then I have several newsletters, newspapers, and every once in awhile a real letter from a real person that didn't send it electronically but actually opened their mouth and licked a stamp just for me! Okay, let's face it....I won't fall behind if I don't know what the latest flash technology has done and I won't lose sleep if I missed out on the fact that the Internet now has a new scratch and sniff screen for purchasing the latest spices. I needed to cut back on this enormous time-hog of mail. So step three would be...

> Step Three: Use superglue found under living room chair to glue mailbox closed. Or...start unsubscribing to all those magazines and newspapers and other junk mail that you receive. Keep one good subscription to a favorite hobby or pastime and save the business subscriptions for reading at the docs office!

ICQ and CHAT are two HUGE time thieves! WHAT in the world can these people find to chat about at 6 am?? After trying to work on web pages and receiving 4 to 5 alerts every hour that someone wanted to chat with me, I promptly uninstalled my ICQ. I wondered if it was that important would they call me on the phone? Nope. Never heard a word from them. Each time the phone rang I jumped at the thought it might be a friend only to find out it was "Kurt's Curl Your Carpet" for $14.95 a room or Jerry's "Jump at the Chance to have Siding Placed over your Brick Home", and even sometimes it was "Mike's Miracle Mow and Garden" who wanted to mow your apartment patio. So step three would entail...

Step Three: Disable your ICQ and Chat, get an answering machine or voice mail and turn your ringer volume down to "is that the neighbor's phone?" volume. Take the time you saved on this step to add to your schedule for "fun" in your daily planner!

After I did a recount of bodies here I found out there were actually 4 people living in my house! That meant I could delegate! Somebody could take over the wash and somebody else could take over the floor cleaning! I wondered who owned all those socks anyway. I asked my older son how old he was and when he said 23, I told him it was time to make his own bed! So step four sends a message of...

Step Four: Delegate some of your work load to others around you or even hire outside help. Less work here and there adds up to a few extra hours a week to spend relaxing and enjoying life as it is happening right now. No longer do you have to look at pictures and say, "When did you all go to Disney World?? How come I'm not in these pictures? Who is that curly headed kid with you? Who is that gray-headed lady? Is that MY mom?? What happened to her chestnut colored hair?"

Now it's time to decide what is important to you BESIDES work. Is it painting, sewing, racing cars, skiing, or maybe tennis? What things do you LOVE to do that you can still do with a right angle hiney?? I decided that painting and ceramics are my thing. So now I have scheduled my fun and playtime in my daily-planner and I schedule family time next and then I schedule my work hours. My work hours might be at 2 am to 4 am, but what the heck... I now have time for ME! Oh... and I found my briefcase... I was sitting on it.

Family Fun

If you read my first book, *Words From Home, How To Start and Operate a Home-Based Word Processing Business,* you know that I started my business when my son was born. I took him to the daycare when he was six weeks old and I knew I just couldn't do it. That's when I decided to start a home-based word processing business. Back then (in 1985) home-based businesses were unheard of and many people thought I was absolutely crazy! Can you imagine? Thinking a WOMAN could start a business and do it out of her HOME — GET REAL!! Well, I'm here to tell you that I did it, by golly, and I'm still going strong.

My son has since graduated college and is going after his Masters. I truly believe he was inspired by my working from home and by my achieving so many goals. I rarely missed any of his school functions and I was able to be here for him when he was sick or WE needed a day off. This is the joy of working from home. This is truly one of the benefits. Seeing him constantly strive to do more is fabulous. I believe I've instilled in him that desire to do more and to be the best.

The good news is that I'm not alone. So many others have similar stories to tell. Julie McMann states, "Keeping a workable balance between family and business is a constant struggle. I try not to make any promises I can't keep. I try to remain as flexible, calm and patient as possible no matter what situation arises. If you remain confident that you can handle whatever comes your way, you will only help yourself reach your goals faster."

Here's what Kelly's daughter had to say, "Hi, I am Kelsey Poelker and my mom has a business. It is called Another 8 Hours and can be visited on the web at www.another8hours.com. I feel that her having this kind of business is challenging for her, but I like it because she can spend more time with my brother and me. But, I don't like it because she is always on the phone." (Little does she know that here at the Ennen's, I'm always on the phone too, but it's not work! I just love to talk!!!)

But do you see our challenges? Once we are aware of them, we can work on them. We make it a point to find out from my kids what they are feeling. But remember, they can also be tricky and try to get their way as well.

Here are some tips from some real pros in the field. I'm sure most of you have already heard of them and we were delighted that they offered some tips for our book. You can catch them online at http://www.mompreneursonline.com. This is an extremely motivating and upbeat site that offers positive suggestions on balancing work and family, and more importantly on being successful in your business.

- Set children up with no-mess crafts materials. Think crayons and markers, not finger paints.
- Give them some construction toys and ask them to make you a surprise. Great attention-getters include Lego blocks, wooden blocks, jigsaw puzzles and beads for stringing.
- Pull out your telephone treasures. Keep a box of goodies by the phone and let the kids open it whenever you've got to be on a business call. Fill it with quiet-time

treats like wind-up toys, trading cards, Silly Putty, Etch-A-Sketch, stamps, stickers and other fun stuff. Don't forget some edible prizes too, such as raisins, juice boxes, fruit roll-ups and animal crackers.

- Use a timer when you have to get something done. Set it for 15 minutes or so of work time, during which your kids must not disturb you. Then let your kids set it for 20 minutes of playtime with you!

As much as we hate to admit it, television, video games, online games, and movies can be wonderful ways to keep your children entertained while you're working. Just use caution and limit the amount of time you expose them each day. I know my pediatrician always tells us to limit this activity to no more than two hours per day.

Be realistic about how much you will be able to accomplish without any childcare. "Many moms underestimate the challenges of tending to business and family tasks simultaneously," the authors say. "If you, like many moms, plan to work around your children's sleep schedules, make sure you have the stamina it will take to pull this off--as you are likely to find yourself pulling the night shift regularly. Many successful virtual assistants find that it is helpful to have some supplemental childcare options—whether it's a preschool program a few mornings a week, a local high school or college kid who comes to baby-sit in the afternoons, or a baby-sitting co-op where you team up with other work-from-home moms to care for each other's kids. There are many creative and cost-effective ways to find childcare and *Mompreneurs*® are great about uncovering them!"

Pat Cobe and Ellen Parlapiano are co-authors of Mompreneurs: A Mother's Practical Step-by-Step Guide to Work-at-Home Success (Perigee, 2002) and Mompreneurs Online: Using the Internet to Build Work@Home Success (Perigee, 2001).

Here at the Ennen household, we started a few things around our house. After a long hard week, we have—*Family Game Night*: We started this about a year ago. We can't do it every Friday, but when we can, we do and really enjoy it. On Friday nights, plan an hour or so to play games with your kids. When we first started this I thought—no way, I'm too exhausted to do this after a busy week. What I discovered was that it had a relaxing effect and put me in the family mode for the weekend. (We recently have added family exercise night as well; although that hasn't caught on quite yet.)

And we do special things with them—like cooking! Kelly and I had the pleasure of writing another book together, *The Bizymom's Cookbook* (available at http://www.www.va-theseries.com) Talk about a lot of fun. We got to try out different recipes and the kids got to help us. Oh, what a MESS!! But what a JOY!! Including your kids in your business makes them feel special. My kids kept trying recipes so that they could put them in the cookbook. If you get the cookbook, you will see that not many of them made it, but the Ennens had a great time! And as the commercial says, that's priceless! When you look through the cookbook you'll see quite a few more recipes from the Poelker family.

Some sage advice--Don't buy your kids off. Many VAs, myself included, feel guilty after an exceptionally busy week and think we can make it up to our kids by buying them the latest game they wanted or their favorite doll. It provides a temporary fix and usually makes the children happy and you feeling not as guilty. The only problem is it often times takes more money to buy these gifts than you made. Also, it teaches your children that they can be bought, and believe me, they will use it to their advantage! Instead, spend some time with them. They will definitely remember that more.

∎∎∎

We'd like to share with you this poem that was provided to us on one of the message boards we used to frequent. It's no longer active but we still wanted to include it.

Oh the excitement of my home office
With the presence here of my rambunctious toddler.

While he's supposed to be watching Toy Story
He's really into something gory.

When I think he's taking a nap
I should have tightened the bottle cap.

I think he's playing basketball
But he's really drawing on the wall.

When I bring him something to eat
I find that he's painted his toilet seat.

I see brown stains on the couch and notice that he's hyper
Then realize he's been playing with his diaper.

It's an extra chore keeping up with this one.
While I'm working on the computer for the company I run.

But I wouldn't trade this experience for a billion
Because my boy is one in a zillion!!

Jackie Ulmer, of StreetSmartWealth.com, sums it up best with this. Can you see yourself in this? We can!!! (Printed with her permission.)

Am I Normal?

It's 3:00AM and instead of sleeping, I'm trying to figure out how to get listed near the top of the search engines. Am I normal?

Am I normal? I pondered that question this morning while I quickly checked e-mail one last time before shuffling the kids in the car and off to school.

Am I normal? It crossed my mind again while racing back toward my home office as I watched a group of moms head to the bagel shop for coffee and a chat.

Am I normal? This afternoon, as my neighbors talked intensely about the latest episode of ER, my mind kept wandering back to my website, and I wondered if that was normal.

My mother tells me I should quit thinking about business so much and just enjoy my children, which I do, but I still wonder, am I normal?

Am I normal? My friends look at me as if they've seen an alien when I tell them that I'm never going back to my corporate marketing career. I'm building an Internet empire from my home, would they like one too?

Now, don't get me wrong. I love life and live it to the fullest, with lots of playtime. But, ambition and the challenge of "building the perfect beast" push me relentlessly sometimes. I figure you can relate if you are reading this article. You are looking to create something bigger than yourself, too!

But, it's a crazy world we live in. A world where people have learned to stifle their dreams, their desires, their creativity. We are taught to "settle" for what we are dealt in life. All too often, when we try to move beyond that, those closest to us try to hold us back, save us from ourselves.

"Consider yourself lucky for what you have."

"It's a good job and the benefits are great."

"The average American family has thousands of dollars in credit card debt."

"It's too risky."

I don't know how you feel, but I want to LIVE my dreams, have my heart's desires and allow my creativity to blossom. I want to be my own boss, work in my pj's if I choose, take a four hour lunch to go shopping and fire myself when I'm not measuring up. (Of course, I'm eligible for rehire tomorrow!)

Normal SHOULD be waking up when your body is rested, not when the alarm clock rings.

Normal SHOULD be taking a vacation when it fits your family's schedule, not when your seniority allows. It SHOULD be having a parent at home when a child comes home from school.

To me, normal ISN'T sitting in rush hour traffic twice a day. It ISN'T working fifty weeks in exchange for two weeks off a year, or five days on for two days off a week. It ISN'T wearing my name and picture attached to my clothing.

Everyone must determine their own definition of what "normal" is and isn't. For those of us who have decided to step outside the box, take control of our lives and build our own business, normal is anything BUT normal!

Life is full of risks, it's true. But, everything great that has EVER happened has done so with some degree of risk. I don't want to get to the end and WISH I had taken just a few risks.

I'm urging you to take some risks with me! Step up to the plate! Decide what it is you want out of your life and your business and GO FOR IT! FORGET ABOUT NORMAL!

Create your own "normal!"

We are at the very beginning of the new millennium!

The Internet is overflowing with possibilities, as it breaks all growth records ever set by anything, and it is just not NORMAL!

As I lay in bed, building my empire (business) on my laptop, I realize just how much I love my other-than-normal life. I wouldn't trade it for anything!
The clock says 10:07 PM.
Ahhh, lunch break!

As we feel that the personal side is just as important as the business side to our VAs, here's a little bit about our contributing VAs and their families...

In Their Own Words:

Tess Strand Alipour: Because my husband is also my business partner and we have worked from home together for nearly the last five years, we have a pretty good system down for making sure the relationship between business and family stays healthy. It took some honest discussions, and it wasn't always easy finding that balance but we seem to have achieved a nice harmony - especially since our daughter was born. We have specific times each week day that each of us can plan on for personal time, family time, and business and client time.

Shane Bowlin: I have a husband, daughter, puppy and kitten. From my husband's previous marriage we also have two daughters and a grandson who lives out of state.

In the beginning I tried to keep my working schedule and ignore what was happening in my household. Now I am more flexible and stop working when Ashley comes home from school, fix dinner, and do a little work in the evening after she goes to bed. It was too chaotic to try to do otherwise. Not sure why it took me so long to realize that I didn't have to keep working til 5 p.m.

My working at home has allowed my family flexibility (especially in the summer) and even if I am working, we have a lot more time together. I can't imagine ever working outside the home again.

Nora Rubinoff: Discipline is huge. Create a routine and stick with it. You will love yourself and your family will love you for creating those boundaries. Resist the urge to do a little additional work in the evening or on the weekend. Creating the separation helps you have time to keep yourself refreshed!

Donna Toothaker: Have boundaries around when you work and when it's family time. When it's family time, be "present" with your family and let work go. Get support in terms of team members to take the pressure off so you can work less and still feel comfortable about how things are running.

Authors Note: One of the things we love to hear from Donna is that on days she has a lot of coaching calls or an important teleseminar, she will take her dogs to doggie daycare. They love it and so does she. See how it all works out!

What Common Childhood Lessons
Have Taught Me About Business Ownership

Alyssa Gregory
avertua, LLC
http://www.avertua.com

As parents, we want our kids to grow up to be productive members of society, so there are a number of universal lessons we teach our children from an early age. When you think about it, it's amazing how much relevance these childhood lessons can have in our adult lives.

Here are some of the things I try to teach my kids that are mirrored in my life as a business owner.

You Can't Always Have Your Way

Productive relationships are built on compromise and a desire to see the other person's happiness. Whether you're working with a business partner, client or colleague, you have to be willing to allow some concessions in order to move your relationships forward.

Sharing is Good

Sharing is definitely not just for the playground. As a business owner and potential expert in your industry, you are in the perfect position to share your knowledge for the betterment of others. And sharing can be more fulfilling than you might ever suspect.

Watch Your Language

Vulgar, crass and offensive language is not acceptable from our kids, and it's also not a good idea in a professional environment. Keeping your language G-rated is a good way to avoid offending anyone or looking foolish in business, and in life.

Treat Others How You Want To Be Treated

The same Golden Rule we try to instill in our children applies in business relationships. Respect is a two-way street, and if you're not being respectful toward others, you can't expect them to treat you with respect.

You Can Do Whatever You Set Your Mind To

Just as we don't want to limit the success of our children, you should allow yourself to aim high in business. With determination, confidence and hard work, you can achieve anything. Set goals that make you stretch, let yourself dream, and go for it.

Preventing Work-Related Injuries

Many work-related injuries could be prevented with proper knowledge and preventive measures. The most common injuries are low back and neck strain, headaches, eyestrain, and Repetitive Stress Injuries (RSI). RSI are terms given to a variety of painful, debilitating conditions that experts believe to be caused by repetitive movements of the hands and arms. Sharon Butler in *Conquering Carpal Tunnel Syndrome* provides an explanation of what repetitive strain injuries are. She states:

> Repetitive strain injuries can occur in many different areas of the body. They are a result of repetitious movement of one or more parts of the body in combination with other forms of structural or physical strain. There are many forms of repetitive strain injury. Common examples include tennis elbow, knee problems in runners and Carpal Tunnel Syndrome.

Home-based workers develop these problems because of bad postural and work-related habits, as well as improper office furniture. Carpal tunnel syndrome (CTS) is one that can actually close down your business (overnight!).

Because we perform duties (typing) requiring prolonged or repetitive movement of our hands, we are more susceptible to getting carpal tunnel syndrome. It can come on very suddenly with symptoms of numbness and pain, especially at night. You can greatly decrease your chances of developing carpal tunnel syndrome with the proper knowledge, including how to set up your office correctly and use of appropriate postural ailment. Your office must be set up in accordance with ergonomic guidelines. Ergonomics refers to the idea of creating a work environment that promotes physical health and comfort while optimizing job performance. It's the science of comfort, convenience, and function. Most office furniture now conforms to ergonomic guidelines. But, you should check before you purchase anything to make sure.

The following suggestions were obtained from these books on preventing carpal tunnel syndrome and setting up an office correctly: *Carpal Tunnel Syndrome and Overuse Injuries* by Tammy Crouch and Michael Madden; *Conquering Carpal Tunnel Syndrome and Other Repetitive Strain Injuries,* by Sharon J. Butler; and *The Home-Office Computing Handbook,* by David Langendoen and Dan Costa.

- Don't have your fingers above your wrists when typing (arching your wrists). Lower the keyboard or raise your chair. Your hands and wrists should be in a comfortable, relaxed position--not too high or held at an awkward angle.
- If you have wrist pain or numbness now, wear a wrist support whenever you type.
- Your keyboard height should be 23-25 inches from the floor.
- Forearms should be at right angles to the body with the forearm parallel to the floor. Seventy to ninety degrees is the ideal angle for typing or data entry tasks.
- Your shoulders should be relaxed without slouching.
- An arm/wrist rest is mandatory. This is placed directly in front of your keyboard and can be obtained at any office or computer store. Also, a mouse rest is required as well.
- Don't lean on your elbows. Don't rest your wrists on your wrist rest when typing.

- Both of your feet should rest flat on the floor or you should use a footrest when typing.
- The lower back needs support through the use of a cushion.
- Purchase the right chair: an uncomfortable chair leads to postural problems, which in turn throws off the alignment of the spine and impairs nerve function to the arms and hands. The ideal chair should be adjustable to a height comfortable for you.
- Your monitor should be positioned at eye level (or *slightly* below eye level) to avoid neck stress. Note: the books differ on this approach. One advises to be at eye level and another slightly below eye level.
- Use a document holder to keep your papers so you are not constantly bending your neck.
- Take breaks every thirty to thirty-five minutes. Rest your hands. Periodically, let your arms fall to your sides and shake out your wrists. This promotes blood flow and relieves tension.

An *ergonomic keyboard* is one preventive item every home-based VA should have. These look as though they would require an extensive period of getting used to, but they don't. In fact, many, including myself, believe they actually improve typing speed.

I also truly believe that positive thinking can help. I'm the type of person that normally has a very positive attitude. As I hope you can tell from this book, I love owning my business. I deeply love my family and friends. And most importantly, I love helping others achieve their dreams of starting a business. That's why I enjoy being so active online. Thus, to conclude this chapter we'd like to leave you with a wonderful article that Sharon Kay Lee wrote and gave us permission to print. It pretty much says it all!!

Sharon Kay Lee

CAN YOU IMAGINE YOURSELF A MILLIONAIRE?

My first introduction to Positive Thinking was 12 years ago when I read "Think and Grow Rich" by Napoleon Hill. The first time I read this book I wasn't sure what to do with the knowledge I had gained. I read it again and then it began to really sink in.

Think and Grow Rich, Could it be Done?? Could you really think and grow rich??

YOU BET YOU CAN!! There are many self-made millionaires that have done just that!!

It starts with DESIRE. DESIRE to be somebody, to do something with your life, to be truly happy.

All of us want these things, so why do so many settle for less? Why do we work year after year at jobs we hate and end up with a meager savings, bad health and unhappiness?

Why do we settle for less than we want? Why do we stand on the sidelines and only wish for what the wealthy have?

Are they smarter than we are? Are they luckier than we are? Did they get all the breaks?

I say NO. The difference between them and you is they took action. They took steps towards financial independence. Yes, there are those that are born rich. There are a lot more that made their own financial independence.

A poem from "Think and Grow Rich" says it all! Read it and really listen to its message.

> "I bargained with Life for a Penny, and Life would pay no more, however I begged at evening. When I counted my scanty store.

> "For Life is a just employer, He gives you what you ask, But once you have set the wages, Why, you must bear the task.

> "I worked for a menial's hire, Only to learn, dismayed, That any wage I had asked of Life, Life would have willingly paid."

IS THIS TRUE?? Have we worked for pennies when we could have worked for millions??

YES IT IS!! How can we translate this desire of riches into its financial equivalent?

The six steps outlined in Napoleon Hill's book are:

1. Fix in your mind the exact amount of money you desire. It is not sufficient merely to say "I want plenty of money." Be definite as to the amount. (There is a psychological reason for definiteness)

2. Determine exactly what you intend to give in return for the money you desire. There is no such reality as "something for nothing."

3. Establish a definite date when you intend to possess the money you desire.

4. Create a definite plan for carrying out your desire, and begin at once, whether you are ready or not, to put this plan into action.

5. Write out a clear, concise statement of the amount of money you intend to acquire, state what you intend to give in return for the money, and describe clearly the plan through which you intend to accumulate it.

6. Read your written statement aloud, twice daily, once just before retiring at night, and once after arising in the morning. As you read - see and feel and believe yourself already in possession of the money.

Follow these six steps and you are sure to achieve your goals. BE true to yourself and make your DREAMS COME TRUE!! YOU are the ONLY ONE that CAN DO IT!!

Don't ask Life for a PENNY, Ask it for MILLIONS!!

You're Not Alone!

Associations and Support Groups

Networking with other virtual assistants can be both fun and beneficial to your business. The general feeling in the VA world is that we are not "competitors" but colleagues promoting collaboration with each other. Consider this: you come across a client who wants a service that you don't provide, or perhaps you are in the middle of a project and you get hung up on the software you're using. Who will you turn to? There is no one sitting at the desk next to you, but there is a whole network of VAs ready to assist you in a matter of moments.

I think Kim Haas, (http://www.kimhaas.com) describes it best when she states, "Find a support group who will help you through the rough times. When you feel like giving up, it's always nice to be involved with a group of women who understand your feelings and who can guide you over the 'bumps.' You'll find that other women in business will tell you to never give up—even when things look darkest."

I hate to say it, but chances are you will have one of these days. I know I've had one or two myself. (Okay, maybe a few more.) Wouldn't it be nice to be able to log online and chat with some supportive friends who could encourage you and motivate you back to your old self? That's why it's such a good idea to get involved with groups right from the beginning. Not only will they provide support on getting started, but friendship and camaraderie. And last, but not least, they are a lot of FUN!!! And I'm all for that!

Home-Based Business Associations/Clubs
Many organizations are available to help home-based businesses succeed. One such organization is National Association of Self-Employed (http://www.nase.org). Even membership in your local Sam's Club or Costco can prove beneficial. The advantages to joining one or more of these associations or clubs include:

- Group health insurance
- Assistance in obtaining merchant account Visa/MasterCard acceptance for your business
- Valuable information targeted for home-based businesses
- Online information
- Phone and travel discounts
- Legislative updates
- Seminars
- Personal consultations

Pick out several that might interest you and call for additional information.

Small Business Resources
There are a multitude of resources available online. We've selected several sites below that we have found over the years to provide a wide array of useful information.

Note: While we do our best to provide up-to-date listings, we cannot guarantee that all sites will remain active over time.

- **Business Know-How(sm)**
  http://www.businessknowhow.com

  Offers a wealth of how-to information and resources that will help you start a business and grow your business, find customers, solve business problems, increase your profits, and succeed. Available on the web at http://www.businessknowhow.com and at keyword "Business Know-How" on America Online, the site provides feature articles, access to experts, community message boards, tools and business-to-business networking opportunities that make starting, running and doing business easier and more profitable.

- **SCORE**
  http://www.score.org
  800-634-0245
  (or under U.S. Government, Small Business Administration in your area)

  SCORE is the "Service Corps of Retired Executives." It is dedicated to aiding small businesses (home businesses as well) to grow and succeed. I've been to several SCORE meetings and I have found them exceptionally worthwhile. In fact, in my area they assign a personal representative to assist you. You can set up a meeting with him/her and go over all ideas you have on starting your business. You can also receive e-mail counseling on the Internet.

- **Small Business Association (SBA)**
  http://www.sba.gov
  800-827-5722

  The Small Business Administration was created by Congress in 1953 with the purpose of helping small-business owners with financial assistance, management counseling, and training. The SBA provides you with a wealth of information, including many seminars and workshops, and publishes excellent literature. Their website can assist you in starting your business, financing your business, business opportunities, offices and services, local SBA offices, etc.

- **American Home Business Association**
  http://www.homebusiness.com
  800-664-2422

  Unique services include a BBS with Internet address; merchant accounts for Visa and MasterCard acceptance; individual insurance, including major medical benefits, term and life insurance, pension plans and IRAs, disability income replacement; and discounts for hotel and long-distance calls.

Industry and Professional Membership Groups

Note: While we do our best to provide up-to-date listings, we cannot guarantee that all sites will remain active over time. Do your research and take the time to find out the philosophy, mission, and vision of each group to match your needs.

- **IVAA**
  http://www.ivaa.net

  International Virtual Assistants Association (IVAA) is an organization for the virtual assisting industry, working to develop and maintain professional standards and help ensure the reputation, growth, and future strength of the industry and its members individually.

- **Elite Office Support**
  http://www.EliteOfficeSupport.com

  Portal and worldwide directory of virtual assistants The site offers a wide variety of resources for professional development.

- **AdminSecret**
  http://www.adminsecret.com

  Provides resources, articles and information for administrative assistants, executive assistants, virtual assistants and office professionals of all types.

- **VANetworking Forum**
  http://www.vanetworking.com

  Virtual Assistant Networking Forum (VANF) is a global networking forum for virtual assistants.

- **Virtual Assistant Forums**
  http://www.virtualassistantforums.com

  To be able to connect with other entrepreneurs who work at the same profession and get exactly where you are, what you do, how you do it, and why is an immeasurable support.

- **Virtual Assistant Hub**
  http://www.virtualassistanthub.com

  A free site for aspiring, new and seasoned virtual assistants, and clients of virtual assistants, to share and receive practical information and high-quality tools to advance their businesses.

- **Home-Based Working Moms**
  http://www.HBWM.com

  HBWM is an online community and professional association for parents who work at home and those who would like to. HBWM offers a unique Work-at-Home Kit for moms, as well as association benefits which include a monthly newsletter, a weekly e-newsletter, member's listserv, panel of experts, online membership directory, support, networking, information and discounts on various products and services.

Some other sites you might want to check out:
- http://www.digitalwork.com
- http://www.elance.com
- http://www.guru.com
- http://www.coworking.com
- http://www.office.com
- http://www.nafe.com
- http://www.nawbo.org
- http://www.allbusiness.com
- http://www.effectivemeetings.com
- http://www.inc.com
- http://www.cwahm.com
- http://www.momstown.com

In Their Own Words:

Shane Bowlin: MacWarehouse.com and OfficeDepot.com. I found the Small Business Administration web site very helpful. WriteDirections.com has a lot of information on business writing (i.e. Business letters, press releases, etc.).

Jeannine Clontz: I've belonged to many, but have found many great resources within my local Chamber(s), BNI, ESPW (Encouraging, Supporting, Promoting Women), ANEW (A Network for Empowering Women), NAWBO (National Association of Women Business Owners), IVAA (Intl. Virtual Assistants Assn.), Kiwanis, Rotary, Optimists, and the eWomen Network.

Susan Totman:
http://www.eliteofficesupport.com
http://www.va-theseries.com
http://www.academyvp.com
http://www.myownbusiness.org

Clara D. Fyffe
All-Write Virtual Office

Note: While IAVOA is no longer an active organization for the virtual assistant industry since the passing of our dear friend and founder, Alfred Gandee, we maintain the reference in the sense of sharing Clara's story and the power of the support you can gain from industry organizations.

The acceptance of my body's inability to function adequately in everyday home and work activities and the trauma of an automobile accident contributed to the decision – the necessity – to set up my home-based business, All-Write Virtual Office.

As a disabled person – I have visual as well as physical problems – I have been classified as homebound, although I can drive in familiar areas when the weather is clear and during daylight hours. I knew that most of my investigations into the proper running of a business would have to be done by phone or by computer.

Through the assistance of the local Small Business Development Center and the State Office of Vocational Rehabilitation, I was able to attend courses and attain equipment that I needed for my home office, which used to be one bedroom of my apartment. But, still feeling isolated and alone and needing more one-on-one mentoring to clearly understand the 'ins and outs' of all the vast areas of operating the business, I started a search on the web.

I first chose to search for a way to market my business. One of the sites the 'net gave me was for another VA who had written articles about the virtual assistant industry. I went to her site, found her number and called her up to ask permission to use some of her material. She, in turn, referred me to others who had joined an online virtual assistant organization in the meantime. Much to my surprise, I was contacted by incredible people and invited to join their group. They told me that their organization had many resources for VAs and that they thought I might find these tools useful.

I grabbed at their invitation, joined the International Association of Virtual Office Assistants, IAVOA, and – BOOM – no longer did I ever feel isolated or alone again! Instant friendship, instant camaraderie, instant and invaluable help. Through the many and diversified members of the IAVOA community, I found that all I needed to do was to post whatever question I had to the list, our very own personal contact forum, and within a matter of minutes, responses come pouring in from all over the world! It's an amazing way to learn. The responses are always encouraging, insightful, and intelligent, and if the answer I need isn't already in someone's realm of knowledge, I am directed to where I might find the answer.

I have found that, in addition to the knowledge and leadership I've found through IAVOA, we also are free to post our successes as well as our insecurities. Always, always, always, we are congratulated and/or encouraged. Since our messages are sent to each member at the same time, we all are aware of what each of us needs or feels, and we, separately yet as a group, all join in to help that individual. I also discovered that I am free to telephone any of these members at any time, without being tossed aside. I've made great friends here, friends who support me and for whom I have great respect. I know that IAVOA and its members have kept me going many a time when I have just wanted to call it quits.

Since joining IAVOA, I have learned a great deal about marketing, client contact, ad writing, proposals, invoicing, bidding, (the list is endless!), and have been able to grow my own business so that I am now beginning to see increased success and finally realize a profit. I have learned the power of teamwork. I feel that one of the most surprising aspects of membership here is that, even though we are all trying to make our own mark in the VA industry, not once has any member refused to help out any of the rest of us to improve our own businesses I think that says a lot for the integrity and compatibility of this group.

For myself and All-Write Virtual Office, I have learned specifically that success does not have to elude the disabled individual. Resources are available everywhere you look, especially with the advent of the Internet and groups such as IAVOA.

Author's note: On June 26, 2010 Clara lost a long and courageous battle with cancer. The outpouring of support continued with notes, prayers, and flowers being extended to her family and friends.

Some Final Thoughts

We hope you enjoyed reading our book as much as we enjoyed writing it. We both feel so fortunate to have had this opportunity to share with you. We also hope that you stay in touch and let us know how your business is going. Remember, we are here to help keep you motivated and informed on how you can start a business and stay in business successfully.

To contact us personally, you can e-mail us at diana@va-theseries.com and kelly@va-series.com or visit us online at http://www.VA-TheSeries.com.

Become a fan of *Virtual Assistant – The Series* on Facebook at http://www.facebook.com/becomeava -- share your success story with us there!

You can also connect with us on Twitter: twitter.com/dianaennen and twitter.com/kellypoelker

We wish you the very best of success!!

Appendix

Checklist for Starting a VA Business

Business Checklist

- Write down your strengths and weaknesses
- Establish business and personal goals
- Determine your financial resources
- Identify any financial risks
- Determine what the start-up costs would be
- Decide on your target market (clients you want to work for)
- Create a business plan
- Create a marketing plan
- Start developing your website

Business operations

- Choose an entity (proprietorship, partnership, or corporation)
- Obtain licenses necessary to start your business
- Open a business checking account
- Look into insurance for your company
- Setup your bookkeeping system

First steps

- Get business cards
- Get furniture and equipment
- Join a professional organization
- Set a starting date

This will get you to Day 1 – your official opening day. You will want to plan out your day, in fact plan for the entire week. Decide what marketing you will be doing, at what time, etc. Your Daytimer or PDA should become a valuable asset to you. You will want to have a complete plan of action outlined before you officially get started.

To have your clients consider you as a professional, you need to have the tools required to look like one.

Tools of the Trade

In most cases, you will need the following:

- Computer
- Word Processing Program
- Database Program
- Spreadsheet or Accounting Program
- Fax Machine

- E-mail Account
- A Website
- A Business Telephone
- High Speed Internet
- A Good Printer
- Transcriber and/or WAV pedal

A reliable computer with a good word processing program and printer is mandatory for your success. Clients do not want to hear that you can't do their work for any reason. They don't want excuses, they want the finished project. That's why it's so important to get a good computer, Internet access and be armed with all the right tools to provide the services you offer. Besides, don't you deserve the best?

A business telephone and fax machine conveys that professional edge. The Internet and an e-mail account are required.

A database program will help you keep track of your customers and even keep track of your clients' clients. An accounting program or spreadsheet program is helpful to keep track of your income and expenses. A website enhances your professionalism and allows you to acquire more clientele by using your website as a marketing and advertising tool.

If you do not yet own a home office, start working on one. A private room in your home is ideal to set up a home office. The kitchen table is a place to begin, but that will not last long because you will need more room to expand and be able to work more efficiently. Besides, your family will want to eat sometime. And you need space to put client's files and other office tools.

Office furniture will also be necessary, which will include at the very least a desk, chair, file cabinet, and open shelves. Office supplies are essential items and should include paper, CDs, DVDs, stapler, paper clips, folders, calendar, etc.

Be thinking right from the start how you plan to back up your information. Get that system up immediately.

Sample Marketing Letter

Dear _____:

Do you need more hours in your day? Week? Year? Well right here in O'Fallon, Illinois, is an enterprise business that can save you time and money and help you grow your business. It's called a Virtual Assistant, or "VA."

A VA provides administrative support and specialized services to businesses, entrepreneurs, executives, sales professionals, and busy people. A highly skilled professional working as an independent contractor, a VA uses leading edge technology to skillfully complete work assignments via the Internet, e-mail, or online file sharing. Traditional methods such as regular mail and overnight shipping are also used.

My name is Kelly Poelker; . I am the founder and President of Another8Hours, O'Fallon's first virtual assistance company. Unlike a full-time employee, Another8Hours is available to you only when you need us. And unlike a temporary employee, we guarantee you the same great service from the same great people every time. Best of all, we save you time and money.

Another8Hours saves you money because we have our own office, use our own equipment, and pay our own taxes. We don't require vacation or holiday pay, medical insurance, or even a 401(k). We do take a sincere interest in helping you grow your business. Another8Hours saves you time because you'll spend less time doing administrative work and more time growing your business, nurturing your family, or just plain relaxing.

Another8Hours virtual services include information processing, spreadsheets, e-mail handling, newsletters, flyers, business cards, presentations, meeting and event planning, advertising specialty items, concierge services, Internet research, web services, mass mailings, database management, bill paying, sales support, and much more. Although our services are virtual in nature, we make it a point to meet with all local clients. Being in close proximity to your business, we gladly offer free pickup and delivery service in O'Fallon and surrounding areas.

Don't be the last one in town to get their own virtual assistant. Find out more by visiting www.another8hours.com or give us a call at (877) 546-7595, and see how you can use Another8Hours to lessen your burden and improve your day.

Kind Regards,

Kelly Poelker
President

Contract Checklist

This is a general checklist of key items to consider when drafting a contract.

(Provide with Permission from Tena Cummings)

1. Identity of Parties

    - Name
    - Type of entity of each party (corporation, LLC, etc.)
    - Addresses

2. Recitals

    - Background of agreement
    - Purpose for entering into the contract
    - Key assumptions for the contract

3. Obligations of the Parties

    - What is each side required to do?
    - By what date?
    - If something has to be delivered, whose obligation is it and at who's cost?

4. Terms of the Contract

    - Is the contract a one-shot situation or will it last for some designated time period?
    - How can the term be renewed or extended?

5. Price

    - What is the price for the product or service?
    - Is it a fixed price, determined by a formula, by a project fee, or some other manner?
    - Who pays any tax?

6. Payment Terms

    - When is payment due?
    - Will there be installment payments?
    - Will interest be charged?
    - Is there a penalty for late payment?

7. Representations and Warranties

    - What representations and warranties are to be made by the parties?
    - Are certain warranties disclaimed (e.g., merchantability or fitness for a particular purpose)?
    - How long are any warranties good for?

8.   Liability

- What limitations of liability exist (e.g., no liability in excess of payment received, or no liability for consequential damage or lost profits)?
- Under what circumstances is one party liable (e.g., material breach of agreement or grossly negligent in performing services)?

9.   Termination of Contract

- When can one party terminate the contract early?
- What are the consequences of termination?
- What post-termination obligations are there?

10.   Confidentiality

- What confidentiality obligations are there?
- What are the exclusions from confidentiality?

11.   Default

- What are the events of default?
- Does a party have a period to cure a default?
- What are the consequences of a default?

12.   Miscellaneous

- Modification of Agreement
- Notice
- Entire Agreement
- Severability
- Execution
- Specific Performances
- Representation on Authority of Parties
- Work Product Ownership
- Independent Contractor Notification

13.   Signatures

- What authority is required for one party to sign the contract (e.g., Board of Directors approval)?
- How many signatures are required?
- Are the signature blocks correct? For corporations, this is a typical appropriate signature block:

ABC, Inc.

By: _____
John Smith, President

Independent Contractor Agreement
(Provided by Tena Cummings)

This Independent Contractor Agreement (the "Agreement") is made and entered between _____, an independent contractor hereafter referred to as "Contractor", and _____, hereafter referred to as "Company".

In consideration of the covenants and conditions hereinafter set forth, Company and Contractor agree as follows:

1. **SERVICES**
    Contractor shall perform the following services for the Company (the "Work").

    _____

    _____

    _____

2. **REPORTING**
    Contractor shall report to _____. Contractor shall provide a weekly written report to the Company on his progress on assignments.

3. **TERM**
    This Agreement shall commence on _____, ____ and shall expire on _____, ____. Contractor agrees to perform services for the Work to Company on or before the expiration of the term set forth above. The Company may terminate the use of Contractor's services at any time without cause and without further obligation to Contractor except for payment due for services prior to date of such termination. Termination of this Agreement or termination of services shall not affect the provisions under Sections 5-11, hereof, which shall survive any termination.

4. **PAYMENT**
    Contractor will be paid for Work performed under this Agreement as follows:

    _____

    _____

    _____

    Contractor will submit an invoice for the Work on _____. Invoices shall be paid by the Company within 15 business days of receipt.

5. **CONFIDENTIALITY AND OWNERSHIP**
    (a) Contractor recognizes and acknowledges that the Company possesses certain confidential information that constitutes a valuable, special, and unique asset. As used herein, the term "confidential information" includes all information and materials belonging to, used by, or in the possession of the Company relating to its products, processes, services, technology, inventions, patents, ideas, contracts, financial information, developments, business strategies, pricing, current and prospective customers, marketing plans, and trade secrets of every kind and character, but shall not include (a) information that was already within the public domain at the time the information is acquired by Contractor, or (b) information that subsequently becomes public through no act or omission of the Contractor. Contractor agrees that all of the confidential information is and shall continue to be the exclusive property of the Company, whether or not prepared in whole or

in part by Contractor and whether or not disclosed to or entrusted to Contractor's custody. Contractor agrees that Contractor shall not, at any time following the execution of this Agreement, use or disclose in any manner any confidential information of the Company.

(b) To the extent any inventions, technologies, reports, memoranda, studies, writings, articles, plans, designs, specifications, exhibits, software code, or other materials prepared by Contractor in the performance of services under this Agreement include material subject to copyright protection, such materials have been specially commissioned by the Company and they shall be deemed "work for hire" as such term is defined under U.S. copyright law. To the extent any such materials do not qualify as "work for hire" under applicable law, and to the extent they include material subject to copyright, patent, trade secret, or other proprietary rights protection, Contractor hereby irrevocably and exclusively assigns to the Company, its successors, and assigns, all right, title, and interest in and to all such materials. To the extent any of Contractor rights in the same, including without limitation any moral rights, are not subject to assignment hereunder, Contractor hereby irrevocably and unconditionally waives all enforcement of such rights. Contractor shall execute and deliver such instruments and take such other actions as may be required to carry out and confirm the assignments contemplated by this paragraph and the remainder of this Agreement. All documents, magnetically or optically encoded media, and other tangible materials created by Contractor as part of its services under this Agreement shall be owned by the Company.

6.   RETURN OF MATERIALS
Contractor agrees that upon termination of this Agreement, Contractor will return to the Company all drawings, blueprints, notes, memoranda, specifications, designs, writings, software, devices, documents and any other material containing or disclosing any confidential or proprietary information of the Company. Contractor will not retain any such materials.

7.   WARRANTIES
Contractor warrants that:

(a) Contractor's agreement to perform the Work pursuant to this Agreement does not violate any agreement or obligation between Contractor and a third party; and

(b) The Work as delivered to the Company will not infringe any copyright, patent, trade secret, or other proprietary right held by any third party; and

(c) The services provided by Contractor shall be performed in a professional manner, and shall be of a high grade, nature, and quality. The services shall be performed in a timely manner and shall meet deadlines agreed between Contractor and the Company.

8.   INDEMNITY
Contractor agrees to indemnify, defend, and hold the Company and its successors, officers, directors, agents and employees harmless from any and all actions, causes of action, claims, demands, cost, liabilities, expenses and damages (including attorneys' fees) arising out of, or in connection with any breach of this Agreement by Contractor.

9.   RELATIONSHIP OF PARTIES
Contractor is an independent contractor of the Company. Nothing in this Agreement shall be construed as creating an employer-employee relationship, as a guarantee of future employment or engagement, or as a limitation upon the Company' sole discretion to terminate this Agreement at any time without cause. Contractor further agrees to be responsible for all of Contractor's federal and state taxes, withholding, social security, insurance, and other benefits. Contractor shall provide the Company with satisfactory proof of independent contractor status.

10. OTHER ACTIVITIES

Contractor is free to engage in other independent contracting activities, provided that Contractor does not engage in any such activities which are inconsistent with or in conflict with any provisions hereof, or that so occupy Contractor's attention as to interfere with the proper and efficient performance of Contractor's services thereunder. Contractor agrees not to induce or attempt to influence, directly or indirectly, any employee at the Company to terminate his/her employment and work for Contractor or any other person.

11. MISCELLANEOUS

(a) Governing Law. This Agreement shall be governed by and construed in accordance with the laws of the State of _____ without regard to conflict of law principles.

(b) Entire Agreement. This Agreement contains the entire agreement and understanding between the parties hereto and supersedes any prior or contemporaneous written or oral agreements, representations and warranties between them respecting the subject matter hereof.

(c) Amendment. This Agreement may be amended only by a writing signed by Contractor and by a duly authorized representative of the Company.

(d) Severability. If any term, provision, covenant or condition of this Agreement, or the application thereof to any person, place or circumstance, shall be held to be invalid, unenforceable or void, the remainder of this Agreement and such term, provision, covenant or condition as applied to other persons, places and circumstances shall remain in full force and effect.

(e) Construction. The headings and captions of this Agreement are provided for convenience only and are intended to have no effect in construing or interpreting this Agreement. The language in all parts of this Agreement shall be in all cases construed according to its fair meaning and not strictly for or against either party.

(f) Remedy for Breach. The parties hereto agree that, in the event of breach or threatened breach of any covenants of Contractor, the damage or imminent damage to the value and the goodwill of the Company's business shall be inestimable, and that therefore any remedy at law or in damages shall be inadequate. Accordingly, the parties hereto agree that the Company shall be entitled to injunctive relief against Contractor in the event of any breach or threatened breach of any of such provisions by Contractor, in addition to any other relief (including damages) available to the Company under this Agreement or under law.

(g) Notices. Any notice, request, consent or approval required or permitted to be given under this Agreement or pursuant to law shall be sufficient if in writing, and if and when sent by certified or registered mail, with postage prepaid, to Contractor's residence (as noted below), or to the Company's principal office, as the case may be.

Company: Contractor:

By:_____   By:_____
Title:_____   [Signature]
                                            Name: _____
                                                              (Print)
Date: _____
                                            _____
                                            Address:_____

WORK FOR HIRE AGREEMENT
(By Tena Cummings with her permission)

This Work for Hire Agreement ("Agreement") is made this <day> day of <month>, <year>, between <enter your business name>, and <enter client name> having its principal place of business at <enter client address>. In this Agreement, the party who is contracting to receive the services shall be referred to as the "Client" and the party who will be providing the services shall be referred to as between <enter your business name>".

1. DESCRIPTION OF SERVICES. Beginning on <enter date>, <enter your business name> will provide the following services (collectively, the "Services"): <enter services provided>.

2. PAYMENT FOR SERVICES. <enter client name> will pay compensation to <enter your business name> for the Services based on <enter fee amounts>. This compensation shall be payable upon receipt of invoice.

3. TERM/TERMINATION. This Agreement may be terminated by either party upon 5 days written notice to the other party.

4. RELATIONSHIP OF PARTIES. It is understood by the parties that <enter your business name> is an independent contractor with respect to <enter client name> and not an employee of <enter client name> will not provide fringe benefits, including health insurance benefits, paid vacation, or any other employee benefit, for the benefit of <enter your business name>.

5. WORK PRODUCT OWNERSHIP. Any works copyrighted, ideas, discoveries, inventions, patents, products, or other information (collectively, the "Work Product") developed in whole or in part by <enter your business name> in connection with the Services shall be the exclusive property of <enter client name>. Upon request, <enter your business name> shall sign all documents necessary to confirm or perfect the exclusive ownership of <enter client name> to the Work Product.

6. CONFIDENTIALITY. <enter your business name> will not at any time or in any manner, either directly or indirectly, use for the personal benefit of <enter your business name>, or divulge, disclose, or communicate in any manner any information that is proprietary to <enter client name>. <enter your business name> will protect such information and treat it as strictly confidential. This provision shall continue to be effective after the termination of this Agreement. Upon termination of this Agreement, <enter your business name> will return to <enter client name> all records, notes, documentation and other items that were used, created, or controlled by <enter your business name> during the term of this Agreement.

7. ENTIRE AGREEMENT. This Agreement contains the entire agreement of the parties, and there are no other promises or conditions in any other agreement whether oral or written.

8. SEVERABILITY. If any provision of this Agreement shall be held to be invalid or unenforceable for any reason, the remaining provisions shall continue to be valid and enforceable. If a court finds that any provision of this Agreement is invalid or unenforceable, but that by limiting such provision it would become valid and enforceable, then such provision shall be deemed to be written, construed, and enforced as so limited.

Party contracting services:

By:_____
<enter client name>

Service Provider:

By: _____
<enter your name>
<enter your business name>

Client Self Assessment Form

1. Describe your business in terms of products, services, targeted market size of operation etc.

2. What are some unique characteristics about your business?

3. What are three short term goals that you hope to accomplish this year?
   Increase my business net worth
   Create E-zines
   Other

4. How do you plan to achieve those goals? Would it help if you had a partner to help with database management or marketing?

5. What are your time cheaters? What do you hate to do?
   Administrative tasks   E-mail   Mailouts
   Correspondence   Voice mail   Other
   Not enough hours in the day to _____

6. What percent of your time do you spend on administrative tasks? Describe some of those tasks.

7. Do you currently have administrative support? Why not?
   Too expensive   Don't know anyone I can trust
   Not enough work   Other

8. What percent of your time do you spend on growing your business?

9. Do you feel that you are effectively operating your business? Why? Why Not?

10. Do you feel like you are effectively managing your time or do you wind up not accomplishing goals because of administrative issues?

11. Do you have a comment or question for the panelists about the VA industry?

    Please provide your e-mail address for response _____

Social Media Tools

Social media is quickly becoming one of the best tools for building relationships online, both personal and professional. Those that embrace it and continue to stay on the cutting edge of the latest technology can reap the rewards. Not only can it improve your business, but also it's a great specialty to add to your service offering. For virtual assistants, it's like money in the bank.

There are a number of tools to help you master social media. Just like most things online (i.e., think computers!), it's important to note that this is ever changing. New and exciting tools will soon replace many of these below. The key is to always look for what would work best for you and stay up to date on these through your VA friends.

Here are some of the tools that are currently available.

Twitter – Is a social networking service that allows you to send and retrieve messages that are up to 140 characters. It allows you to stay connected with your friends, clients, and potential clients and easily follow those who can help with your business. Through the use of hashtags (#), you are able to not only chat with others, but also find new business connections.

- TweetDeck –Allows you to easily access Twitter, follow your mentions, direct messages, search, connect with Facebook & LinkedIn.
- TweetChat - Allows you to easily follow hashtags for chatting on Twitter.
- TweetLater – Allows you to program your tweets and send them at a later date.
- Qwitter – Tells you who quits following you and after what posting. Very valuable to see which posts are annoying your followers.
- TwitterSearch – Allows you to post keywords and search those terms.

HootSuite – Is a Twitter Tool that makes keeping up easy. It allows you to manage multiple Twitter profiles, pre-schedule postings, send to multiple places, and so much more. It also interfaces with other social media applications to bring it all under one roof.

Facebook – Is a social networking site that allows friends to connect with one another, share photos, etc., but that's only the beginning. For businesses it can be invaluable. Among the many benefits of Facebook to your business include: branding, driving web traffic to your site, connecting with clients, associates, and potential clients, posting events, advertising, and that's just the icing on the cake.

LinkedIn – Is often considered a more professional site than the others. It allows you to connect with other professionals, give recommendations, chat with others, etc.

Ping.fm – allows you to easy connect to all your social networks from one place. Great for social bookmarketing.

SocialOomph – Productivity tool that allows you to manager multiple aspects of social media together for posting in one.

YouTube – The largest and most well-respected means of posting videos.

TubeMogul –For video uploads and syndication, this allows you to upload a single video to dozens of video sites, not just You Tube.

Tweetie – A great tool for Mac users to manage their social media with the look and feel of true Mac interface.

Flickr – This allows you to download photos and easily add them to your blogs and presentations.

Sample Disaster Recovery Plan

[Company} maintains regular backups of client files on an external hard drive. The external hard drive is removed from the corporate offices located at [Address] on a daily basis. The drive remains in the possession of the owner, [Owner's name]. Backup of software files has not yet been finalized but will be located off-site in a binder.

In the event of a disaster at the corporate office where [Company name] could not operate the business, the corporate offices will be temporarily relocated to [Address]. The temporary office is the home of owner, [Your name].

Alternate contact numbers for [Owner's name]:

Cell phone:
Home Number:
Toll-Free Voice and Fax:
E-mail:

In the event that Internet access is down, [Company name] has access available at the temporary office through cable modem, as well as a dial-up back up in the event that main cable modem is inactive. Dial-up access is available through Sysmatrix – www.sysmatrix.net. Telephone number:

In the event of a disaster, [company name] will follow these steps to set up operations in the temporary facility, or continue operations in the event [Owner's name] becomes incapacitated:

1. Call the phone company to have phones forwarded to temporary office or cell phone number.
2. Contact [contact name and details of your backup VA] and advise status of situation, request any necessary assistance. [Backup name] has access to pertinent passwords for accessing data. Access to client files is only available by shipping external hard drive to her at: [insert backup VA address]
3. Contact insurance company:
   a. [Agent's Name] – State Farm Insurance (Phone Number)
      Business Policy # : (original policy located:
      Life Insurance Policy # : (original policy located:

4. Key people to be contacted with status:
5. Attorney [insert attorney's name] maintains Corporate Book at [attorney's office location]
6. Computer operations can resume through use of laptop. In the event the laptop is not accessible new computer would need to be purchased.
7. Purchase items, depending upon time for recovery of primary office location:
   a. Computer, printer, and necessary peripherals
   b. Additional phone line and fax setup at temporary location
   c. Computer network established
   d. Utilize online resources
8. Additional pool of virtual assistants who could step in to assist clients include:

Vendor information:

Web Hosting for clients and [your company name] is handled through –
Domain management and registration handled through www.domainofmyown.com
Contact Michelle Nations for assistance.

Dos And Don'ts For Starting A Virtual Assistant Business

DO -- Decide on a targeted market and initially focus your marketing efforts in that area. By developing a "niche" in your field, your reputation spreads quickly and soon you become a recognized expert. There are several specialties, including medical, legal or business transcription, resume consulting, desktop publishing, manuscript preparing, academic typing, computer tutoring, etc.

DO -- Be creative about where you can find business. Look in the want ads for those seeking help and offer your assistance until they hire someone. If you see a new business opening, approach them to help with not only their typing needs, but also their marketing efforts as well. Actively network and don't limit your marketing to simply placing a few ads in newspapers or the Yellow Pages. You want to find where there might be a need -- and go fill it!

DO -- Write a complete plan of action for your marketing efforts. For example, I plan to 1) stop by local businesses in the area and drop off my card, 2) advertise in my local weekly paper, 3) send a marketing letter to doctors, new businesses, etc. Having everything written down ensures that you stay on track in developing your business.

DO -- Develop promotional material that looks sensational! Your business card alone is often the only connection a potential client has with your services. It should have the POWER to draw them to you. Spend the time to review cards that have caught your interest in the past and then design yours with that in mind. With your letterhead, brochures, flyers, etc., add color and style by purchasing specialty paper at places such as Office Depot, Office Max, or specialty paper stores. Occasionally change your letterhead and cards as you develop your business. With a few years experience under your belt, you can develop a much more professional marketing tool that emphasizes your current word processing capabilities and added strengths.

DO -- Learn everything you can about starting a business. Knowledge is power and the more you know, the fewer mistakes you are likely to make. Look to online services, message boards and chats to talk with other word processors operating a business. Join associations that are targeted for your industry. And read, read, read. By frequently continuing to increase your skills and your knowledge of your profession, the end result is a more confident, satisfied you.

DO -- Provide your clients with more than they ask for. When clients leave your office and get more than they expected, they come back. And best of all, they refer others. This is how businesses grow. Also, it's easier to keep a client than it is to get a new one. By providing your clients with excellent services, you do just that.

DON'T -- Under-price your services. The average VA today makes $25-$35/hr, depending upon location, specialty, and years in business. (Some a lot more, but for start-ups, this is a good average).

DON'T -- Overextend yourself. One of the common mistakes many word processors make is to accept too much work and then not be able to accurately complete it. Learn to say NO or have a back-up helper who can assist you with any overflow work. One of the most important ingredients for success is keeping your clients satisfied. If you overextend yourself and make a lot of errors, it will jeopardize your business.

DON'T -- Get discouraged. It takes time to get a business going. Plan ahead and have money saved in reserve. Don't buy items until you have found the best possible price and there is an absolute need. This advance planning takes the pressure off of having to make money NOW. If things are slow and the phone just isn't ringing ... MAKE IT RING!! There's plenty of work out there, you just need to aggressively pursue it.

Virtual Assistants Who Contributed To This Book

Tess Strand Alipour
Codehead, LLP
http://www.virtualassistantforums.com

Tina Armillotto
Ft. Lauderdale, FL

Gretchen Berg
Berg Business Solutions
http://www.gberg.com

Shane Bowlin
AskShane.com
http://www.AskShane.com

Ginger Brown
The Writer's Typist
TheWritersTypist@yahoo.com

Jeannine Clontz
Accurate Business Services
http://www.Accbizsvcs.com

Tena Cummings
A Page In Time Designs
(also Blackwater Media)
http://apageintimedesigns.tripod.com

Bernadette Davis
Virtually Yours
Office Assistant Services
http://www.virtuallyours-oas.net

Lee Drozak
My Office Assistant
http://myofficeassist.org

Nina Feldman
Nina Feldman Connections
http://www.connections@ninafeldman.com

Stephanie Fish
Buckeye VA
http://www.buckeyeva.com

Clara D. Fyffe
All Write VA
Alyssa Gregory
avertua, LLC
http://www.avertua.com

Janet Ann Janowiak
http://www.ezonesecretary.com

Patsy LaFave
The Write Place
writeplace@earthlink.net

Dawn Mayo
Absolute Document Services
http://www.yourremoteoffice.com

Ruth Martin
Maplewood Virtual Assistance
http://www.maplewoodva.com

Julie McMann

Jan Melnik
Absolute Advantage
http://www.janmelnik.com/

Andrea Pixley
Andrea M. Pixley, Virtual Assistant
http://andreapixley.com

4MilitaryFamilies.com
http://4militaryfamilies.com

Kathy Ritchie
Ritchie Secretarial Service
RSS Herald
http://www.thebestva.com
http://www.rssherald.com.

Barbara Rowen
Virtually Everything
http://www.virtuallyeverything.net

Nora Rubinoff
At Your Service Cincinnati Ltd.
http://www.aysweb.com

Nancy Seeger
Arts Assistance
http://www.artassistance.com

Patty Shannon
The Wordstation

Kimberly Thomas-Catanzaro
Bookkeeping and Secretarial Services
http://www.on-linesecretary.com

Donna Toothaker
1st VA
http://www.1stva.com

Susan Totman
Elite Office Support
http://www.eliteofficesupport.com

Vivian Vican
Nerd World Productions
http://nerdworld.scriptmania.com

Index

ORDER FORM

Name: _____   Date: _____

Contact: _____   Phone #: _____   Fax #: _____

Street: _____   Email: _____

City, State, Zip:

Item/ Description	Quantity	Unit Price	Total
Virtual Assistant – The Series: Become a Highly Successful, Sought After VA		32.95	
BUNDLE: Virtual Assistant – The Series: Become a Highly Successful Sought After VA, Workbook & Financial Statements Template for Business Planning On CD-ROM		59.95	
Financial Statements Template for Business Planning CD-ROM Only		14.95	
Virtual Assistant – The Series: Become a highly Successful, Sought After VA Workbook Edition		29.95	
Sub-total			
Shipping & Handling: Domestic - $11.20; Int'l - call			
Sales Tax - IL orders only add 7.75%			
GRAND TOTAL			

Payment Type: (check only one) ___ Sending Check ___ Mastercard ___ Visa ___ American Express ___ Discover

_____   Authorized transaction amount: $
_____

Purchaser's Signature (required on all orders)

If paying by credit card: Card Number _____   Exp Date _____
CVV _____ (three digit number on back of card)

Billing Address on Card (if different from above) _____

Mail order form and payment to:
Another 8 Hours Inc., 106A East Fourth Street, O'Fallon, IL 62269,
FAX: (618) 624-3081 • E-mail: orders@va-theseries.com
Visit us online at http://www.VA-TheSeries.com for upcoming e-books and new additions to our book collection.

CPSIA information can be obtained
at www.ICGtesting.com
Printed in the USA
FFHW011947190119
50141498-55033FF